KNIGHTS UNHORSED

KNIGHTS UNHORSED

Internal Conflict in a
Gilded Age Social Movement

Robert E. Weir

WAYNE STATE UNIVERSITY PRESS   DETROIT

Library of Congress Cataloging-in-Publication Data

Weir, Robert E., 1952–
Knights unhorsed : internal conflict in a gilded age social movement /
Robert E. Weir.
p.   cm.
Includes bibliographical references and index.
ISBN 0-8143-2873-3 (cloth : alk. paper)
1. Knights of Labor—History.   2. Labor unions—United
States—Biography.   3. Powderly, Terence Vincent, 1849–1924.   I. Title.
HD8055.K7 W46   2000
331.88'33'0973—dc21   00-009733

Contents

Acknowledgments 7

Introduction: Unhorsing Terence Powderly:
The Knights of Labor as a Social Movement 9

CHAPTER 1: To Rule or Ruin: The Revolt of the Home Club 23

CHAPTER 2: The B & B Affair 47

CHAPTER 3: In the Larger Field: The Fate of Joseph R.
Buchanan 73

CHAPTER 4: Portrait of a Difficult Man: Charles Litchman
and the Problem of Personality 97

CHAPTER 5: The View from Below: The Trials and Tribulations
of Obscure Knights 117

CHAPTER 6: A Dubious Equality: Leonora Barry and
Women in the KOL 141

CHAPTER 7: "We Have to Get Rid of You": The Fall of
Terence V. Powderly 161

Afterword and Conclusion 179
Notes 185
Select Bibliography 211
Index 219

5

Acknowledgments

This book went through many false starts and iterations before it came together. The final product is as much due to the insights and assistance of those who have graciously lent their talents as to my own efforts.

Bruce Laurie of the University of Massachusetts took an early look at the manuscript and made suggestions for tying together what were then disparate strands. More than decade after Bruce was my dissertation advisor, he continues to be a friend and first-class mentor.

Richard Schneirov of Indiana State University read several chapters of this work and put me onto sources and interpretive schemes that especially enhanced the chapters on Joseph Buchanan and Thomas Barry. Richard Oestreicher of the University of Pittsburgh generously provided a copy of his unpublished work on Barry and made several fine suggestions. Thanks also to Jonathan Garlock, whose work on Knights of Labor courts enhanced my approach to that thorny subject.

Leon Fink of the University of North Carolina read the entire manuscript several times and offered invaluable advice on sources, unifying threads, and avoiding potential interpretive pitfalls. Leon was supportive of the project, generous with his time, and shrewd with his advice.

A big thank-you goes to Daniel Horowitz of Smith College. Dan's friendship through the years has helped sustain my academic career, and our periodic brainstorm lunches forced me to clarify half-baked ideas. Through his gentle questioning and genuine interest, Dan prodded me to think beyond surface observations.

I also owe a debt to Larry Leavitt of Holyoke Community College and numerous colleagues at Bay Path College who made wonderful suggestions on works to consult on social movement theory. A special thank-you goes to Shirley Johnson, the academic dean, and to Carol Leary, president of Bay Path College, who gave me valuable release time to work on this book. Without the breathing space they created, I doubt I could have brought this book to completion.

Wayne State University Press has been a dream to work with. Director Arthur Evans has been supportive from the start and pushed the board to consider my work. His cheerful staff of editors, designers, and production assistants has done a great job. They also went out of their way to make me feel at home. I especially appreciate the efforts of Adela Garcia in bringing this project to completion.

The guiding spirit of all that I do is my wife, Emily. She has endured enough of my complaints, exasperated desperation, long-winded stories, and shoptalk to qualify for sainthood. She is one of the best editors I've ever seen, and she patiently read multiple, often rambling, drafts and helped me organize chaos into coherence. Above all, her good humor, enthusiasm, and love kept me on the path to both completing this book and maintaining a life outside of academia. She is, simply, my rock and anchor.

I dedicate this book to my parents, Archie and Sarah. Neither went to college, but both toiled hard for many years to ensure that I could. Both were also longtime union members in their pre-retirement years and instilled in me the importance of collective action. Luckily their respective unions—the International Printing and Graphics Communication Workers for Dad, and the United Food and Commercial Workers for Mom—were considerably less contentious than the Knights of Labor!

Robert E. Weir
Northampton, MA

Introduction
Unhorsing Terence Powderly:
The Knights of Labor as a Social Movement

In August 1875, *Scribner's Monthly* turned its attention to preparations for America's upcoming one hundredth birthday. According to the magazine's editorialist, centennial festivities would be in vain unless the opportunity was seized to bind wounds leftover from the Civil War. Americans needed to "recognize the fact that, for richer or poorer, in sickness and health, until death do us part, these United States constitute a nation; that we are to live, grow, prosper, and suffer together, united by bands that cannot be sundered." It was the writer's fervent hope that nothing less than a "reunion of the great American nationality" would emerge and that a new era of "national freedom, concord, peace, and prosperity" would result.[1]

When Edward Bellamy surveyed the American social landscape a mere thirteen years later in his classic novel, *Looking Backward,* he supplied numerous hints as to how little the centennial accomplished. Bellamy's protagonist, Julian West, is hypnotized, falls into a deep trance, and is revived in the year 2000. The utopia in which West awakens is rendered all the more remarkable in contrast to his remembrances of the age from which he was magically transported. In the book's prologue, West recalls the discontent of nineteenth-century laborers, "Strikes had become so common . . . that people had ceased to inquire into their particular grounds. In one department of industry or another, they had been nearly incessant ever since the great business crisis of 1873. In fact, it had come to be an exceptional thing to see any class of laborers pursue their avocation steadily for more than a few months at a time." Though most Americans concurred that society was in turmoil, few could agree on how to address its myriad ills. West confessed that many from his upper-middle-class strata knew "they had made a sad mess of society." Nonetheless, "they had the votes and the power to do so if they pleased and their leaders meant that they should."[2]

Bellamy's fictive alter ego was West's twentieth-century benefactor, Dr. Leete, who blamed the strikes of West's day on "the concentration of capital in greater mass than had ever been known before. . . . The individual laborer, who had been relatively important to the small employer, was reduced to insignificance and powerlessness . . . against the great corporation."[3] Much of the novel is given to cataloging the social wrongs of the late nineteenth century as justification for the Leete/Bellamy formula for recasting American society according to collectivist and communitarian principles.

The Noble and Holy Order of the Knights of Labor (KOL) emerged from obscurity, reached its zenith, and began its decline in the years between America's centennial fete and the publication of *Looking Backward.* Just two years before Bellamy's work appeared in 1888, a substantial number of laborers would have looked to the Knights to fulfill utopian fantasies. With a platform embracing everything from abolition of the wage system to the establishment of cooperative enterprise and social harmony, the Knights promised to shift the task of remaking America away from the elites who controlled the centennial's planning and into the hands of those journalists dubbed the "hoary hands of toil."

This work examines one aspect of why the Knights faltered: internal conflict. The context for conflict and collapse, however, was the same for the Knights as it was for centennial architects and for Edward Bellamy. None could overcome the enormity of challenges facing post–Civil War American society. As America enters the twenty-first century of Bellamy's imagination, utopia remains elusive. Nonetheless, as historians look backward, the musings of *Scribner's* seem the most naive of the three visions. The *Scribner's* editorialist missed the mark widely because he assumed that sectional discord was America's most pressing social problem when, in fact, it was class conflict. Prior to the Civil War, politicians assiduously avoided both chattel slavery and the degradation of free labor dubbed by many of its advocates as "wage slavery." As black abolitionist Frederick Douglass graphically put it, "The difference between the white slave and the black slave is thus: the latter belongs to one slaveholder, and the former belongs to all the slave owners, collectively."[4]

The Civil War rendered black indenturedom moot, but wage slavery remained. As Terence V. Powderly, the general master workman of the KOL from 1879 to 1893 recalled:

> When the Civil War was in progress, if the President of the United States called for troops, the workingmen patriotically responded. If more troops . . .

were necessary, a draft was ordered and more men were taken from the forge, factory, mine, and farm. . . . While the workingmen were enlisting in the service of their country, the bankers and owners of gold were working their way into Congress. . . . These men enacted such legislation as was beneficial to themselves; they diminished the volume of currency and reduced the price of labor and property. . . . Monopolies were born and nourished, and the Congress of the United States gave them millions of acres of the nation's land.

Working-class soldiers mustered out into a world of business speculation, economic instability, and periodic unemployment. In a poignant turn of phrase, Powderly concluded that patriotic workmen "were forced to the conclusion that, while the war for the preservation of the union was over, the battle for the preservation of life itself was still being waged with unrelenting fury."[5]

The period known to historians and contemporaries alike as the "Gilded Age" (roughly 1870–1901) was one of great promise and equally great disappointment and disillusionment. Post-1865 economic expansion was so feverish that by century's end the United States' national wealth was rivaled only by that of Great Britain and Germany. Coal production, which stood at 14 million tons per annum in 1860, increased to 100 million tons per year by 1884. Annual steel production increased eightfold, from 1.25 million tons to 10 million, in the single decade from 1880 to 1890; this greatly accelerated rail expansion. By 1900, the nation was crisscrossed by 193 million miles of railroad track.[6] As the twentieth century dawned, the United States had gone from being a second-rate military and industrial power to a nation in a position of world leadership in the span of thirty years.

That said, the social cost of economic expansion was enormous. As both Bellamy and Powderly observed, the fruits of American prosperity were harvested mostly by elites. Rags-to-riches sagas notwithstanding, a study conducted in the 1870s revealed that 90 percent of America's richest businessmen were born into either upper-class or upper-middle-class families. This fact was conveniently hidden from the public; as historian Howard Zinn notes, dreams of upward mobility were "a useful myth for control."[7]

Dreaming was the only affordable outlet for many Gilded Age workers. A male presser in the garment trades of New York's Lower East Side averaged $9–10 per week in the 1880s, while women earned about $7. The 1870 census estimated that some 700,000 children toiled for under $2 per week, numbers that hardly improved in the early twentieth century, despite child labor laws passed during the Progressive Era. Even with entire families working, many laborers found the meanest comforts of life difficult to obtain. It was estimated that over half a million New Yorkers lived in substandard housing in 1875, with as many as eight people crowded into tenement apartments of under two hundred square feet. As late as 1882, only 2 percent of New York's homes had running water.[8]

Work was as arduous and dangerous as it was unremunerative. Coal mining—dubbed "a disaster-prone industry" by anthropologist Anthony F. C. Wallace—exacted a heavy toll with its industry-standard twelve-hour days. According to Wallace's calculations for four Pennsylvania counties in 1870, one miner died and two more were badly injured for every 49,174 tons of ore exhumed.[9] Railroading was equally deadly. By 1890, accidents claimed the life of one of every 306 workers, while one in thirty was injured.[10]

Moreover, America's overall economic climate was fragile. The Gilded Age gave rise to the modern corporation but also to price- and wage-fixing pools, trusts, holding companies, and both vertical and horizontal monopolies. Coupled with an unsound monetary system resting on a gold standard that made credit expensive and cash scarce, it took little to topple the U.S. economy into recession. Major depressions struck in 1873–74, 1877–78, 1884, and 1893–97, with several short-lived downturns plaguing the intervening years. In 1874 alone, more than six thousand businesses failed. During the 1877 downturn, approximately three million workers were jobless; during the harsh winter of 1893–94, over four million.[11] Even when the overall economy was sound, individual industries engaged in boom-and-bust cycles and others, like meatpacking, were notoriously seasonal. Workers found themselves at the mercy of a system that worked them like draft animals for months on end and left them to fend for themselves when work was slack.

Nor could workers expect succor from their political leaders. As Powderly reminds us, Gilded Age politicians were a self-interested lot. Many were also corrupt. Scandals like the Crédit Mobilier railroad fraud and the Star Route mail scam prompted Mark Twain's barb, "I think I can say with pride, that we have some legislatures that bring higher prices than any in the world."[12] Local and state government was, if anything, worse. New York's infamous Tammany Hall was but the most famous urban political machine selectively doling out spoils from ill-gotten power bases. Rare was the city or state that did not sport the "boss" system wherein political favor was traded for votes and cash. Even more rare was the solon with the political will to place collective interests over individual privilege. When the United States drained its gold reserves in 1895, twenty-six New York banks held more than $129 million worth of bullion; no serious effort was made to divert these reserves to restoring the nation's economic health.[13]

To this sorry social scenario one must add the racism from which

African Americans and other minorities suffered, the sexism that plagued women, and the nativism that dogged new immigrants. Not even the vaunted yeoman farmer of Jeffersonian myth fared well. By the 1880s, more than one-third of the nation's farms were heavily mortgaged, and foreclosures were common. These problems, plus crippling railroad freight rates and high grain-elevator storage costs, placed farmers in a precarious situation. A dip in commodity prices of several cents could spell disaster. For African-American sharecroppers and tenant farmers, it often meant a permanent descent into debt peonage.[14]

Denied the opportunities of and entrance into mainstream political, social, and economic institutions, humbler Americans created their own paths to power. The Gilded Age was a crucible in which the downtrodden attempted to forge new institutions or dramatically recast older ones. The student of social movements has no shortage of nineteenth-century case studies: Grangers and farmers' alliances, suffrage and feminist organizations, civil rights groups, scores of fraternal institutions, Greenback and free silver crusades, single-tax clubs, Bellamyite nationalists, antimonopoly societies, temperance leagues, third-party attempts, and the labor movement.

In fact, the modern labor movement was born in the Gilded Age. To be sure, Gilded Age unions owed much to their antebellum forebears. Nonetheless, it was only in the postwar period that unions truly became centralized mass movements. The trailblazing organization in this regard was the Knights of Labor. The KOL built on foundations provided by the National Labor Union (1866–73) and the ubiquitous labor congresses of the late 1860s and early 1870s. It also borrowed freely from fraternal organizations, fringe labor groups, and decades-old reform agendas. At the time of America's centennial celebration, the seven-year-old Knights of Labor had fewer than 10,000 members; when *Looking Backward* was published in 1888, that number had risen to nearly 260,000. The Knights were in decline by that date, having lost as many as three-quarters of the members it commanded in 1886. By the early 1890s, the KOL was a lean, largely rural organization, and by century's end it was anemic. The KOL officially disbanded in 1917, though a few locals held on until the 1940s.[15]

The rapid rise and slow demise of the KOL has long fascinated historians. In fact, there is something of a teleology concerning the Knights. Derived largely from the criticisms of ex-Knight and first president of the American Federation of Labor (AFL), Samuel Gompers, some critics maintain that the KOL was founded on archaic principles that became increasingly obvious to workers once the modern craft union federation model of the AFL became available. A variant view blames the incompetence of Terence Powderly for the Knights' demise. I have voiced my disagreement with both groups elsewhere, and in this study I wish to suggest a different tack.[16]

This study focuses on leadership—but not leadership per se, though I will raise questions about the nature of authority in the Gilded Age. Instead I wish to give context to the Knights of Labor by treating it as a social movement and its leaders as individuals struggling with problems inherent in most social movements. This book is titled *Knights Unhorsed* because it focuses on leaders who were suspended or expelled from the Order. Like jousting paladins, these erstwhile wielders of power were tumbled from their leadership saddles and left to curse their fate and those who bested them. I see their outcomes as having deeper resonance beyond the portrait they provide of internal nastiness.

Each chapter will focus on specific individuals to reveal some of the inner dynamics of the KOL. Given the overemphasis historians have placed on the figure of Terence Powderly, little is known about the KOL's other national leaders, let alone some of the local and regional power brokers who appear in these pages. In the interest of illuminating some of the KOL's second-tier leadership, I will give brief biographical sketches, but the main goal is to highlight what individuals teach us about issues and struggles within the KOL. To that end, I will focus on why each figure generated supporters and followers and how individual conflicts impacted the Knights institutionally.

One of the things I will highlight is the KOL's organizational complexity. For most of my academic career I have railed against making too many generalizations about the KOL, an enormously labyrinthine, diverse, and interesting organization. For the most part, this work explores levels of power within the Knights and seeks to illuminate the dialectical relationships between those layers. Gilded Age labor leaders seldom operated under the parameters of modern union structures, nor were their concerns restricted to the exigencies of bureaucracy.

The KOL had an organizational flowchart, and the general master workman spent hours each week ruling on procedural matters that were duly printed and distributed. That said, local Knights were adroit at adaptation and selective application of "official" pronouncements. This should not surprise us. As Jonathan Garlock shows, there was scarcely a town or city of consequence that did not sport a KOL local at some point in the late nineteenth century, and there were a substantial number of hamlets and backwaters of little consequence that did the same. In all, the KOL spawned over 12,000 locals between 1869 and 1918.[17]

The KOL was so spread out that local and regional concerns, not its leaders, often determined individual fates. We will encounter men stripped of officially sanctioned authority who continued to assert it on the local level, just as we will see those conferred with power on the national level be denied its application by local and district assemblies. We will also see individuals who were either wisely or foolishly stripped of power by central administration. But even those decisions were subject to local adherence, or lack thereof.

Power was diffused across the KOL and within each level of authority. To some extent, my research validates an underappreciated analysis of the Knights completed by William Birdsall in 1953. Birdsall noted that the KOL's organizational chart created local, district, state, and national trade assemblies that shared power with its national bodies: the general assembly conventions, the general executive board, and the general master workman. Each level of authority had its own bureaucracy staffed with individuals holding administrative, legislative, and judicial powers. This made clashes between levels inevitable when, say, a local court suspended a member and the district reinstated him. Birdsall noted that the KOL was torn between the "brotherhood of man" concept on one hand and "particularism" on the other. Among members, the clash between the two ideals was "not always confined to the highest ideological plane." Further, some KOL assemblies were trade assemblies, while others were "mixed" ones that were often little more than "association[s] of study circles or labor lodges." In all, Birdsall thought, the KOL's structure was "more complicated than it should or needed to be." Left with unclear lines, too many individuals and assemblies were left to "improvise."[18]

Before one can appreciate fully the KOL's complexity or come to grips with the enormity of what the organization tried to accomplish, the first Knight one needs to "unhorse" is Terence Powderly. As Birdsall reminds us, the KOL was far too complex to associate it with single individuals. This study refutes those historians who overemphasize Powderly's authority. Many studies ignore the KOL altogether until Powderly assumed leadership of the Order, and too many others focus on his failings as a leader. Several—including Norman Ware's classic survey—go so far as to blame Powderly for the Order's demise.

The search for what I call the "failure thesis" invariably involves a gaze at Powderly, who has come under fire from nearly every historian who has written about the Knights, myself included.[19] I will sample some of their comments in my final chapter, but I have little quarrel with those who see Powderly as a vain, pigheaded, unyielding, difficult man—hard to like even from the safe distance of an archive one hundred years after his prime deeds. That said, I do not believe that Powderly was the reason the KOL faded. I am equally dubious of the claim that a "Powderly machine" controlled the KOL, much as the ever-vain Powderly might have longed for this to be true. Powderly was usually at the center of KOL disputes, but he was more the lightning rod than the storm. High public visibility made him the pole around which some Knights rallied and from which others fled, but he did not create most of the Order's tensions, many of which were inherent in the KOL's makeup.

I do understand the fixation with Powderly. To employ an anachronistic label, he was labor's first media "superstar." Through the 1880s and into the 1890s his portrait and speeches were found in the mass and labor press alike, and his opinions were sought by journalists, ministers, industrialists, politicians, and educators, as well as by workers and reformers. Powderly's face and name graced everything from chewing tobacco packages and haberdashers' trade cards to an entire town in Alabama. Fathers even named sons in his honor.

But one should not confuse omnipresence with omnipotence. As noted above, the KOL struggled with tensions inherent in its conception. First, it was both a fraternal and a labor organization. The emphasis given to each shifted over time, with each reorientation producing varying degrees of stress among members. A second set of tensions emerges from the principles the Order formalized in its 1878 constitution. That document contains much of the fiery rhetoric one would expect from a document produced less than a year after the cataclysmic railroad strikes of 1877. But practice was often a different matter. On the one hand, the KOL was a defiant organization whose stated purpose was to destroy society as currently constituted; on the other hand, it appealed to existing authority to reform the nation. Like social movements before and after it, the KOL struggled with the competing pulls of revolution versus reform and with maintaining ideological purity versus the lure of tactical and pragmatic compromise. These tensions remained as unresolved as the fraternal/labor split.

These comments point to the major analytical thrust of this study: the Knights of Labor as a social movement. As the nation's largest labor organization at a time when the wage-earning classes were increasing exponentially, the KOL commands special focus. In 1860, there were approximately 5.3 million nonagricultural wage earners; by 1900, there were over 17.4 million. In the two decades before 1900, the nation was wracked by 2,378 strikes involving nearly 6 million workers.[20] Many of these involved the Knights.

I began this introduction with a look at the Gilded Age rather than the KOL because it is important to ground the Order within a specific framework instead of treating it as a discrete entity. The KOL was just one of many movements seeking to address the gross inequities and structural deficiencies of its time. Very few such movements have survived to the present day; some became antiquated, but most no longer exist because it is the nature of social movements to pass away. Sociologists Gary Marx and Douglas McAdam state flatly, "Most social-movement organizations are unsuccessful in institutionalizing their goals."[21]

Theorists argue over why social movements emerge. Some argue in favor of deprivation theories, which postulate that when individuals perceive inequity between what they have and that to which they feel they are entitled, they will mobilize. Mass-society theorists build on the pioneering works of Ferdinand Tönnies and Emile Durkheim to argue that the impersonal nature of industrialized societies creates alienated, anomic individuals who are more likely to seek political and associational redress for perceived ills than are those living in traditional, personal societies. Structural-strain theorists—most of whom cite Neil Smelser's pathbreaking 1962 study—note a complicated six-step process through which movements emerge. Smelser factored in everything from first perception of a problem to the responses of established power to make the point that social movements are most likely to emerge when the structure of a given society is under stress and its ability to respond is weakest. Finally, resource-mobilization theorists argue that no group can hope to succeed unless it has at its disposal the necessary material and human capital.[22]

Historians of the Gilded Age need not be overly concerned with resolving sociological debates; to some degree, all of them apply to the late nineteenth century. Workers both felt and were deprived; they were also alienated, prone to associational action, and increasingly concentrated in anomie-producing industrial cities. To state that Gilded Age society was under stress is to belabor the obvious. Moreover, resource mobilization was a constant struggle for the Knights of Labor and other late nineteenth-century groups.

Theorists draw a distinction between emergent and mature social movements that is crucial to locating the KOL as a social movement. Emergent movements tend to be spontaneous and generate great excitement among early adherents. But they also tend to be vague about membership criteria. Broad principles and high-sounding rhetoric are often the fodder for recruitment campaigns, with mere survival and the building of an operational base the primary aims. By contrast, the mature movement is bigger, more structured, and more concrete in its articulation of goals and regulations. Frequently, mature movements stifle ideologues, are less likely to operate by consensus, and are more likely to compromise principles for pragmatic gain. Battles over organizational direction take place in both phases, but damaging internal conflict is more common among mature movements. The KOL exemplified, at different points in time, one of three types of social movements: revolutionary, resistance, and reform movements. The constitution and principles articulated at the Order's 1878 convention read like a revolutionary manifesto advocating a near-total social, political, and economic makeover of American society. The KOL contained radicals of all sorts, a few of whom committed revolutionary deeds, but for the most part, once it gained a critical membership mass in the early 1880s, it fought for what was later dubbed "pure and simple" unionism: higher wages, fewer working hours, and better workplace conditions. But unlike the AFL, the KOL never fully jettisoned its idealistic goals. Instead, it adopted a take-now/work-for-a-future-utopia approach. In doing so, however, it removed pursuit of utopia from the rank and file and put it in the hands of leaders, lobbyists, and political allies. In that regard, the KOL functioned like a reform movement that sought to amend society through existing legal and political channels.

The KOL went through the normal phases typical of all social movements: emergence, coalescence, bureaucratization, and decline.[23] By the time it fully articulated its structure—that dizzying array of local, district, and state assemblies augmented by a general executive board and national trade districts—it began to look, on paper, like a modern bureaucracy. As we shall see, there was a gap between de jure and de facto authority, with official procedures being violated with great regularity.

My study refutes Norman Ware's thesis that the KOL was "a study in democracy." The KOL's version of democracy often resembled Plato's nightmare, a system of demagoguery and mob rule bordering on anarchy. Depending on the issue and the leaders involved, the rule of law within the Order was ignored with impunity or applied with rigidity approaching anality. Many of the internecine battles are dark walks into what Greg Kealey and Bryan Palmer called the "underside" of the KOL.[24]

But as Marx and McAdam caution, "Social movements are seldom the masters of their own fate. Instead, they must rely on the power, resources, and political support of other groups in society. At the same time, they are also subject to the power, resources, and political clout of groups that oppose them."[25] Social movements can decline for a number of reasons: internal strife, incompetent leadership, dwindling resources, member fatigue, competition from other social movements, a hostile state, repression by power elites, negative public perceptions, encounters with countermovements designed specifically to thwart progress, the co-optation of key leaders (or of the entire organization), and even success. Most of these factored into the KOL's decline, providing still more reasons to unhorse Powderly and gaze more deeply into the organization.

This work takes a look at the internal workings of the Knights of Labor, as refracted through the internal conflicts endured by a Gilded Age social movement. Chapter 1 further destroys the myth of a Powderly machine and recaps problems associated with both ideology and the shift from a fraternal to a labor perspective among key KOL leaders. I reveal a shifting alliance of malcontents, ideologues, and power seekers called the Home Club who wreaked havoc within the Order during a crucial period of its development.

Chapter 2 deals with the disruptive debate over trade unionism through the eyes of Thomas Barry and William Bailey. The "B & B Affair" also highlights battles over broad versus narrow principles as well as those problems inherent in an unwieldy organization in which freelancing leaders in the field struck deals without clearing them through proper channels.

Chapter 3 looks at the man who was perhaps the KOL's most capable leader, Joseph R. Buchanan. He embodied many of the Order's inherent tensions: Buchanan was simultaneously an ideologue, a pragmatic trade unionist, and a utopian, yet he was drummed out of the Knights. His tale underscores the KOL's inability to reconcile its revolutionary, resistance, and reform strands.

In the person of Charles Litchman, in chapter 4 I tackle head on the problems associated with bureaucratizing the Knights. In his case we will see how personality overrode chains of command and how selective application of bureaucratic machinery had the potential to undermine any structure the Order built.

Chapter 5 applies the Litchman dilemma to the local level and raises questions relating to the de facto decentralized nature of the Knights. Henry Sharpe's views on cooperative industry and distribution struck some Knights as so zealous that they used his marital discord as pretext for striking him from the membership rolls. John Brophy's fervent trade unionism made him a prime target for Home Club advocates, while Massachusetts Knight Daniel Hines was chased from the Order because of his invidious personality and bourgeois pretensions. Each case demonstrates the potential for abuse when social movements mature and begin to articulate rigid membership standards.

Chapter 6 highlights a problem to which social theorists have not paid enough attention: sexism. It focuses on Leonora Barry, a victim of sexual harassment, and showcases the KOL's inability to match its actions to its rhetorical stance on gender equality.

My final chapter unhorses Powderly in earnest, through a look at his 1893 ouster from power and his subsequent expulsion. Powderly was done in by the very forces that denied him the "machine" he craved: ideologues, proceduralists, trade unionists, and radicals.

Through all of this the open question is the degree to which internal conflict mattered. In other words, had the Knights of Labor become a model of fraternal bliss, could it have radically transformed American society? I don't think so. For all the many shortcomings in the KOL's structure, its decision-making processes, and its leaders, I believe the KOL was done in by opposition, not primarily by structural and ideological ineptitude. Once again I return to the Gilded Age context in which the Knights emerged, flourished, and foundered. The problems facing that age were so enormous that one should applaud the Order's courage in tackling them rather than belabor its failings. There were many mistakes made, but even had the KOL been a flawless organization filled with competent and altruistic leaders, it would have struggled to overcome the fury of capital's counterassault, the blows delivered by its myriad enemies (including those within labor's own ranks), and from the hostility of the state, courts, and press. The KOL faced forces that were better financed, better organized, institutionally entrenched, and more determined.

Where internal conflict *did* matter lay in the KOL's ability to transform itself. Many social movements never get beyond the emergent stage, but those that manage to mature then face the dilemma of where to turn next. How much bureaucracy is necessary to sustain the organization? What should be done with factionalists? Which principles can safely be compromised and which are essential to the soul and identity of the movement? To what degree should co-optation of goals and leaders be encouraged? What relationships, if any, should be forged with institutionalized power? What is the proper balance between idealism and pragmatism? The Knights of Labor never resolved most of these dilemmas. Like most social movements, the questions were rendered moot when the movement faltered.

I am convinced that the challenges of the age were such that the KOL had little chance of effecting the goals articulated in 1878 and to which the Order paid lip service for its entire existence. Had the KOL been less scathed by the chaotic days from 1885 to 1888 known to historians as the Great Upheaval, it is likely it would have changed to such a degree that the Knights of 1878 would not have recognized those of 1896. As it was, they recognized them far too well. In the latter year, the KOL general assembly voted to return the organization to the oath-bound secrecy rules under which the men of 1878 operated. In my view, it is at this moment that critics who decry the Knights as anachronistic have a point.

Speculating on what never happened is intellectually intriguing but analytically useless. Though it limped into the twentieth century, the Knights of Labor was primarily a Gilded Age social movement. Late in his life, Powderly himself recognized this. He was keenly aware that "young men fresh from college" would try to "apply logic and scientific research" to the study of the KOL and that they would find "motives, ambitions, and intentions that I never dreamed of." He even admitted that he had been "inconsistent," but pleaded that "the only really consistent man I ever saw was an inmate of the asylum for the insane." No matter how the KOL's history was "dissected and vivisected . . . its history was the history of the day in which it moved and did its work."[26] It is with this in mind that I turn to those days.

CHAPTER 1

To Rule or Ruin:
The Revolt of the Home Club

Both contemporary critics and modern scholars who have "dissected and vivisected" the Knights of Labor have noted that Terence Powderly, the Order's general master workman from 1879 to 1893, was a difficult man. He could be petty, crude, and authoritarian. But those who confuse these traits with wielding unlimited power run into a major analytical obstacle: his power seldom went unchallenged and at several junctures it was little more than theoretical.

Discontent with leaders and grumbling among the rank and file are common in most social movements, but the Knights faced more than the usual dose of factional discord. The Order faced numerous splinter groups that claimed to speak for "true Knights." These usually emerged just before or just after a general assembly, and they labeled themselves as "advanced," "improved," or "independent" assemblages of Knights. Most of these came to naught and ended after a few ringleaders were judiciously expelled. The followers were then left in limbo for a suitable period of chastisement and then quietly returned to the fold.[1]

This was not, however, the case with the New York–based Home Club, an ever-shifting group within District Assembly (DA) 49 determined, in the words of its detractors, "to rule or ruin." To some extent, the Club did both. From the time the Club coalesced in 1882 until its final demise in 1889, Powderly was never entirely free from it, and on occasion, it controlled the KOL through him. One of its creations, John W. Hayes, ultimately deposed Powderly and held the dubious distinction of being the last general master workman of the Order.

The Home Club's life span is crucial, as it corresponds to the KOL's most vital period. The KOL was founded in Philadelphia in 1869, and its small membership was confined mostly to the City of Brotherly Love and its immediate environs until the mid-1870s. Much of the pre-1880s membership outside Philadelphia consisted of miners living in isolated areas or workers in small cities like Powderly's hometown, Scranton, Pennsylvania.

It is telling that the KOL's first convention was held in the railroad/ coal town of Reading, Pennsylvania. Although the KOL had a globe as one of its symbols, indicating its intent to organize worldwide, its pre-1880s power base was a triangular slice of Pennsylvania whose outer limits were Philadelphia in the east, Scranton in the north, and Pittsburgh in the west. Of the thirty-three delegates to the Reading convention, only nine came from large cities, two-thirds of them from Philadelphia and Pittsburgh. Only Brooklyn shoemaker Thomas Crowne represented the greater New York City area.[2]

But change was on the way. By 1880, there were eight local assemblies in New York; by 1883, at least seventy-six. Expansion into New York brought the Knights into contact with a million potential working-class recruits. By 1886, New York DA 49's 65,000 members made it second in size only to Massachusetts DA 30, and that body covered most of the commonwealth, whereas DA 49 was a metropolitan entity. Expansion into New York exposed the Order to cosmopolitan ideas and to radical political ideologies that shocked more parochial men like Powderly. In 1887 he complained, "I am sorry that the order ever found a foothold in New York, for no good has ever come from large cities which are prolific in whiskey and crime."[3]

The story of the Home Club's rise and fall is embodied in the careers of four men: Peter J. (P. J.) McGuire, William Horan, Theodore Cuno, and Victor Drury. As ideal types they represent four competing tendencies within the KOL: trade unionism, ritualism, Marxism, and anarchism. How these played out inside DA 49 was, to some extent, a microcosm of what occurred throughout the Order. At its core, the Home Club was Lassallean and anarchist, but its modus operandi was opportunism. As such, it was an ever-shifting alliance that served as a gathering ground for those who opposed KOL leaders or policies.

It is common for social movements to experience tension between radicals and moderates. Men more inclined to temper official rhetoric and principles with pragmatism and strategic compromise led the KOL, while the rank and file often contained ideologues. This is true of most labor organizations, but the KOL had an unusually diverse membership, excluding only bankers, lawyers, gamblers, land speculators, drunkards, and liquor tradesmen from its ranks. Home Club leaders developed fungible methods to attract malcontents to the fold, at least temporarily. Thus, there were usually plenty of recruits Home Club leaders could utilize in its search for power.

Of this chapter's four major players, P. J. McGuire is the most familiar. McGuire is well known to labor historians for his role in cofounding the AFL, but in 1881 he was a young carpenter affiliated with Brooklyn's

Uriah Stephens. Courtesy of the
Catholic University of America.

ultrasecretive Local Assembly (LA) 1562. He had high hopes for the KOL, and early on he gravitated toward New York's Marxist trade unionists. By the mid-1880s, McGuire was at odds with DA 49 leaders over their anti–trade union policies. He was suspended or expelled from the KOL on several occasions before leaving the Order to cast his lot with the AFL.[4]

William Horan was the reason why McGuire's LA 1562 was clandestine. Born in 1849, he worked as an engineer and a brassworker. Like many men of his generation, he developed a passionate love for fraternal societies and belonged to several. He joined the KOL around 1880, when Local 1562 was founded, and he served as its master workman for much of the decade. Although there is no record of his having met KOL founder Uriah Stephens, Horan idolized both Stephens and the ritual he fashioned. Horan quickly mastered the KOL's dense, quasi-masonic ritual embodied in the *Adelphon Kruptos* (*AK*), treated it as a sacred text, and insisted that no one should tamper with it. When the KOL became a public organization on January 1, 1882, and adopted an amended *AK,* Horan refused to accept either change. LA 1562 remained a secrecy-cloaked, ritual-bound assembly, and Horan became the KOL's most vociferous critic of modernizing reforms. He died in November 1889, leaving behind a wife, several children, and nearly a decade's worth of opposition to Powderly's policies. For Horan, the Home Club was the logical abode it never was for McGuire.

Nor did Theodore Cuno find succor there, though he sorely longed to be a power broker among New York City Knights. Cuno accepted Karl Marx's dictum that trade unions were agents of revolutionary change and the building blocks upon which a utopian socialist society would be constructed. This necessitated a mass movement best recruited through open, public organizing, a belief that put him on a collision course with Horan and the ritualists. Cuno was a passionate but humorless man who was easily aroused to anger and prone to rash behavior. Of his dedication to radicalism, however, there can be little doubt. His very radicalism made him a useful pawn for Lassalleans and anarchists seeking to control DA 49.

Of the four men, Victor Drury was the most shadowy and complex. Born in France in 1825, he was already a seasoned radical by the time he came to the United States in 1867, having helped overthrow the government of King Louis Phillipe in 1848. He was a delegate to the 1864 radical gathering in London at which Marx proclaimed the first International Working Peoples' Association (IWPA), and Drury immigrated to New York City for the express purpose of establishing French-speaking sections of the IWPA. That work went slowly; meanwhile he acquired a reputation as an erudite writer. He briefly edited a French-language journal before penning English editorials for *The Socialist*. His 1876 lectures on land, labor, capital, exchange, and insurance were so popular that they were reprinted in book form as *The Polity of Labor*. The *Polity* ranges far and wide, but draws largely from the works of Marx, Charles Fourier, and Arthur Brisbane.[5] It is a sometimes rambling work, but Drury's sharp critiques of social and economic theory established him as New York's leading intellectual, Henry George excepted.

The above sketch suggests that Cuno and Drury should have been fast friends and allies. That was not the case. By 1880, Drury had abandoned his youthful Marxist precepts. He joined New York City's Social Revolutionary Club, befriended anarchist Justus Schwab, and espoused the anarchist cause with vigor. In late 1882, he and Schwab cosponsored famed European anarchist Johann Most's first American speaking tour. The next year, Drury served as the principal author of the Pittsburgh Manifesto, an anarchist screed that advocated using violence to overthrow capitalism.

Drury's conversion led him to reevaluate Marx's views on trade unions. He readily embraced Frederic Lassalle's assertion that only political activity could liberate the masses and came to see all craft unions as exclusionary and their wages/hours/conditions agendas as antithetical to revolutionary change. Moreover, he came to embrace the importance of secrecy, as articulated by theorists like Bakunin and Proudhon.

The latter idea ingratiated Drury to Horan. Both Horan's LA 1562 and Drury's own LA 2234 were typical of many DA 49 locals in that they were "mixed" assemblies that organized across craft lines, although each contained trade unionists. Most city locals were also divided along ideological grounds and, by logic, ought to have self-destructed. This did not happen for several reasons. First, most locals were small; LA 1562, for example, averaged thirty-two members between 1880 and 1885.[6] Such intimacy increased the likelihood of leaders holding together factions by charm, persuasion, and compromise. Second, the ritual of which Horan was so enamored bonded workers in a common activity and reinforced the broader principles upon which the KOL rested. Mystic and psychic connections were forged in practices that took Knights through symbolic birth, death, and rebirth and insisted that all initiates were members of a "Universal Brotherhood." Third, though DA 49 contained many trade unionists, they never constituted a controlling percentage as they did elsewhere. Anecdotal evidence also suggests that many of them took KOL principles seriously and subsumed their craft ideals. Nor should one underestimate the cohesive potential embodied in New Yorkers' mutual distaste for Terence Powderly. The city was a fertile ground for radicals of all stripes, and Powderly's moderate views often appeared reactionary to such individuals.

There is, finally, the structure of DA 49 itself and the manner in which Drury was able to exploit it. In theory, KOL district assemblies were little more than coordinating bodies charged with disseminating decisions made at annual conventions or planning district-wide events pertinent to all Knights. In an area as concentrated geographically as New York, however, locals were small and diverse, and district assemblies functioned as de facto executive boards. Because DA 49 was one such district, Drury was able to orchestrate opposition to central leadership and develop methods to advance that opposition beyond the city. Moreover, Drury's tactical use of secrecy insulated him from close scrutiny and facilitated his scheming. To that end, Drury avoided holding formal offices within DA 49, preferring to be the power behind pliable men like James Quinn and Thomas McGuire. He occasionally gave fiery speeches at public rallies but, for the most part, Drury's public popularity was established by his widely read *Polity of Labor.*

A key to Drury's proselytizing efforts were his "Spread the Light" clubs, a term en vogue among Irish Land League nationalists. To Drury, however, "Spread the Light" meant to hold the Order accountable for its rhetorical emphasis on educating the masses. He and Horan established Spread the Light clubs across the metropolitan area. Each was essentially a debate, discussion, and lecture series on political economy using Drury's *Polity* as the primary text. Several local assemblies, as well as a few Social Revolutionary clubs, began life as Spread the Light classes. At first the clubs were confined to greater New York City, but Horan and Quinn soon advanced them beyond the metropolitan area.

Victor Drury. Courtesy of the Schlesinger
Library, Radcliffe College.

Ironically, Theodore Cuno paved the way for the Druryites by engen-
dering a controversy that made the latter seem voices of reason. When DA
49 was formally chartered on July 1, 1882, New York Knights were embroiled in a controversy of Cuno's making. Cuno was the KOL's grand
statistician, a post that gave him easy access to the executive board. In
April 1882, Cuno convinced Grand Secretary Robert Layton to issue a
boycott of the Duryea Starch Company of Glen Cove, New York, alleging
that the company was dismissing KOL members and that pressure from
Duryea cost him his job with the German-language journal *Staats-Zeitung*.

By calling a boycott, Layton invoked the KOL's harshest sanction
against an employer, given that the Order was opposed to strikes. There
were, as yet, no labor laws forbidding secondary boycotts, and the action
against Duryea proved a major irritant to the company when retailers complained of a falloff in trade. When Duryea threatened to sue the Knights in
July, it was the first time Powderly had heard of the matter. He promptly
contacted co-owner John Duryea, who invited an investigation and pledged
to pay a thousand-dollar penalty for each of Cuno's allegations verified by
independent investigators. Subsequent inquiry led the KOL executive
board to call off the Duryea boycott.

Another Cuno action sealed his fate. After losing his job at *Staats-
Zeitung,* Cuno was down on his financial luck. He earned seventy-five dollars from the *New York Herald* for an anonymous piece titled "The Knights
of Labor: American Workingmen United for Self-Protection," a thumbnail

sketch of the KOL's evolution from oath-bound secrecy to its current public posture. The article created a stir within the Order for three reasons. First, Cuno aired some of the KOL's inner tensions over opposition to abandoning secrecy. Second, he quoted bits of the *Adelphon Kruptos,* a work that was still unavailable to non-Knights. Finally, he printed an ironic out-of-context Powderly remark in which Powderly appeared to advocate that workers should use rifles and Gatling guns against their enemies.[7]

Powderly took Cuno to task and told him that many members were demanding that "the traitor who exposed the secret work be . . . expelled." To Layton, Powderly referred to Cuno as "the most malicious man in the Order"; to Gilbert Rockwood he added, "I feel sometimes like bouncing the whole socialistic element out of the Order." That comment stirred New York Knight Phillip Van Patten, who was also president of the moderate Socialist Labor Party, and he, too, demanded Cuno's head. When an investigation revealed that Cuno's dispute against Duryea was personal, Powderly called off the boycott and suspended Cuno pending an expulsion hearing at the September grand assembly.[8]

The matter might have died there except that LA 1562 threw its support behind Cuno. In August, it issued unauthorized circulars urging continuation of the Duryea boycott and charging the KOL executive board with suspending Cuno without due process. This placed the entire local beyond the pale, but newly chartered DA 49 unexpectedly supported the local and even helped distribute its circulars. Horan, unaware that Cuno was the author of the *New York Herald* article, leaped to Cuno's defense, as did LA 1562 colleagues P. J. McGuire, William Cowen, and John Caville. As the local's master workman, Horan simply refused to recognize Cuno's suspension. For his part, Drury saw the entire matter as a golden opportunity to smear Powderly at the upcoming convention.

That gathering was a donnybrook. Horan reintroduced the previous year's resolution—put forth by Cuno—that the KOL abandon its public mission and return to oath-bound secrecy. The proposal failed, but it was resurrected in slightly altered form twice more, once by DA 49 Master Workman James Quinn and again by Baltimore's John Elliott, both of whom were staunch Drury allies. When all else failed, Horan proposed that the word "grand" be stricken from all KOL business and be replaced with "general." He intended this as a caustic gesture, but the convention complied after being swayed by Horan's satirical remarks that the term "grand" denoted imperial power.

The newly christened "general" assembly next took up the Duryea matter. On the surface, it was a Powderly rout. Cuno's authorship of the *Herald* article was revealed, and he was expelled from the Knights. Caville, the KOL's auditor, was expelled for issuing an unauthorized circular and, along with P. J. McGuire, Cuno, and three others, was "forever debarred" from the KOL. LA 1562's charter was revoked and DA 49 was directed "to hold no intercourse" with any remaining members until such time as they were transferred to another local.[9]

All of this was easier said than done. Although Cuno was vilified, he nonetheless touched a raw nerve when he accused KOL leaders of an anti–New York bias. Noting that all of New York state had but three organizers while Philadelphia and Pittsburgh had eight each, he railed against "bum politicians" who wanted to keep the KOL "concentrated in Pennsylvania." He defied his expulsion and proclaimed, "I shall organize as many locals without a commission as I did with one," and called Powderly a "miserable hypocrite," a "skunk," and the leader of a "lying, sneaking gang of scoundrels."[10]

Even those outraged by Cuno's breach of secrecy agreed that the Order was overly controlled by Pennsylvanians. Horan went to the Midwest and Canada in search of support, where he set up several Spread the Light clubs. More disturbing, LA 1562's expulsion was ignored by DA 49. Van Patten warned Powderly of the "likelihood that the whole Order in this neighborhood will separate from the rest of the Order" unless the executive board acted decisively. Van Patten's warnings seemed warranted when, in January 1883, both Cuno and Caville served as delegates at DA 49's convention, the latter being elected recording secretary. All spring he communicated with the executive board on DA 49's behalf, as if nothing were out of the ordinary.[11]

Drury skillfully exploited the Cuno affair to unite dissident Knights. By the end of 1882, an inner coterie known as the Home Club took over DA 49's decision-making processes. The Club began with nine members over whom Drury presided, the most important being Edward Kunze, Thomas McGuire, James Quinn, and Timothy Quinn. Officially, these nine were the first Spread the Light educational club. In truth, it was the base for what Drury dubbed "concentric circles," though they were actually interlocking groups in which an individual from each nine-member study group also belonged to another circle. In effect, each member was also a recruiter and reporter through whom Drury could scrutinize other groups. These interlocking circles formed the structure—such as it was—of the Home Club.

The Club was not a cabal as current-day conspiracy theorists understand the term, but a core of mostly Lassalleans and anarchists for whom Drury was an intellectual role model and for whom opposition to Powderly and other moderate leaders was a cause célèbre. The foot soldiers for Home Club schemes came and went, with the group attracting administration dissidents like a lightning rod attracts electricity.

One of the Home Club's earliest recruits was Horan, and some of its earliest victims were Marxists. Cuno's betrayal of his oath made Horan suspicious of Marxists, and Drury massaged those fears. He also took advantage of mainstream fears of socialism, all the while clandestinely championing anarchism. J. Mulhane, a Brooklyn Knight, warned Powderly that "this cry about socialism in the labor ranks is being used now as effectively as the 'rebel yell' was used in Democratic and Republican politics." He suggested that Powderly stop the infighting and refocus the Order's attention on its capitalist enemies.[12]

Powderly ignored Mulhane's sage advice and embarked on a course that ultimately weakened him. In February 1883, Powderly suspended DA 49. By then, however, New York had more than seventy locals, most of whose members thought more of Drury than they did of Powderly. The general master workman's pronouncements had little effect on day-to-day affairs in New York. Powderly recognized R. H. Cook as the district master workman of what the administration saw as the "official" DA 49, but most New York Knights ignored it and Cook. The old 49, headed by James Quinn, continued to meet and send correspondence to the Order's general secretary. When the Home Club grew bored with the Cook faction, it simply deposed it. Cook showed up to preside over a meeting on May 1, 1883, only to find Quinn seated in his chair and a host of burly men advising him to leave the hall.[13] Shortly thereafter, in an obvious act of defiance, Caville requested organizer credentials for three suspended members of the Home Club, including Tom McGuire.[14]

As in 1882, the 1883 general assembly was dominated by New York affairs. The convention upheld Powderly's decision to revoke DA 49's charter, but it shied away from harsh punitive action. Rather than disband 49, the assembly ordered a "reorganization," with locals temporarily attached to the general executive board. Further, Local 1562 was reinstated, and all six of those "forever debarred" one year earlier were readmitted to the Knights. Delegates realized that New York was too important to alienate, especially given that total KOL membership actually declined the first year it operated as a public order, and nearly 10 percent of the entire membership resided within DA 49's sphere of influence. Moreover, it was all that modernization advocates could do to ward off renewed attempts to return the Order to secrecy. To clamp down too hard on New York would run the risk of splitting the Knights.[15] By early 1884, Cuno, Horan, and P. J. McGuire were officially Knights once more. DA 49's "reorganization" was laughable, its major feature being the removal of Drury ally James Quinn as district master workman in favor of Drury ally Tom McGuire. All the locals attached to the executive board were reassigned to DA 49, including several from Brooklyn who opposed Drury and wanted to form their own district. The wily Drury continued to expand his interlocking circles and soon commanded over four thousand members. He also cultivated Horan's support. One DA 49 correspondent boasted to the *Journal of United Labor,* "The names of D.A. officers have not . . . been obtained by the venal press, so as yet none have been victimized, which shows the advantage of our secrecy." This was no idle brag; when a New York writer requested information on how to join the KOL, *John Swinton's Paper* admitted ignorance and advised that the city's Knights "maintain a degree of secrecy unknown . . . in any other part of the country."[16]

Drury's grip over DA 49 affairs allowed him to dispense with ideological foes whose services were no longer required. This made Cuno and P. J. McGuire marked men. Cuno was easy. As a Marxist among Lassalleans and anarchists, he had precious few soul mates. Ritualists despised him, with Horan feeling personally betrayed after having defended Cuno at the 1882 general assembly. Cuno remained on the fringes of LA 1562, where he complained of being excluded from the Home Club. Soon he was so distanced from fellow Knights that he was reduced to the humiliation of seeking a job reference from Powderly. Given the general master workman's thin skin and keen memory, there was little chance of Powderly's aid. The volatile Cuno responded to the slight with a new round of insults that further isolated him, and he remained marginalized until both Powderly and the Home Club waned.[17]

The situation of P. J. McGuire was a different matter altogether. In 1881, he cofounded the Brotherhood of Carpenters and Joiners (BCJ). He joined KOL Local 1562 in late 1881, when he moved the BCJ headquarters from St. Louis to New York. He spent much of the time he was under suspension from the KOL in advancing the BCJ. As it expanded, the upstart union got into jurisdictional disputes with KOL carpenters. Moreover, McGuire angered the Order's more idealistic members when he voiced public skepticism over KOL cooperative production plans.[18] To top it off, he alienated Socialist Labor Party (SLP) boss Phillip Van Patten, although he himself was a lifelong socialist and a card-carrying SLP member. The infuriated Van Patten began to blame McGuire, not Cuno, for the Duryea debacle. He even accused McGuire of holding "fraudulent" KOL membership in New York, as he was under suspension in St. Louis.[19]

While McGuire pondered the usefulness of the KOL for trade unionists like himself, Drury advanced the notion that the trades were enemies to class solidarity. This put Drury on a collision course not only with McGuire, but also with a young KOL cigarmaker named Samuel Gompers. Though the Duryea boycott and secrecy disputes consumed the energies of convention delegates from 1881 to 1883, it was a minor squabble among New York City cigarmakers that ultimately proved more important.

In 1880, a group of Lassallean socialists led by Samuel Schimkowitz grew disenchanted with the Cigarmakers International Union (CMIU), a body founded in 1875 by Gompers, Adolph Strasser, and Ferdinand Laurrell. When the Schimkowitz faction failed to abide by CMIU directives, it was expelled from the CMIU. But in the complicated world of overlapping Gilded Age labor organizations, things were seldom resolved this simply. Both Gompers and Schimkowitz were also Knights of Labor as, in theory, were all CMIU members. Both groups appealed to the KOL executive board for support. The issue lay unresolved into 1882, the year DA 49 was chartered.

In the interim, Lassalleans outflanked competing socialist groups among Knights who formed DA 49. In addition, Drury was furious with Gompers and P. J. McGuire for their 1881 roles in establishing the Federation of Organized Trade and Labor Unions (FOTLU). In Drury's eyes, FOTLU's embrace of the particularist precepts of craft unionism imperiled the universal emancipation of labor. Strasser and Gompers demanded that DA 49 expel Schimkowitz, only to face questions about their own commitment to class solidarity. Instead, the district sided with Schimkowitz. By 1883, most of the CMIU rebels were reorganized in the Progressive Cigar Makers' Union (PCMU), which was simultaneously chartered as KOL Local Assembly 2458. From 1883 on, the CMIU and PCMU battled for the hearts, minds, and membership fees of New York City cigarmakers. Their struggles framed a looming battle between the KOL and trade unionism. In 1886, when the Home Club reached its pinnacle of power, the KOL general assembly was persuaded to both expel all remaining CMIU members and to demand that all Knights quit either the Order or their international trade unions. By then, both McGuire and Gompers were working to supplant the KOL, not reform it.[20]

Despite the long-term ill effects of the clampdown on Cuno, McGuire, Gompers, and trade unionism, in the short run it provided the Home Club with the opportunity to influence KOL policy. By 1884, all the ingredients of the Home Club agenda were in place: secrecy, opposition to Powderly, education and recruitment of new members, ideological commitment to anarchism, and anti–trade unionism. Further, Drury's views and methods were spreading. Dyer Lum—a Spread the Light advocate—told Detroit's Joseph Labadie, "It is our duty to take hold of our Locals and D.A.—organize schools, etc. . . . We have permitted locals to be organized without instruction as to the economic lessons contained in the great seal [of Knighthood] and symbols. . . . Go back to the old style of the order. . . . Organize classes to study the 'polity.' "[21]

By mid-summer, executive board member John McClelland warned

Powderly that DA 49 was gaining in strength and would likely try to embarrass Powderly by forcing him to demonstrate his knowledge of KOL ritual. McClelland told Powderly to "brush up on your mummery," and joked, "Bless your heart, you haven't the *solution to the labor problem. . . .* Drury has it and I believe that the shimmering iridescence of the effulgence of his mystical erudition has played fanciful flashes on the imaginations of the wise men of 49 to such an extent that they actually believe *they* have it."[22]

McClelland poked fun, but Drury remained keenly aware of the potency of ritualist sentiment within the Order. DA 49 sent ten delegates to the 1884 general assembly, including Drury, Caville, Horan, Tom McGuire, and James Quinn. Once again they introduced resolutions to return the KOL to secrecy, as well as ones that would forbid the wearing of KOL badges and dismantle the *Journal of United Labor.*[23] When all three failed, Drury quietly retreated to the recruitment field. He did his work so tactfully that the 1885 convention was comparatively calm. It was, however, the lull before the storm.

By late 1885, Drury's "concentric rings" included several executive board members and recruits across Michigan, New York, Ohio, Ontario, and Virginia.[24] General Secretary-Treasurer Frederick Turner left no doubt where his sympathies lay; in 1885, he published Drury's *Polity of Labor,* thereby exposing a new generation of workers to his ideas. Throughout 1885, the Home Club slowly gathered strength, waiting for the proper moment to strike. That came in the fall, when the KOL won an unexpected and dramatic strike against the Southwest Railway conglomerate. That system was owned by Jay Gould, infamous for his remark that he could hire one half of the working class to "kill the other half," one of capital's grossest (if most honest) public pronouncements about labor.

Victory over such a foe led many workers to embrace the Knights as the long-awaited labor messiah, with new members pouring into the Order at an astonishing rate. By early 1886, the executive board was so swamped with requests for new assemblies that it declared a forty-day moratorium on new charters, just so it could process existing paperwork. Officially, the KOL had nearly 730,000 members, but it may have had as many as a quarter million others claiming KOL affiliation and meeting without benefit of charter. Most new converts were unfamiliar with KOL principles, and many were unaware that the Order was opposed to strikes and sanctioned few of them. Neither Drury nor his Home Club allies did much to disabuse workers seeking action. The Lassallean and anarchist core of the Club was at odds with KOL's antistrike policy and hoped to change it as soon as possible.

Ominously for Powderly, New York DA 49 swelled to over 65,000 members. The Home Club used the pretext of uncontrolled growth to push for a special convention to address the Order's logistical problems. In June 1886, a KOL "special assembly" elected six "auxiliary" executive board members to facilitate the Order's bureaucracy. Four of them were Home Club sympathizers. Given that four existing general executive board members were Home Club partisans, Drury's allies now controlled eight of the KOL's top fourteen administrative posts.[25]

It was enough to give the Home Club control of KOL bureaucracy but not to dispense with Powderly without a ruinous internal fight. Drury doubtless reasoned that he had checked Powderly's real power and could bide his time. He may also have felt he could force Powderly to cooperate with the Home Club as a way to hold on to his master workman position. The more immediate goal was to consolidate the Club's power, integrate new members into an Order that bore a Home Club imprimatur, and begin the process of transforming the KOL into a radical, activist labor organization.

The first step was to exonerate the Home Club and quash vicious rumors about its activities, including an absurd charge that it had tried to assassinate Powderly. The Home Club was investigated at both the special assembly and the fall general assembly. Predictably, both reports were whitewashes of the Club. Placed in the position of either cooperating in the cover-up of the Home Club or resigning his post, Powderly chose the former course.[26] He denied any knowledge of a Home Club power clique and told an investigating committee that so far as he knew, its "purpose was to create a fund to build a home for aged members." Powderly even went so far as to blame all Home Club rumors on "enemies of the labor movement."[27]

Drury could not have written Powderly's script better himself, but he soon got a taste of the problems involved in trying to run an organization as unwieldy as the Knights, let alone integrate the hordes of new members whose knowledge of the Order was minimal. One New York local complained that an organizer initiated several new Knights because "his boss ordered him to" and that he had performed the Order's secret rites "in a room behind a saloon." It was also alleged that eight women were initiated against their will and that they "publicly gave away the signs and passwords." A group of Brooklyn sawyers charged that Caville showed up four hours late to instruct their new assembly and "only" taught them about the ritual. Obviously, these new Knights had little idea of the centrality of ritual in KOL assembly life.[28]

Nor was the Drury clique successful in keeping its affairs out of public view once it was in power. Prior to 1886, DA 49 affairs and leaders were seldom mentioned in either the public or the labor press; by mid-1886, they were often the focal point of both. Whereas Home Club leaders once donned pseudonyms, their names were printed freely after 1886, and even the occasional profile of Victor Drury made the rounds. Both the *New York Times* and the *Chicago Tribune* printed news of the Home Club, while KOL editors in Boston, Denver, Detroit, and Philadelphia railed against Club machinations.[29] Notoriety, of course, was the last thing that Horan-led ritualists wanted. The Home Club no sooner grabbed power than it found its ritualist alliance unraveling.

Despite a shaky start, the Home Club regrouped in time for the 1886 general assembly, held in Richmond, Virginia, the home of Club sympathizer William Mullen. As previously noted, it was here that DA 49 exacted its revenge on Gompers, Strasser, and the CMIU. General assembly actions in effect abrogated a "peace treaty" between the Knights and trade unions hammered out at the June special assembly. A principal architect of that deal was P. J. McGuire, and the Richmond convention drove McGuire into vocal opposition against the Knights.

The Home Club favored disbanding all KOL trade assemblies in favor of mixed assemblies in which workers of all crafts would meet in class solidarity. To do so overtly would have been folly, however, as the KOL contained more trade than mixed locals, even within New York City. Instead, the general assembly was given over to speeches and discussion of how the KOL was superior to trade unions. With the rhetorical high ground seized, the convention then promoted an expansion of National Trade Districts (NTDs).

NTDs had been in place since 1879, but until 1884, they were largely confined to glassworkers, telegraphers, and trunk makers. KOL National Trade Districts differed from arrangements between constituent trades and the soon-to-be-born AFL in several important ways. First, NTDs were theoretically subject to the general executive board and the general assembly and thus did not enjoy total trade autonomy. Second, members could belong to an NTD even though their KOL local might be a mixed assembly. Third, NTDs could not depend on KOL sanction or support for strikes and boycotts. Finally, in most matters, NTD decision-making authority could be overruled on the district level and, in some cases, also by local assemblies.

The Home Club's attempted dodge of the trade union question fooled few. Complaints of general assembly actions resonated in Boston, Detroit, and Philadelphia—where the KOL had a heavy trade assembly presence—while the convention was still in session, and more criticism was on the way. Forced to choose between a pragmatic loyalty to their trades and an idealistic commitment to class solidarity, thousands of Knights chose the former. In December, Gompers and Strasser coaxed the AFL to life. They found immediate recruitment success among disenchanted KOL craftsmen.

The depth of Home Club miscalculations concerning trade unions was not yet apparent, however, and it scored a public relations triumph in the area of racial equality. One of DA 49's delegates to the Richmond assembly was Frank Ferrell, an African American. When the segregated hotel booked for DA 49 delegates refused to house Ferrell, his New York comrades marched out en masse and camped in tents until taken in by KOL families associated with the city's all-black DA 92. Tensions elevated when the convention's keynote speaker, Virginia governor Fitzhugh Lee, learned he was to be introduced by Ferrell and refused to take the stage. A quick compromise was hammered out in which Ferrell introduced Powderly, who then turned things over to Governor Lee. But the governor had to first squirm in his seat while Powderly delivered an impassioned speech on the KOL's commitment to racial justice for African Americans.

Neither Drury nor his Home Club allies were content to let the Old Confederacy off that easily. While the convention was still in session, DA 49 delegates decided to attend a local stage performance of *Hamlet*. Ferrell accompanied his colleagues, and the entire assemblage sat in the previously segregated orchestra section of the theater. All of this made Drury and his associates heroes within Richmond's black community. It threw a banquet in their honor at which Drury gave a speech comparing the European revolutions of 1848 to DA 49's struggles for racial equality.[30]

On the heels of the convention, DA 49 embarked on an experiment in equality that went beyond what it attempted in Richmond: Drury authorized Timothy Quinn to organize New York City's Chinese workers. Anti-Chinese sentiment was a given for millions of Gilded Age workers, especially those west of the Rocky Mountains. Ministers, politicians, pseudo-scientists, moralists, and labor leaders alike tended to conform to a Victorian hierarchical view that ranked the Chinese below all other "races." KOL District 49 extended the Order's commitment to black equality to the Chinese. By mid-1887, it claimed to have brought five hundred Chinese into the Knights, with Quinn being assisted in his work by none other than Frank Ferrell. When western Knights complained that these assemblies violated the Order's Chinese exclusion policy, Drury and Quinn simply transferred the two Chinese assemblies—dubbed the Patrick Henry Club and the Victor Hugo Labor Club—into mixed assemblies and argued there was no constitutional provision forbidding this. Powderly, though himself an anti-Chinese xenophobe, was forced to agree.[31]

In retrospect, the Home Club pushed too hard. It was never a "club" as such but more of a loose assemblage of diverse ideas and individuals whose mutual distrust of central leadership gave it a cohesion it otherwise would have lacked. William Mullen, for example, distrusted Powderly, but he was a trade unionist and a white Southerner. Provocative acts like forced desegregation, the expulsion of the cigarmakers, and the organization of Chinese assemblies were bound to produce a backlash, and any notoriety made the ritualists nervous. Drury had little time to savor his lionization in Richmond. By 1887, the Home Club was besieged by enemies from within and without the KOL.

American radicals were deeply divided, despite their mutual goal of dismantling capitalism. Powderly complained bitterly of Home Club policies; if he had not foolishly refused to endorse a clemency plea for the eight men condemned for the May 4, 1886, bombing in Chicago's Haymarket Square, he would have found willing radical allies for his fight against the Home Club. Instead, his condemnation of anarchism was so broad it made radicals of all persuasions nervous. Thus, self-professed anarchists who were also opposed to the Home Club—such as Joseph Buchanan, Burnette Haskell, and Joseph Labadie—divided their energies against both the Drury faction and the Powderly-led alternative. Nonetheless, anti–Home Club attacks from fellow radicals relaxed the group's grip on the KOL.

Joseph Buchanan declared himself "an indefatigable fighter against rings and conspiracies" and vowed to oppose the Home Club until it was broken "or I am dead." He lambasted the group as "union haters" and urged Knights across the country simply to ignore the general assembly's directive on cigarmakers. He bragged that in his own Denver DA 82, "not one man was forced out of the order . . . and not one gave up his union."[32] In Detroit, Labadie published similar attacks, and he singled out Drury to blame for the Home Club's ruinous policies. There, as in New England, Philadelphia, Milwaukee, and elsewhere, the general assembly's order concerning the CMIU was reinterpreted as applicable only in New York.[33]

The Home Club was able to dispatch critics like Buchanan, and it might have endured criticisms leveled against it had it been able to deliver more successes akin to the 1885 victory over Jay Gould. Lost strikes, however, reversed Home Club fortunes. New members gained in the wake of the Southwest Railway strike expected to march behind KOL banners, not find solace in ritual. Their militancy was consonant with Home Club ideology, but not its ability to deliver. The new executive board dutifully authorized scores of strikes from 1886 through 1888, most of which were dismal failures. As a portent of what was to come, the KOL's greatest triumph quickly became a disaster. In the spring of 1886, workers on Gould's railroads struck again, charging that Gould reneged on 1885 agreements. This time, Gould crushed them and most of the gains from the previous fall vanished. This was followed by lost strikes in the Chicago stockyards, in New England textile and shoe mills, and along the rails and in the mines controlled by the Reading Railroad. These setbacks emboldened critics of KOL trade-union policies. By 1887, thousands of craft workers were deserting the Knights.

The Home Club also witnessed defections within metropolitan New York. City telegraphers who had quit the KOL after losing a strike against Western Union in 1883 rejoined in 1886 as DA 45. Just as abruptly, they turned against the Order in 1887, partly over a perceived lack of commitment on the KOL's behalf to support the telegraphers' experiments with industrial unionism.[34]

A more serious defection came from Brooklyn, where none other than LA 1562 initiated matters. In February 1887, Matthew Maguire, a former Drury protégé, petitioned the general executive board to form a new district assembly in Brooklyn. In the interim, he requested that LA 1562 be decoupled from DA 49 and attached to the executive board. As in all matters pertaining to LA 1562, exact motives are shrouded, but discontent seems to have arisen from a combination of feeling that Brooklyn concerns were being ignored and dissatisfaction with the erosion of secrecy and ritual within DA 49.

Others assemblies followed 1562's lead. By April, eight breakaway locals combined to declare the formation of Montauk Assembly. In defiance of DA 49, one of Montauk's first actions was to support John Morrison, leader of NTD 126 and a sworn enemy of the Home Club. At the time, NTD 126 was on the cusp of settling a bitter strike against several carpet manufacturers. In May, the executive board declared Montauk an illegal assembly and, in June, the board expelled Morrison and NTD 126, then imposed a settlement it had forged with the carpet firms. Seventeen locals and some ten thousand workers were slated for "reorganization" and placed under DA 49's jurisdiction. But it was a hollow victory for the Home Club. When the board's contract with manufacturers gained less than Morrison had previously negotiated, droves of workers quit the Order. Those Montauk Assembly workers who remained in the KOL simply refused to submit to DA 49.[35]

Montauk Assembly was rife with ex–Home Clubbers who knew how to forge alliances and how to embarrass their former leaders. At a benefit for striking coal miners, twenty rebels interrupted a theater performance by marching single file into the theater and sitting in a box directly opposite the Home Club leaders who had sponsored the event. Each sported a silk top hat, a provocative act understood by most laborers to represent the "labor fakir," an opportunist whose alleged commitment to labor was a ruse for self-aggrandizement. Moreover, three of the protesters—William Martin, George Murray, and Ralph Robb—were former Home Club power brokers who withdrew from the Club because of its opposition to trade unions. To underscore that point, also present were members of New York DA 64, which was committed to trade unionism, and both John Morrison and George McNeill. The latter's presence was calculated to attract notice. In addition to being perhaps the most universally admired man in the Order, McNeill—who represented Massachusetts DA 30—was also its staunchest defender of trade unionism.[36]

Drury realized the Club was in trouble and attempted a deflecting subterfuge. In June 1887, he dissolved the Home Club—or so it appeared. In truth, he reorganized a loyal rump as "The Class" and began anew the concentric circles recruitment process. No key Home Club leaders were purged. From the beginning, however, Drury's plans went awry. Some New Yorkers even demanded Drury's ouster, something not even Thomas McGuire, in the midst of shifting toward Powderly, could stomach. The Class was so unsettled that for a brief moment in July, a coup led by George Murray and George Dunne toppled DA 49's executive board and placed eight tradesmen on its nine-member panel. A countercoup dislodged them two weeks later, but factional posturing and positioning consumed the rest of DA 49's summer.[37]

It was Powderly himself who saved the Home Club in 1887. When self-described DA 49 "kickers" tried to suspend Drury, McGuire, and Quinn, Powderly reinstated all three and cut a deal that left the old guard with remnants of its power. Powderly's seemingly incomprehensible actions become more clear in letters exchanged with Thomas O'Reilly. The rebels were not only anti–Home Club, they were also anti-Powderly. By choosing to cooperate with the conspirators for over a year—no matter what his hidden motives were—Powderly was subject to innuendo that Murray and Dunne clamored to unleash. Further, Morrison's presence among the kickers was problematic since Powderly had personally ordered his expulsion and loathed him. Powderly attempted to appease both groups, hoping that neither could risk scapegoating him to further its cause. He feigned loyalty to each, then played one side against the other. When DA 49 elected an anti–Home Club faction to the 1887 general assembly, Powderly exchanged a series of jocular letters with several delegates in which he humorously referred to "The Homeless Club" and forcefully denounced the Druryites.[38]

But he also maintained good relations with the pliable Tom McGuire, and apparently cut some sort of compromise with Murray and Dunne, as neither man pounced on charges from those claiming the general master workman had coddled the Home Club. If anything, the convention came out better than Drury could have hoped. His nemesis, Joe Buchanan, was refused a seat and his two shrillest defenders, William Bailey and Thomas

Barry, were shouted down and suspended shortly thereafter. Still, Powderly temporarily shook loose from the Home Club. The 1886 expulsion order of CMIU members was rescinded, anti–trade unionism was repudiated, and Powderly's call for a peace conference between unions and the KOL was applauded.[39]

But the damage was not easily undone. Within days of the convention's close, disgruntled Knights supporting Buchanan and Morrison rallied to a splinter group known as the Provisional Committee of the KOL. The committee continued to tar Powderly with an anti–trade union brush, while Buchanan charged him with "moral cowardice" for continuing to support the "crumbling cause of his crooked pals."[40] Everyone understood this to mean the Home Club, and George Murray's presence among the Provisionals left little doubt of it, his silence at the general assembly notwithstanding. Powderly struck back by countermanding Murray's renewed suspensions of Quinn and Drury. He even stooped to authorizing John Hayes to purloin documents from Murray that could be used to control him. By August 1888, the Home Club had revived enough within DA 49 to block substantive reform efforts from the Murray faction.[41]

Powderly got precious little out of saving Quinn and Drury. At the 1888 general assembly, each supported resolutions to return the Knights to secrecy, to adopt a simplified *AK,* and to sanction the chartering of Chinese assemblies. Although each proposal failed, fully one-third of the delegates supported each, an indication that the Home Club's grip was weakened though its reach remained long. Powderly finally moved against the Club at the convention and a pro-administration board, purged of most Home Club sympathizers, was elected. The convention also downgraded the suspensions of Bailey and Barry to expulsions, thereby ridding Powderly of two potential embarrassments who could reveal his previous cooperation with the Home Club.[42]

The Home Club was down, but not yet out. In 1889, Drury and Horan resurfaced in the Founders' Order of the KOL, a splinter organization pledged to oath-bound secrecy and opposed to recent reforms. Although never powerful, the cachet of having endorsements from four of the KOL's surviving cofounders—Robert Keen, Joseph Kennedy, Robert McCauley, and James L. Wright—gave the renegades prestige. Powderly was worried enough to authorize the use of treasury funds to pay spies to apprise him of Drury's and Horan's movements. By mid-summer, however, the Founders' Order was little more than a paper tiger. When McCauley withdrew his support, Horan died, and Thomas McGuire pledged allegiance to Powderly, the group fell apart. In the aftermath, Quinn and Drury were expelled from the Knights and Powderly was at last free of the Home Club.[43]

But the price was high. The Founders' Order siphoned members the rapidly declining KOL could ill afford to lose. Moreover, the internecine battles crippled the KOL's presence in New York, the nation's largest industrial city. Within DA 49, Drury was out and George Murray was the man of the hour, but his triumph was Pyrrhic and short-lived. Murray was unable to stem DA 49's erosion. In August 1889, DA 49's Pythagoras Hall and its contents were sold at auction. Murray penned a rosy "D. A. 49 Again on Top" article for an 1890 *Journal of the Knights of Labor,* and h led a parade that laid a conciliatory wreath on William Horan's grave, bu the erosion continued.[44]

After the KOL lost a strike against the New York Central Railroad 1890, the task of rebuilding DA 40 fell to a rising star, Daniel DeLeon climb to power closed the circle of DA 49's history as he brought wit an ever-deepening commitment to Marxism, and his cadre quietly remaining Lassalleans. By 1891, even Theodore Cuno's reputation had been rehabilitated and he was once again active in district affairs. In 1893, with Cuno at his side, DeLeon finally accomplished what Drury never managed: he assembled a coalition that unseated Powderly.[45]

It is obvious that the Knights of Labor was no Powderly machine. It is equally evident that the KOL achieved little success in mediating among internal advocates of resistance, revolution, and reform social movements.

Of the four men highlighted in this chapter, none accomplished what he set out to do within the KOL. William Horan died prematurely in 1889, at the age of forty-nine. But the KOL that Horan championed died in 1882, the year in which it voted to become a public organization, and the year in which Horan's idol, Uriah Stephens, passed away. For seven years Horan struggled in vain to restore the dream. In this sense, he was a resister—a social movement advocate seeking to undo change. He embodied the KOL's inability to finalize the shift from fraternal ideals to pragmatic labor action. The faction he represented was small and waning, but it was never vanquished. Most of the KOL's splinter groups appealed to ritual fraternalism and, in 1896, the official Order retreated to that sanctum. The persistence of men like Horan helps explain why the KOL never fully articulated a modern bureaucratic structure.

For Horan, KOL fraternalism was an article of faith that led him into uneasy alliances with the Order's revolutionaries and reformers. In many respects, Horan belonged to what sociologists dub "expressive" social movements.[46] Like a member of a religious group, Horan viewed the KOL's ritual as an end in itself. He took seriously those symbolic actions that reenacted birth, death, and rebirth.[47] Horan lived just long enough to see the KOL rituals he so cherished decline into irrelevancy. In what must have been a bitter pill to swallow, he also witnessed his own LA 1562 lead a revolt against the Home Club, which had pledged to preserve ritualism.

Theodore Cuno was a difficult man who spoke like a revolutionary but often behaved like a self-seeker. While the Home Club controlled DA 49, he was persona non grata. In his second go-round after Drury's expulsion, Cuno remained a loose cannon. He organized Knights for New York City's 1891 Labor Day parade and authored a series of fiery articles for *The Weekly People* promoting the Knights as a revolutionary Marxist vanguard, proving he had learned little about the organization during his long exile. In 1894, he renewed his personal vendetta against the Duryea Starch Company and launched a new boycott. That year, he also worked for Socialist Labor Party candidate Lucien Sanial in his bid to become mayor of New York City.

None of Cuno's ventures met with success. The sagging Knights no longer posed a threat to Duryea, which simply ignored the boycott, and Cuno generated precious little enthusiasm for Sanial, who lost the election handily. And it was patently obvious that reformers had vanquished revolutionaries and that the Knights were no vehicle for radical change, Lassallean or Marxist. In 1895, DeLeon reached that conclusion and split what was left of the KOL. His reconvened faction dubbed itself the Socialist Trade and Labor Alliance and organized along KOL lines, but it proved even less able to effect positive change. Without the encumbrances of dissenting or numerous members, however, Cuno and DeLeon were free to split ideological hairs.[48]

Trade unionism thrived, but not within the KOL and not to the benefit of Peter J. McGuire. Despite his bitter attacks against the KOL, McGuire retained more fondness for it than most of his new comrades within the AFL. McGuire even patterned the ritual for his BCJ after that in the *Adelphon Kruptos*. Further, he participated in several inconclusive "peace" conferences held between the AFL and the KOL, often siding with the Knights.

McGuire gained only the distrust and disrespect of both organizations. As late as 1898, his BCJ battled KOL carpenters in bitter jurisdictional disputes in Chicago. Three years later, his beloved BCJ suspended him in what one historian called a "palace revolution."[49] Although McGuire breathed life into the early AFL, Gompers proved a less reliable ally than Powderly and a more dangerous foe than Drury. Gompers did not help his onetime friend regain his standing among the carpenters, and McGuire died in poverty in 1906, at the age of fifty-four.

McGuire's story reminds us that the KOL policy toward trade unions was as complicated as it was ill considered. Not all Gilded Age trade unionists adhered to the Gompers program of "pure and simple" unionism. Very few trade unions survived the Panic of 1873, the Molly Maguire scare of the mid-1870s, and the railroad strikes of 1877. When trades revitalized in the 1880s, many unionists felt that only a class-wide organization like the Knights of Labor would ensure their survival. Roughly speaking, trade unionists themselves were split into those who held craft consciousness and those with a broader class solidarity consciousness. The latter group was further divided into those with a revolutionary perspective and those of a more cautious reform bent. Some revolutionary trade unionists were lured by the appeal of Lassalleanism, as opposed to Marxism. In their view, Lassalle's emphasis on political action and cooperative enterprise made more sense, and they believed that Marxist craft unions were unlikely to topple the iron law of wages.

Trade-unionist divisions help explain how it was possible for the anti–trade union Home Club to have trade advocates in its ranks. Outside New York, such prominent trade unionist supporters as Hugh Cavanaugh of Cincinnati, John Elliott of Baltimore, David Gibson of Hamilton, Ontario, William Mullen of Richmond, and Frederick Turner of Philadelphia at least temporarily supported the Home Club. Even Michigan's Thomas Barry, later one of the Club's harshest critics, briefly flirted with the Home Club. What all these men held in common was the belief that leaders like Powderly were not fully committed to class solidarity. In essence, some Gilded Age trade unionists felt that in the best of all possible worlds the very craft-based organizations to which they belonged would wither away. This sentiment also found expression in the KOL's near obsession with cooperative enterprises.

Victor Drury outlived his adversaries. He returned to the KOL fold in 1895, as DeLeon and Cuno exited. By then, Drury was seventy years old and his vitality was waning. Nonetheless, fifteen new locals formed in the New York metropolitan area the year Drury reemerged. His main achievement, however, was mentoring Leonora O'Reilly, the future Women's Trade Union League leader and his pupil since she was a wide-eyed sixteen-year-old in 1886. Drury tutored O'Reilly in French and on political economy, much like an elderly, radical grandfather.

Drury's fiery days lay behind him. In his declining years he wrote sentimental poetry, dabbled in Christian socialism, and penned musings on the cooperative ideals of Charles Fourier and Albert Brisbane with nary a mention of anarchism. He spent more time at the O'Reilly household than in KOL lodges, and when Leonora and her mother moved to Brooklyn in 1909, they invited Drury to be their permanent houseguest. He served as companion to O'Reilly's mother, and Leonora was his nurse in sickness and his posthumous archivist. Drury passed away on January 21, 1918, one month short of his ninety-third birthday. O'Reilly lovingly gathered Drury's few remaining writings, copied several in her own hand, and deposited them with her own effects.[50]

Victor Drury outlived the KOL as a national movement. The year before his death, the last general master workman and ex–Home Clubber, John Hayes, closed the KOL's national headquarters and locked its papers in a Washington, D.C., garage. Some locals lingered, but the best available evidence suggests that there were no New York City locals after 1914.

The Home Club affair went to the grave with Drury. Scholars have argued over its importance and its very existence.[51] It was real enough, and its significance was broad. Joseph Labadie accused the Home Club of a "rule or ruin" policy, and it is tempting to conclude he was right.[52] But doing so may be confusing symptoms with the illness. The Home Club did more than its share of damage to KOL internal harmony, but one should not underemphasize the conditions that made it possible in the first place.

The Knights of Labor was one of the most broadly based labor organizations in American history—a characteristic that was both a source of strength and an exposed Achilles' heel. The Home Club forged alliances with anarchists, ritualists, Lassalleans, agrarian radicals, select trade unionists, social reformers, and a few self-promoters like John Hayes. Add Marxists, union bureaucrats, single-issue reformers, small employers, Greenbackers, and a host of others to the volatile mix and one has a fair cross-section of KOL membership in the mid-1880s. With moderate reformers in official leadership positions, schisms were inevitable. The Home Club's genius was parlaying division into a power base.

The case of the Home Club underscores the fragility of KOL structure. Depending on the individual, Knighthood could mean holding on to the past, seeking modest gains in the present, dreaming a producerist utopia based on universal brotherhood, or espousing a radical makeover of society: resisters, reformers, or revolutionaries. One can fault the Home Club for sowing the seeds of discord, or one can admire its zeal in promoting KOL principles. Its record toward women, African Americans, and the Chinese were beacons in the Gilded Age darkness, and even the Home Club's detractors admired its discipline and solidarity. In its heyday, DA 49 did what the rest of the Order talked about doing but seldom managed: it educated the working classes. And, for all the allegations laid at the Home Club's doorstep, the two years (1886–87) it "ruled" the KOL correspond with its historical high-water mark.

Did Drury and his followers also "ruin" the KOL? Theodore Cuno, P. J. McGuire, Terence Powderly, John Morrison, Joe Buchanan, Jo Labadie, and a host of others certainly thought so. Objectively speaking, though, it bears repeating that the Home Club only exacerbated existing tensions within the Order. It did, however, severely compromise all who came into contact with the Home Club. Powderly never regained the trust of the Order, and his plans to transform the KOL into a more modern, centralized bureaucratic organization had to be scuttled. Numerous well-intentioned members were ruined in fights against the Club. Even Marxists suffered, with moderate Knights lumping all radicals together and ignoring the ideological distinctions over which they clashed.

As we shall see in subsequent chapters, the Home Club interfered in matters near and far from New York City. From 1882 through 1889, Home Club affairs occupied crucial KOL energy and resources. If these had led the Order to resolve its tensions, better define itself, and complete inchoate transformations in its focus and structure, the Home Club controversy would have been worth the pain. KOL moderates won the battle against the Order's radicals, but in doing so, they jeopardized the war effort.

CHAPTER 2

The B & B Affair

Norman Ware subtitled his classic 1929 study of the Knights of Labor "a study in democracy."[1] As the Home Club debacle of the previous chapter reveals, the internal life of the KOL as often resembled a culture of contentiousness as a model of democracy. Gary Marx and Douglas McAdam note that "collective behavior can mean a challenge to unjust authority, and liberation and renewal. It may demonstrate humans at their most moral and heroic. But it can also involve . . . the least honorable of human qualities."[2]

Factionalism often embodies such lesser traits. No matter how focused a given organization might be on achieving its goals, few escape some sort of factionalism. In a study of fifty-three separate nineteenth- and twentieth-century social movements, sociologist William Gamson detected rank-and-file disorder in most of them and formal schism in 43 percent of his sample.[3] This means that organizations routinely spend much of their time and energy putting out factional fires. As sociologist Samuel Friedman discovered, "worker opposition" groups are as likely to turn against union bureaucrats as against employers. Moreover, as both Friedman's and Gamson's data reveal, the more decentralized the organization, the more difficulty it has mollifying its factions or healing its splits.[4]

Ideological, tactical, structural, and personal disputes combined to create what Knights of Labor dubbed the "B & B Affair," a vicious round of accusations and counteraccusations involving general executive board members William H. Bailey and Thomas Barry. Both were expelled from the KOL in 1888 for "conduct unbecoming a Knight." That high-sounding charge aside, their removal was the culmination of over two years of feuding among Bailey, Barry, Powderly, and the board. Home Club policies provided the context for much of the dispute, but other factors also played a part.

The Knights' chain of command could be maddeningly ambiguous. In theory, power flowed from local assemblies whose will was made manifest at annual representative general assemblies to its district assemblies and elected officers on the local, district, and national levels. In practice, the Knights functioned as if the executive board were a legislative as well as executive body. But the relationship lines on all levels were blurry. As we have seen, DA 49 often rode roughshod over the will of its local assemblies, just as locals defied decisions of the general assembly and its elected officials. This sort of de facto decentralization encouraged freelance leaders, of which Bailey and Barry were exemplars. Given that the latter also possessed an autocratic streak every bit as wide as that of Powderly, it is difficult to assess to what degree Barry's problems within the Knights were ideological versus structural or personal.

The B & B Affair was fraught with irony. Both men were once extolled as pillars of the KOL's new generation of leaders, especially by the very Home Club opponents of Powderly who expelled them. Norman Ware claimed each was an early executive board supporter of the Home Club.[5] Neither was ever a Home Club insider, but Bailey and Barry clearly shared the Club's disenchantment with Powderly's leadership. Both men had considerable numbers of allies within the KOL; thus the B & B Affair disrupted several KOL general assemblies. It also spurred disgruntled members to flee to splinter groups and to trade unions hostile to the Knights.

There was little in either man's background to suggest he would become the center of a maelstrom, and both were loyal Knights prior to 1886. William H. Bailey was born in Hamilton, Ontario. Little is known of his life until he moved to Shawnee, Ohio, and began coal mining. By the 1870s he was an active labor organizer in Ohio mines, and he was deeply involved in that state's Greenback Labor movement. He joined the Knights of Labor some time around 1880, and he took part in the Order's traumatic 1884 Hocking Valley strike. Although the mine owners won and crippled area KOL organizing efforts, Bailey's admirable deportment led to his election to the general executive board. His star rose higher when he was part of the 1885 negotiating team that wrung favorable concessions from Jay Gould after the Southwest Railway strike.[6] Bailey continued to organize miners and, in 1886, became master workman for the newly created miners' NTD 135.

Thomas Barry was born in Cohoes, New York, on July 17, 1852, the son of Irish immigrant parents. Family poverty prevented him from attending school and he received no formal education. At age eight, he began work in J. H. Parsons and Company knitting mills, often working fourteen-hour days. Although he was a mere youth, Barry saw action in the Civil War, was wounded, and lost partial use of an arm. He returned to the mills and despite long work hours, taught himself to read and write.

He also immersed himself in union activities, joining the carder's union when he was fifteen. At the age of sixteen, he apprenticed himself to an ax polisher but was blacklisted for union organizing and forced to leave Cohoes before completing his apprenticeship. Barry assumed the life of a peripatetic journeyman polisher and managed to finish his ax-polishing training while in Baldwinsville, New York, where he also mastered ax making.

In all likelihood, Barry joined the KOL while in Pittsburgh, some time around 1874. He drifted to Dundas, Ontario, where, in 1875, he married Maggie Devaney, a farmer's daughter. Barry's union activism cost him one job after another, and eventually the young couple drifted to Cleveland. Ironically, he had never taken part in a strike until he reached Cleveland and struck the Powell Tool Company.[7]

Barry's dedication to labor led Cleveland Knights to elect him master workman of DA 47. This made him an even greater target for blacklisters, as did his leadership of ax-maker strikes in Ohio and western Pennsylvania in 1880. The collapse of the ax makers' nine-month strike cemented Barry's place on the blacklist and reduced him to poverty. He toiled as a day laborer on the Cleveland waterfront and managed to organize new KOL locals. In October 1882, Barry left Cleveland for East Saginaw, Michigan, lured by a job offer from an ax maker not part of the consortium blacklisting Barry. He only worked there for about six months before the company joined the Association of Manufacturers and fired him. He never again worked as an ax maker.

By then, Barry was firmly entrenched in the city. Dubbed by comrades "the one-armed veteran," Barry's tireless organizing on behalf of the KOL gained him respect. By 1883, nine KOL locals met in the East Saginaw area where none had met previously.[8] He attended the KOL's 1883 general assembly and was elected to the general executive board that year. Barry managed to eke out a living as a professional labor organizer and his wife took in boarders to help support their family of five.

Barry was also attracted to the Greenback Labor movement. In 1882, Gilbert Rockwood, the KOL's assistant grand secretary, groused that Barry was "a damned socialist" plotting "to tear the Officers of the G[rand] A[ssembly] apart." Rockwood also dropped heavy hints that Barry had made contacts with the New York City dissidents who subsequently headed the Home Club.[9]

Rockwood's discomfort notwithstanding, in 1884, Barry rode a Democratic/Greenback fusion ticket to electoral victory and the Michigan state legislature. Michigan laborers applauded as he sponsored bills to establish a ten-hour workday, abolish payment in scrip, and to employ factory and mine inspectors. By 1886, his name was bandied about as a possible candidate for lieutenant governor. Barry's political career proved to be a short one, but his reputation was such that when he moved to nearby Bay City, friend and foe alike dubbed him the de facto "mayor of Bay City."

Barry's harassment by Michigan manufacturers sealed his reputation among workers. Representative Barry's ten-hour bill was watered down with a clause allowing employers to "contract" with workers willing to work more than the legal limit. Bay City lumber mill workers refused to work the extra hours and struck when employers subsequently docked their pay. Barry personally took charge of their strike. Owners retaliated by hiring scabs and Pinkerton detectives to guard their interests. They also convinced state authorities to arrest Barry under a little-used conspiracy law. Between July and August 1885, Barry was arrested, posted bail, and rearrested no fewer than six times. Despite his personal woes, Barry hammered out an agreement that allowed striking Knights to save face and return to work. In gratitude, the KOL returned Barry to the executive board at its fall convention.[10] Barry's fortunes revived somewhat in January 1886, when he was acquitted on conspiracy charges in a trial widely covered in both the labor and popular press.[11]

Prior to the lumber mill strikes, Barry's labor activism was marked by autonomy and freelancing. An 1886 strike in his hometown of Cohoes marked the first time he was dispatched officially by the KOL and the first time he worked with Bailey. Long-festering troubles in area knitting mills precipitated short strikes in 1884 and 1885; by 1886 other Hudson River towns experienced problems. In March 1886, DA 104 ordered a strike when employers slashed wages and dismissed workers belonging to the Knights. The towns of Amsterdam, Cohoes, Little Falls, and Schenectady were particularly hard hit, and Bailey and Barry were sent to mediate a settlement. Both men delivered fiery speeches at an impromptu rally held in a Cohoes skating rink, sharing the dais with DA 49 representatives who journeyed from New York City to harangue the crowd. Bailey and Barry brokered an agreement that was more symbolic than substantive but enhanced each man's reputation within the KOL.[12]

In the ensuing euphoria, few Knights bothered to take a hard look at what was, in reality, a replay of Barry's lumber mill settlement. Mill owners agreed to little more than a cooling-off period, one in which they organized as the National Association of Knit Goods Manufacturers, a united front that later crushed the KOL. Nor did Knights pay much attention to the fact that both Bailey and Barry overstepped their charges by inflaming and inciting before they bothered to mediate. And Powderly could not have been pleased by the presence of DA 49 speakers more than a hundred miles from their New York City base.

In October 1886, lockouts and strikes broke out anew. Once again Bailey and Barry were sent to intervene. For over a month, manufacturers refused to meet with them or with Florence Donovan of the New York State Board of Mediation. Several tentative agreements fell through before a compromise was finally signed in December 1886. It was little more than yet another repeat of the Michigan lumber mill treaty, though it was widely hailed as a victory.[13]

Although the reputations of both Bailey and Barry rose among the rank and file, KOL leadership suspected both men were undisciplined free-lancers. Further, Home Club ideologues grew increasingly uncomfortable with what they perceived to be Bailey and Barry's uncompromising trade unionism, a suspicion exacerbated by their public criticism of the KOL's handling of the Chicago stockyards strike. Both would subsequently face repudiation by the very faction of which they were early supporters. But neither man found solace among craft unionists either.

Both Samuel Gompers and Adolph Strasser identified Bailey and Barry as anti–trade unionists, an accusation tantamount to Home Club membership in their eyes. In truth, each man held something of a middle position wedged between the wide-open mixed-assembly views of the Home Club and the craft unionism of Gompers and Strasser, views akin to what Dorothy Sue Cobble calls "occupational unionism." That is, they held a hybrid view that championed craft organization, stringent skill re-quirements, and restrictive membership clauses, but also demands for closed shops, union hiring halls, and portable benefits that "stressed em-ployment security rather than 'job rights' at an individual worksite."[14]

Gompers also had an ax to grind with former polisher Barry and ex-miner Bailey. Both men had sided with Progressive Cigarmakers Local 2814 in its dispute with Gompers' Cigarmakers International Union. Barry, Bailey, and John Hayes drafted the very March 1886 report that exonerated the actions of the Progressives. Moreover, historians Norman Ware and Stuart Kaufman accuse the three of sabotaging a reasonable CMIU com-promise and opening the animosity floodgates between craft unions and the KOL.[15]

Why would Barry and Bailey engage in such actions? Both were troubled by what they saw as the exclusivity of international trade unions. As occupational unionists they were more concerned with industry-wide standards than with individual shop-floor bargaining. Moreover, the AFL was yet to rise, and the FOTLU appeared moribund. For all of their craft rhetoric, both men also charged that international trade unions were insuf-ficiently committed to the ultimate dismantling of capitalism. Both men simply felt that the KOL's broader federation concept was superior to the parochial concerns of groups like Gompers's CMIU.[16] Bailey and Barry were also increasingly at odds with the romantic mixed-assembly views of the Home Club. Both spearheaded moves with the KOL to expand NTDs, craft organizations empowered to negotiate rates and conditions across geographical boundaries. They took their cue from the misnamed LA 300, a glassblowers' organization whose membership spread from Pittsburgh to Belgium. At the KOL's 1884 general assembly each spoke on behalf on NTDs. By 1886, Bailey headed the miners' NTD 135 and Barry the ax makers' NTD 153.

NTDs differed from international craft unions in their conceptions of authority and goals. Neither Bailey nor Barry accepted the principle of total trade union sovereignty. As formalized at the 1886 special assembly, NTDs could negotiate on behalf of their members, but they were subject to the discipline of the general assembly and its elected officers. One clause laid down rigid conditions under which the executive board would sanction or support strikes. In theory, locals could engage in unauthorized actions, but they could not command logistical support from the KOL if they chose to do so.

Nor did Bailey and Barry support anything that smacked of "pure and simple" unionism. Both men endorsed the KOL's broad reform agenda and spoke of transforming American society along radically different social and economic lines. They insisted that local, craft, and personal agendas sometimes needed to be sacrificed in the name of long-term gain for all workers. In essence, Bailey, Barry, and NTD enthusiasts advocated a parallel structure in which trade districts sought immediate gains for members, while the organization as a whole worked toward broader reform goals.

Advocacy of such a pragmatic-gain-today/eliminate-the-wage-system-tomorrow plan was fraught with ambiguity and factional potential. By wanting it both ways, Bailey and Barry were seen as anti–trade unionist from the perspective of men like Gompers and Strasser. But they were also out of sorts with prevailing attitudes within the KOL. In essence, Bailey and Barry were too trade unionist for the Home Club, and too tainted by the Home Club for trade unionists. This helps explain why both men, though enormously popular, lacked allies during their subsequent battles with KOL leaders.

Bailey was the first to discover his isolation. NTD 135 was first proposed in 1884 but not chartered until May 20, 1886. By then it faced competition from the National Federation of Miners and Mine Owners, a union founded along classic international trade-union lines, though its founders included old Knights like John Davis, Chris Evans, John McBride, and Daniel McLaughlin. Jurisdictional disputes quickly arose, with KOL miners placed in the unenviable position of having to decide which group to join.[17]

Bailey's estrangement from the Home Club also surfaced. He told fellow NTD 135 members, "Our Order demands and our own interest compels us to have an intelligent and thorough knowledge of matters pertaining to the mining interest. . . . The time had arrived to unite all of our calling into a district body based upon the principles of the world's education—the Knights of Labor." Bailey should have left matters there, but he went on to tout the virtues of miners instructing other miners, remarking that mixed assemblies conformed to "primitive meanings" of Knighthood.[18] NTD 135 was strong in western Pennsylvania and in Ohio, but elsewhere it clashed with other KOL assemblies. When Bailey pleaded his case before the executive board, Home Club allies turned a deaf ear.

Tom Barry made a similar mistake. When reporters asked his views on trade unions, he regaled them with an encapsulated history of craft unionism and the Knights. He predicted that "ultimately all trades will be organized into trade districts, under the general order of the Knights of Labor," but rashly acknowledged that there were advocates of mixed assemblies who disagreed. Barry boldly predicted that "notwithstanding [mixed assembly] opposition," trade districts would eventually dominate.[19]

Bailey and Barry also got into difficulty for trying to have it both ways concerning strikes, the linchpin of trade-union tactics but opposed by the KOL. At the 1886 special assembly, each reaffirmed the KOL's official disapproval of strikes except in rare circumstances, yet both men threw themselves into strikes with vigor and enthusiasm. Barry's zeal for shop-floor action was such that Toronto Knights charged him with violating a cardinal principle of Knighthood by emphasizing strikes over cooperation and education.[20]

The 1886 Chicago stockyards strike was a turning point in the KOL careers of Bailey and Barry, and their conduct during it paved the way for their eventual ousters. Historians generally skewer Powderly for his handling of the work stoppage, with a few accusing him of selling out.[21] The problem with that assessment is that so much of it entails a noncritical acceptance of charges leveled by Barry and other Powderly opponents. Although Powderly no doubt made mistakes during the strike, the historical record is more ambiguous than Barry made it out to be, and Barry's own conduct was no more exemplary than Powderly's. The Chicago packinghouse strike was indeed a fiasco, but it was one in which manifest personal animosities unfurled themselves against an institutional backdrop involving ideology, local power struggles, chains of command, and timing.

To be sure, there was already bad blood among Powderly, Barry, and Bailey. Like many Knights, Bailey and Barry were infuriated by Powderly's refusal to endorse the May 1, 1886, general strike for the eight-hour day and appalled when he denounced the eight men scapegoated for the Haymarket bombing and refused to endorse clemency pleas on their behalf.

William Bailey. Courtesy of the
Catholic University of America
Archives.

Thomas Barry. Courtesy of the
Labadie Collection, University of
Michigan.

Both interpreted Powderly's blanket condemnation of radicalism as an act
of cowardice. Powderly's rigidity likely explains why Bailey and Barry
supported the Home Club coup at the June special assembly.

But neither man had much appreciation for the local situation in Chicago. The Windy City, like New York, proved difficult to absorb into a
structure largely constructed at the KOL's 1878 convention in Reading,
Pennsylvania, at a time in which the Order had fewer than ten thousand
members. Chicagoan Richard Griffiths joined the KOL in 1877, but for a
time he was the only Knight in the city. By the end of 1878, Griffiths had
recruited enough allies to warrant the chartering of DA 24. Nonetheless,
the affable Griffiths represented an older view of Knighthood forged in the
values of ritual fraternalism and the provincial mentalities of Chicago in
its pre-boom prairie market town days. He was fifty-nine at the time of the
stockyards strike, a veritable elder statesman by the youthful standards of
most KOL leaders. By then, he held the largely ceremonial post of general
worthy foreman and was charged with safeguarding the Order's ritual.[22]

Griffiths was a loyal Powderly ally who faithfully adhered to KOL
principles and general executive board directives. Rising DA 24 leaders

Richard Griffiths. Courtesy of the Catholic University of America Archives.

like Elizabeth Rodgers, Albert Parsons, and George Schilling viewed Griffiths as old-fashioned, but they respected him enough to tread lightly when disagreeing with him. Both Parsons and Schilling ignored Powderly's order for Knights to forego the May 1, 1886, general strike on behalf the eight-hour workday, with Parsons playing the role that eventually cost him his life and Schilling helping the packinghouse workers secure an eight-hour day in May.

The actions of Parsons and Schilling notwithstanding, Griffiths had the ear of the KOL's central leadership, and his personal reputation bolstered by a battle against cancer commanded influence in Chicago. Griffiths enthusiastically embraced a rule change at the June special assembly requiring two-thirds of all workers to approve a strike vote before the KOL executive board would consider approving it. The fact that Griffiths and DA 24 ruled the Chicago roost is crucial, as the packinghouse strikes were, in fact, a DA 57 affair.

DA 57 formed in 1882, when Knights in the city's south and southwest split from DA 24.[23] Although it was more vital than DA 24 by 1886, its very existence was resented by some area Knights, as was Michael Butler, district master workman for DA 57 after July 1886. Griffiths viewed him as an upstart, even though he had been a Knight since the early 1880s.

Butler's spectacular success worried DA 24 power brokers. In June, he brought six hundred beef butchers into the KOL as LA 7802, in hopes that KOL membership would protect their fragile one-month-old, eight-hour-day victory. He and John Joyce continued to organize packinghouse workers and by mid-1886, DA 57 had mushroomed from three thousand to over fifteen thousand members. If Illinois Bureau of Labor Statistics figures are to be trusted, total KOL membership in Chicago was just over eighteen thousand.[24]

Neither Bailey nor Barry was party to the summer-long jockeying for position among Chicago's packinghouse workers and the city's district assemblies, or that between workers and packers. Among stockyard workers, beef dressers saw themselves as more skilled than their counterparts in pork, while the latter demanded and received a separate local assembly (7654). More serious was DA 57's inability to get all of the packinghouses to agree to paying ten hours' wages for eight hours of work. This caused those who did to complain they were being placed at a competitive disadvantage. They sought a compromise in which workers would receive nine hours' pay, not ten. Moreover, an ineffective KOL boycott against Armour over the practice of shipping pre-dressed beef to eastern markets via refrigerator cars served mostly to unify battling employer associations. By summer's end the National Cattle Growers Association was allied with the National Butchers Protective Association in what would prove to be a solid front against the KOL.[25]

On Labor Day, KOL executive board member Albert Carlton addressed a festive rally of over twenty thousand, but turmoil broke out soon thereafter. On October 4, beef workers at several large firms—including Swift, Cudahy, and Morris—finally hammered out a definitive eight-hours-work-for-ten-hours-pay deal. Their triumph soured three days later, however, when a consortium led by Armour announced that as of Monday, October 11, all pork workers would return to a ten-hour day. When the day arrived, pork workers threw down their knives and walked off, the first act of the 1886 packinghouse strikes. Act two came four days later when Michael Butler called out Armour beef workers to pressure the company. Armour was seen as the key to the entire industry, but Butler's sympathy strike had the effect of causing other packers to back off agreements to which they had acceded just eleven days earlier.[26]

The matter could not have come at a worse time for the KOL. The strike broke out while the Knights were gathered for their annual general assembly, held in Richmond, Virginia, some eight hundred miles to the east. It was the KOL's largest and longest assembly, convening on October 4 and adjourning October 21. During that time the assembly took up the Home Club investigation, resolutions to expel the cigarmakers, and proposals to increase the size of the executive board. It also authorized the purchase of a new headquarters, elected officers, and appointed a special investigator for women's work. Dozens of resolutions were debated, and public demonstrations were organized on issues ranging from racial equality to women's suffrage. Butler had to leave the convention, and Powderly assigned Tom Barry to go with him when DA 24 representatives insisted the executive board investigate the situation.

Many observers credit Barry with skillfully negotiating separate agreements among the packers and dividing their associations. They pay less attention to Barry's violations of his charge and of KOL policy. Because of rules adopted in June, the KOL executive board did not authorize the packinghouse strike. Barry was dispatched at DA 24's request and as a courtesy to DA 57, but he was not empowered to take tactical control of the strike. His agreements must be seen as those of a free agent, not those of an executive board member. As Powderly put it, his only charge was to "restore harmony" in the yards.[27] Such procedural fine points may have been irrelevant to the twenty thousand men on strike, but Barry bears the blame for much of the ensuing confusion.

Very little of what was going on in Chicago made its way back to Richmond, and it is doubtful the assembly would have approved of Butler's strike call for Armour beef butchers. Nor in all likelihood would Barry have approved it. He made a brief visit to his home and left Butler in charge of a five-man strike committee. Historian Louise Wade charges that Butler ran roughshod over the strike committee: "[T]he 'leading spirits' in District 57 had taken the opportunity to flex their muscle . . . at a time Powderly, the General Executive Board, and Thomas Barry were looking in another direction."[28] Fewer than half the Armour workers honored Butler's call.

On October 15, Barry wired to tell Knights that he was negotiating with Armour and several other firms. Four days later he unilaterally called off all the strikes except that against Armour, against whom he also called for a boycott. Apparently Barry also made a secret pact with both Fowler Brothers and the Chicago Packing Company to send men back to work under a ten-hour arrangement through November 7. At that time, Barry told them, he would call a new strike and demand nine hours' pay for eight hours' work. Barry gambled that he could isolate Armour before that time.

If Barry thought he was on the verge of victory, he failed to make it apparent to KOL leaders. He wired Powderly, "The people here were fighting a losing fight. The packers set a trap for them and they fell into it."[29] On October 22, he left Chicago to consult with Powderly. In that meeting, Barry warned of the presence of Pinkertons in Chicago and of Armour's intransigence. His report did little to convince Powderly that Armour was close to surrender. Barry went home to Michigan.

Barry was in East Saginaw when he learned that matters were rapidly deteriorating. Armour categorically refused to consider an eight-hour day, though it offered the KOL a potentially face-saving gesture of a fifty-cent daily raise. On October 28, those few Armour beef men remaining on strike accepted the money and returned to work. Morris and Swift immediately demanded the same deal. On November 1, an agreement was signed and the firms ended their eight-hour experiment.

Morris and Swift workers were furious about the return to a ten-hour day, and they streamed into the streets rather than to their stockyard posts. Ominously, however, Armour workers stayed on the job. Barry returned to Chicago on November 2, though there is no record he was dispatched by the executive board. On November 4, he and Butler ordered the Armour men to strike and some of them obliged the next day. By then, Pinkertons, Chicago police, hastily commissioned deputies, and the Illinois National Guard ruled the streets.

On November 7, Barry sent two telegrams to Powderly. In the first he told Powderly that all negotiations had failed and that twenty-five thousand men were out. In the second, he contradicted himself and stated that Fowler Brothers and the Chicago Packing Company were again willing to sign a nine hours' pay for eight hours' work contract. But he added that the strikers were "headstrong men . . . unwilling to yield" and he feared matters were at an impasse. At long last, he asked for instructions.[30]

Executive board member Albert Carlton hastened to Chicago, but before he arrived, Powderly received a wire from DA 57 official William Degnan informing him there was no chance for a peaceful settlement. Powderly convened the executive board and on November 10, 1886, it issued a back-to-work order and demanded Barry and Carlton lift the charters of any locals that refused to comply. Both men were stunned and wired to ask if the order was accurate. Powderly confirmed it. According to Powderly, he did not receive Barry's request to stay the order as a packers' conference was in session until *after* he confirmed his order. If true, it was a cruel twist of fate. On November 12, Barry and Carlton telegraphed: "We obey in opposition to our judgment. Will caution meeting and transmit the order. Our lives in danger, but we face the matter as Knights of Labor. Don't give to the press before we do."[31]

Historians have been overly quick to condemn Powderly's handling of the packinghouse strike, though the historical record suggests that bad timing and misinformation guided his decision making more than his legendary opposition to strikes. Nor was it Powderly's decision alone; the order to lift the strike came from the executive board of which he was but one member. Powderly justified the board's action on the basis of side agreements Barry claimed to have negotiated that would have saved striker jobs and allowed time for the KOL to reorganize and truly isolate intransigents like Armour. Perhaps Powderly thought at the time that no better deal was possible. In his defense, most of the strikers did get their jobs back, though under ironclad contracts that did the KOL little good.[32]

The contemporary record is far more favorable to Powderly. John

Albert A. Carlton. Courtesy of the
Catholic University of America Archives.

Joyce and Sylvester Gaunt, members of the DA 57 strike committee,
blamed Barry. Gaunt bluntly told Powderly he thought Barry a bumbler
and pleaded that if he ever sent another board member to the area, "for
pity's sake . . . give us a man that has some brain and [is] capable to cope
with any trouble he may find."[33] DA 24's Elizabeth Rodgers sided with
Powderly, as did Griffiths, who denounced the entire strike as an unconstitutional debacle evolving out of eight-hour agitation Knights were ordered
to avoid.[34] Among contemporary historians, Richard Oestreicher is among
the few to suggest that Barry acted hastily. In his view, Barry was motivated increasingly by the "belief that the industrial system could only be
changed through direct militant action," a "revolutionary position" that
was increasingly "out of step" with the views of other KOL executive
board members.[35] Although Oestreicher perhaps overstates the conserva-
tism of the KOL's executive board, those who wish to fault Barry's actions
can find evidence for doing so. Barry poorly represented the KOL in the
negotiations: he made promises, assumed powers, and struck deals that
were not his to make, take, or execute. Further, his cables to Powderly were
so vague that there was no way he or any member of the executive board
could have known what Barry was plotting.

For his part, Barry did not initially blame Powderly for the strike's
collapse. In remarks delivered to the *Chicago Tribune* the day after the

strike collapsed, Barry accused Butler of "treachery" and belittled his competence.[36] Many Chicago workers apparently agreed. DA 24 leaders and some within DA 57 denounced Butler as a political self-seeker, an attitude that spilled over into the polls. When Butler ran for sheriff in the November elections, he was soundly defeated. Barry did not openly criticize Powderly until well after the strike's end, and not until men like George Schilling and Joe Buchanan, angered by Powderly's views on Haymarket, took up the charge.

Barry's behavior following November was more petty than heroic. As packinghouse workers quit the KOL in droves, Barry opted to take the aggressive lead in the blame game. He sounded a series of minor complaints, hinted at a sellout, regaled Powderly haters with how workers howled in protest when he read Powderly's back-to-work cable, and helped spread a rumor that Powderly called off the strike to appease the Catholic Church. That accusation stemmed from a communiqué dated October 16, from Father P. M. Flannigan of St. Ann's Church of Lake, Illinois, imploring Powderly to call off the strike. Barry must have known this to be a baseless charge, as Flannigan's telegram was sent nearly a month before the strike ended, and Powderly never even read it until the strike was over. Barry and Butler, not Powderly, ordered all lulls in the strike.[37]

Instead of working to stop DA 57 hemorrhaging, Barry donned the martyr's mantle. He asserted that the back-to-work order was a "mistake," though for a time he avoided scapegoating Powderly and noted that he was no more responsible "than any other member of the board." By December, rumors flew that Barry planned to challenge Powderly for the general master workman's post, discussion flamed by Chicago radicals reeling under the double blow of the stockyards debacle and Powderly's refusal to join the Haymarket clemency drive. Among Powderly supporters there was substantial sentiment to sanction Barry for his disobedience and "conduct unbecoming a Knight."[38]

Barry drew support from board members Bailey and Carlton. The latter had a legitimate beef with Powderly's interference in the Chicago stockyards strike. He first learned of the back-to-work order from an Associated Press story and was miffed that some stockyard workers accused him of pressuring the executive board to call off the strike. Carlton lashed back by vilifying Powderly.

Bailey and Barry renewed their friendship when they revisited New York knitting mills in December 1886 and worked out another temporary agreement. However, it was just as ephemeral as their past efforts and soon collapsed. By April 1887, the two men were back in New York state for a third round of negotiations, where they did little but brew more controversy. Several months earlier, John Morrison of NTD 126 negotiated a closed shop and a pay raise for carpet weavers in Pennsylvania and New York, only to have his efforts undermined by the Home Club. Morrison was later expelled from the KOL.[39] Barry equated Morrison's fate with his own betrayal in Chicago and spoke out on behalf of Morrison and NTDs. Though the Home Club, by then reorganized as The Class, was weakened, it retained enough clout to isolate Barry.

Barry was portrayed as an undisciplined lone wolf defiant of majority will. Such a charge contained elements of truth, but it was Barry's alliance with Bailey that proved his undoing. Neither man was prepared for the startling accusation that they were guilty of fostering ill will with, of all things, trade unions.

Bailey's zeal to advance the miners' NTD 135 occasionally led him into jurisdictional disputes with other organizations, including those affiliated with the Knights. Many Knights in isolated mine patches belonged to mixed assemblies laced with miners, railroad men, and iron and steel workers. Those occupations were closely related, but solidarity among them was fragile. Bailey believed that moving laborers into the correct national trade districts would obviate loyalty questions.

In his haste to effect change, Bailey precipitated a jurisdictional dispute in Mingo Junction, Ohio, where workers at the Laughlin and Junction Steel Company were on strike. In late 1886, Bailey negotiated an agreement for KOL workers there but signed a contract that excluded the rival National Amalgamated Iron and Steel Workers (NAAIW). The NAAIW accused the Knights of scabbing for lower wages, while the KOL countered that NAAIW members crossed jurisdictional boundaries and barred its members from KOL membership.[40] Soon, the two organizations battled for the membership dues of the miners. In addition, the KOL's own Mine and Mine Laborers branch called for the abolition of Bailey's NTD 135, and Powderly's own Scranton DA 16 got involved in a turf battle with NTD 135. The latter squabble cemented Powderly's personal dislike of Bailey.[41]

In the spring of 1887, Powderly handed Bailey several Sisyphean tasks. First, Bailey was placed on temporary "leave" from the executive board to "investigate" the dispute between Brooklyn's renegade Montauk Assembly and DA 49. In the midst of this no-win situation, Bailey was dispatched to salvage the KOL's "official" position in the carpet weavers' strike. In April, he joined Barry in Cohoes. Bailey dutifully denounced John Morrison, an act that put a momentary strain on his relationship with Barry, but which he repudiated at the 1887 general assembly. Bailey's activities won him more enemies than kudos and in June, he was eased out as master workman of NTD 135. His replacement, William Lewis, proved no more pliable than Bailey, but The Class had Bailey where they wanted him. Bailey was charged with "waging war" against trade unions, a position reiterated by Morrison, who felt Bailey betrayed him.[42]

Bailey drifted closer to Barry and the two came to see themselves as executive board rebels. Barry convinced Bailey that he was wrong about Morrison and that DA 49 set him up. The two counterattacked by raising questions about KOL finances, with Charles Litchman as their first target. Bailey accused the general secretary of squandering KOL resources and hinted that he might be robbing the till. On July 18, he complained that Litchman had already drawn over $1,900 of his $2,000 yearly salary and that he had not yet repaid a $500 advance from 1886. Powderly advised Litchman to get his accounts in order and suggested scrutinizing Bailey's financial records as well.[43]

Barry joined the fray with a claim that the Order was awash in money but was spending it unwisely. In the next breath he floated a "practical" plan to implement cooperative production for striking Knights, complete with funding figures based on inflated membership figures. The scheme was so half-baked that it is hard to believe Barry was serious about it. In all likelihood, Barry hoped to exploit the Order's downturn in membership by appearing to be proactive. Some Knights took it seriously enough to debate it at the 1887 general assembly.[44]

Bad timing hurt Bailey and Barry. The Class came undone on the eve of the 1887 assembly, and DA 49 elected a reform slate to represent it at the convention. Rumors abounded that the convention would turn out all those most closely associated with the Home Club, including Powderly, Litchman, Hayes, and Thomas McGuire. Powderly desperately needed scapegoats to deflect criticism of his leadership. He deftly allied himself with the reformers and called upon all general executive board members to resign. None were compelled to do so since all had been elected to two-year terms in 1886.

Bailey and Barry saw Powderly's ruse for what it was: an attempt to purge them while reinstating the rest of the board. Other board members compliantly tendered their resignations, but when Bailey and Barry refused they quickly withdrew them. The convention floor erupted into chaos. Powderly faced down resolutions from George Schilling and Charles Seib condemning his handling of the stockyards strike. But both Bailey and Barry voted in favor of it and were promptly tarred with the anarchist's brush.

When Hayes charged Barry with anarchism, he leapt to his feet to call Hayes a liar and assert, "I am as loyal . . . [to] the republic as any man on this floor. No man can call me an Anarchist on the outside." After he calmed down a bit, he told a reporter, "The cry of anarchy, which is being continually kept up by the representatives of this administration . . . is entirely uncalled for, as there were to my knowledge, only two or three Anarchists present, and they were manly enough to proclaim themselves as such. I never countenanced anarchy in my life, but if to differ with my colleagues is anarchy, then surely I am an Anarchist."[45] It was Bailey's turn to take the hot seat when Morrison and DA 126 came up for an expulsion vote. Bailey defended both to no avail. Like Barry, he too took his position to the press and denounced the vote as a travesty. He returned to the convention floor to join Barry in charging board members with financial misappropriation. This was a tactical error. Litchman had indeed taken Powderly's advice to scrutinize all the accounts. He dramatically unveiled figures revealing that only Powderly, whose base salary was $3,000 higher, had drawn more money from KOL accounts than had Bailey and Barry.[46]

Pro-Powderly forces won the floor battles, forcing malcontents to take their battles elsewhere. Two days after the general assembly adjourned, Schilling and Seib convened a Chicago-based reform movement, the Provisional Committee of the Knights of Labor. Bailey and Barry soon joined the Provisionals, as did KOL treasurer Frederick Turner. By December 1887, the Provisionals had spread east to Philadelphia and as far south as Charleston, South Carolina. One estimate claims that up to one-third of all KOL members had ties to the Provisionals by year's end. Powderly's friend Tom O'Reilly complained, "Turner, Bailey, and Barry are entirely responsible for the present condition of affairs in the Order. The first pair are fools, the latter a tremendous knave."[47]

The Philadelphia and Reading Railroad strike aided Provisionals' recruitment. Company president Austin Corbin broke promises made to KOL trainmen and miners, precipitating a strike. Bailey threw himself into the struggle. His activities in northeastern Pennsylvania suggested that the KOL executive board endorsed the strike. In February 1888, Powderly instructed Hayes to squelch such rumors, claiming "the men of the Reading system [do] not want to allow the G.E.B. to have any voice in their affairs." He insisted that it was not a KOL strike and that the Order should do little more than pass a resolution of sympathy for the strikers.[48]

The strike ended badly and bitterly. Violence erupted and there was full-scale scabbing by members of rival miners' unions and by the Brotherhood of Locomotive Engineers. On February 17, William Lewis ordered NTD 135 miners back to work, and though a few other groups held out for several weeks, the strike ended in a near-total victory for the Reading corporation.[49] For KOL critics, the Reading strike was yet another confirmation of the incompetence of current leadership. Many of those who stayed with the Knights were drawn into the ranks of the Provisionals. The Provisionals were an internal reform group, not a secession movement, though Powderly and his cronies labeled it as such and declared it illegal. Stripped of legitimacy, the Provisionals inadvertently provided an opportunity for the moribund Home Club to be revived once again. By early 1888, erstwhile reformers like George Murray and Ralph Robb were on the defensive, and James Quinn, Thomas McGuire, and Victor Drury held enough sway to divert KOL funds to spies investigating the Provisionals.[50]

Bailey continued to charge the KOL executive board with misappropriation of funds. He penned a defiant note to Powderly in which he crowed, "You did not hear the something drop at [the convention in] Minneapolis that you expected to hear drop—with all your infamy." That "something" was Bailey's head and, cranium intact, Bailey demanded that Powderly submit an itemized list of KOL expenditures. When Powderly ignored his request, Bailey threatened to sue. Powderly crafted a careful reply in which he claimed he could not provide the list since the assembly had voted against it. He piously asserted, "I am therefore obliged as a true Knight to bow to the vote of that body. . . . You are obliged to do the same." As for the lawsuit, Powderly reminded Bailey, "The KOL is not chartered or incorporated and is thus not obligated to throw its books open to the public." He chided Bailey for being "rude" and for allying himself with a "rule or ruin" faction. Bailey was not chastised. He countered that at least $5,000 was missing from KOL accounts and added, "[Y]ou had better apply the rule or ruin term to some of those dear friends of yours where I think it belongs."[51]

Strike failures and rumors of financial malfeasance kept the Provisionals alive. Barry toured the South and issued reports of employer brutality and racism that cast doubts about the KOL's effectiveness in the region. Powderly's patience, always thin, began to fray. In a letter to Hayes he wrote:

I cannot stay on the board with two brutes like Bailey and Barry. . . . If the Order will require my services next November and will pass laws to keep down strikes and incipient and foolish resolutions, I will take the reins again with a decent set of officers. But to ask me to suffer the torments which attend associating with men who routinely insult every noble sentiment by which the patient worker for the Order is actuated by the grossest and most licentious conduct . . . is asking too much. You are tired of it, so am I. Let us quit until the Order will either place men instead of brutes on the board or until they approve the actions of such men.[52]

As usual, Powderly chose a subterranean plot over the high moral path. When Bailey lectured on the West Coast in June, Powderly spies reported his every movement and proclamation. When Bailey revealed KOL internal disputes and asserted that actual membership was lower than the Order's public claims, Powderly charged Bailey with violating his obligation as a Knight by divulging secret matters. Bailey was ordered to return to Philadelphia to explain himself.[53]

Powderly frightened Bailey into temporary silence, then turned on Barry by resurrecting an old charge that he held an unauthorized hearing on the status of Morrison. Barry took the bait and defended Morrison, a tactical error as technically Morrison was out of the KOL by his own accord. After the carpet weavers' debacle Morrison was ordered to give up his leadership of DA 126 and return to LA 1899 to face charges regarding his conduct during the strike. When he refused to do so, he automatically forfeited KOL membership. Morrison was not a member in good standing at the time he joined Bailey, Barry, Turner, and others in the Provisionals.

Powderly had Barry in a procedural trap. If Barry pushed for Morrison's reinstatement, Morrison would face charges in LA 1899; if he insisted this was unfair, he showed contempt for procedure. Barry choose the second path and was immediately accused of seeking to circumvent the will of the general assembly. The executive board upheld Powderly's charge, with a chastened Bailey voting with the majority.[54]

Barry realized he was losing ground and once again sought to recover it publicly. An outburst concerning Powderly's "do-nothing policy" became the centerpiece of a Michigan newspaper story. Powderly, in Barry's words,

> has told the Order many things not to do, but very little as to what it should do. He has told us not to strike, not to boycott, and when members have taken political action as a means of relief . . . that again was displeasing to him, and in some instances he threatened to take their charter away for participating in politics.

He called the KOL a "ship without a compass," in need of complete "reorganization" in which districts and locals would have "complete jurisdiction" over their own affairs.[55]

Barry was promptly threatened with suspension. He boldly told Jo Labadie, "I have made up my mind to fight the gang and I shall do so regardless of the consequences," but he was such a marked man that even Bailey backed away from him. Exasperated, Barry told Labadie that Bailey "can go to the big dung hill. I shall go it alone." The two patched up their differences in the early fall, after both Carlton and Litchman quit the executive board. Barry acidly remarked, "Great God . . . if they all resign who will spend the boodle for the gudgeons?"[56]

On October 5, 1888, Barry also resigned from the board. Powderly and Hayes used the unexpected breathing space to compromise Bailey.

Hayes pilfered a letter from Bailey's desk that revealed that Bailey, Barry, and Buchanan had been recruiting for the Provisional Committee as late as September. Hayes forwarded it to Powderly and gloated, "It is the winning card if presented at the proper time to the G.A. . . . It proves beyond a doubt that Innocent Bill was and is working in the interests of the Provisionals."[57]

Barry was momentarily liberated by his resignation from the executive board. He unleashed charges against Powderly ranging from cronyism in central office hiring policies to financial mismanagement and sabotaging strikes. He even tried to turn the tables by accusing Powderly of bungling peace negotiations with trade unions. Barry shared his wild accusations with any reporter willing to take notes and forwarded a detailed list of allegations to the Associated Press, along with a copy of his resignation letter.[58] Hayes was livid and lampooned Barry as a "chimp." Barry kept up the pressure by unveiling Michael Breslin, a Home Club apostate who became Barry's shadow on the lecture circuit. Breslin told all who would listen of the perfidy of James Quinn, Tom McGuire, and their ally, Terence Powderly. Barry followed with his own indictments of the KOL's "body of professional tricksters" who squandered membership dues living in hotels owned by "industrial lords at poverty's expense." Barry called Hayes a man so removed from the working class that his "only possibility of hardship . . . is that he may die of dyspepsia or the gout." The Breslin/Barry lectures took on the look of a public confessional, with both Breslin and Barry admitting they once held cavalier attitudes about the Order's money, but now wished to atone. Even more damaging to the KOL's reputation was their insistence that the Order had fewer than two hundred thousand members, not the half million it publicly asserted.[59]

On October 18, the *Journal of United Labor* informed Knights that Barry had been expelled from the Order. The story was supplemented by carefully selected letters from Powderly's files of Knights complaining of Barry's behavior. It also gave an expurgated version of his activities at the 1887 assembly. The expulsion order charged Barry with betraying the Order to pursue political ambitions, slandering fellow board members, being active in the illegal Provisional Committee, and publicly criticizing KOL policy. Given that at least the latter three charges were true, Powderly was able to claim the high moral ground.[60]

All that was left was for the general assembly to rubber-stamp Barry's expulsion. The 1888 gathering in Indianapolis was as contentious as Minneapolis had been a year earlier. As if Bailey and Barry were not enough, Powderly's old nemesis, Victor Drury, reemerged to introduce failed resolutions to return the KOL to oath-bound secrecy and to charter Chinese assemblies. The convention turmoil should have confirmed Barry's basic assertion that the Knights needed new leadership. Powderly was forced to concede one of the Bailey/Barry charges: the KOL contained just over half (256,000) the 500,000 members claimed in press releases. The convention took up the question of how to control travel expenditures, reduce operating costs, and transfer account moneys to pay bills.[61]

Barry showed up at the convention, though he must have known his fate was sealed. Barry had little left to lose and laid his remaining card on the table. He accused board members of spying and produced an affidavit in which executive board stenographer F. F. Donnelly admitted spying on Bailey, Barry, and Carlton. Donnelly also confessed he removed letters from each man's files and withheld others addressed to them. The charges, though true, were old news. The 1887 assembly had previously dismissed Donnelly's affidavit, and the 1888 convention was not about to reopen it.[62]

Barry played out the string and submitted to an investigating committee hearing. His behavior was more laconic than defiant as Powderly and Hayes pressed charges of treason and disobedience. Barry interrupted on just a few occasions to offer what were, in essence, small corrections to the record. In one such moment he mentioned, in passing, the word "decentralization." Powderly immediately launched a defense of existing KOL structure and parodied Barry's views. "I would not give a cent for an organization in which every man has the right to act for himself," Powderly thundered. "What would an army be with every man acting on his own judgment and according to his own ideas? This is an army—it is not child's play." When Barry tried to return to policy issues, he was rebuffed to the point of frustration. After numerous interruptions from Hayes, who insisted on moving the expulsion question, Barry blurted out, "Oh, do as you have a mind to." The committee unanimously ruled against Barry, and the assembly upheld it by a vote of 122 to 24. The same vote also removed Bailey from the Order.[63]

The assembly twisted the knife in Barry's back by revoking the charter of his ax makers' trade district, an act of wanton revenge that served no one well. On November 23, Barry addressed his NTD 154 colleagues and advised them that the assembly had established the KOL as a "one man power" ruled by "czar" Powderly. He advised the ax makers to quit the KOL and reorganize as an international trade union rather than paying dues to "keep up the czar's palace in Philadelphia." The ax makers took Barry's advice and quit the KOL before the year was out.[64]

Bailey's expulsion ended his career as a national labor leader. He returned to Shawnee, Ohio, and dropped from view; not even local papers record his whereabouts after 1889. Nonetheless, his removal rippled through DA 135, whose 16,782 members made it the KOL's largest district by 1888. After the general assembly, many members quit the KOL for rival organizations. Powderly got on no better with Bailey's successor, William

Lewis, and NTD 135 fell into disarray. In late 1889, what was left of NTD 135 joined forces with the American Miners' Federation to form the Miners' Progressive Union (MPU). In January 1890, the MPU merged with several other miners' bodies, reorganized as the United Mine Workers of America (UMWA) and joined the AFL.[65] KOL mining locals that had once formed the backbone of the Order deserted to the UMWA in droves, including those in Powderly's northeastern Pennsylvania backyard. By 1893, the once-powerful DA 16 was reduced to a single operating local assembly, Powderly's own Scranton LA 222. When the 1893 convention ousted him as general master workman, even LA 222 surrendered its charter.

Barry made it his one-man mission to demean the Knights of Labor at every turn. He formed a rival organization, the Brotherhood of United Labor (BUL). Although the BUL accomplished little, it hastened KOL decline in several regions. By December 1888, Barry was crisscrossing the nation in search of support for the Brotherhood. At his side were Breslin and T. J. Wallace, a former clerk at KOL headquarters. In January 1889, they raised ire in Pittsburgh's DA 3 when several officials lobbied to have Barry address them. That request was denied, but Barry formed a Brotherhood branch in the Steel City; most of its members were ex-Knights. This proved a hardship within a city where total KOL membership had declined from over eleven thousand in 1886 to fewer than forty-five hundred in 1888. Within six months of Barry's visit, a dozen KOL locals collapsed in Allegheny County.[66]

More damaging was Breslin's success in New York City. DA 49 had once again overthrown the Home Club, and its new leaders were unfavorably disposed toward Powderly after his years of cooperation with Quinn and McGuire. DA 49 defiantly formed a committee of nine to study the BUL and to write a new DA 49 constitution. The committee emphasized DA 49's independence from the KOL's central leadership. That committee, patterned after Drury's concentric ring model, was headed by George Dunne, who routinely corresponded with other Powderly critics like Buchanan, Labadie, and Morrison.[67] Although DA 49 never officially endorsed Barry's Brotherhood, it maintained cordial relations with it.

Barry's Brotherhood was a decentralized version of the Knights of Labor; even its platform was cribbed from the Order. Like the KOL, it contained mixed and trade assemblies organized on local, state, and national levels. It allowed for the creation of "central" branches consisting of five or more locals—essentially district assemblies under a different name—but insisted that each local be attached also to a national trade assembly which set dues, created its own rituals, and determined its own strike policy. Each trade was autonomous and the powers of officers were

greatly curtailed. A general secretary, whose role was "advisory and cleri-
cal," headed the BUL. At its core, the Brotherhood sought to be a hybrid
of the KOL and the AFL, though Barry invested so little power in the
umbrella organization that one wonders what purpose affiliation with it
would have served.[68]

Barry's organization was more impressive on paper than on the shop
floor. Its raison d'être was lambasting the KOL. Although BUL letterhead
was emblazoned with a KOL triangle and the slogan "Equal and Exact
Justice to All—Special Privileges to None," Barry's private motives were
less noble. To Labadie he wrote, "I have learned to hate this man Powderly.
And I have sworn to drive him out of the labor movement in disgrace."[69]

Barry was destined for a shorter labor career than his nemesis. Moreover, Barry's correspondence reveals him to be just as thin-skinned, petty,
and vindictive as Powderly. In a subsequent letter he railed against a proposed unity conference among Powderly, P. J. McGuire, and Gompers.[70]
Barry's hatred for Powderly clouded his judgment to the point where personal issues superseded the best interests of labor. He failed to convince
Labadie to establish a Brotherhood branch in Detroit. By then, Labadie
was already president of the Michigan Federation of Labor and no doubt
suspected that Barry was a better critic than organizer.

It was clear by May 1889 that the Brotherhood was a stillborn flop.
For the rest of 1889, BUL organizers continued to attack Powderly, and T. J.
Wallace created a stir when he lodged formal corruption charges against
Powderly at the October general assembly, but the press soon ignored the
Brotherhood.[71] Barry carried his futile efforts into 1890, before quietly
laying the Brotherhood to rest and drifting away from labor leadership.

In 1907, Barry again contacted Labadie. The note featured Barry's
picture on the letterhead of "Barry's Lyceum Specialty Co.—Introducing
High Class Specialties with the Latest Illustrated Song Hits." He told Labadie of some articles he had written for *The Socialist* in which he turned his
guns against the AFL. He called the "trades union movement a rope of
sand" and accused the AFL of scabbing on the Western Federation of Miners. Much of the rest of the letter was filled with laments for Albert Parsons
and August Spies.[72]

For much of the 1880s, Barry was accused of being an anti–trade
union anarchist when he actually endorsed both international trade unions
and the ballot box. It was thus poignant irony that Barry spent his final
years advocating a vague anarcho-syndicalism. He was not very successful
at either selling sheet music or the socialist cause and died in 1909, his
fifty-seventh year.

*   *   *

Gary Marx and Douglas McAdam are correct: social movements can bring out inglorious as well as admirable human qualities. As Samuel Friedman noted, when these are turned inward, labor opposition groups can be as vicious against perceived labor bureaucrats as against employers. Because union bureaucrats like Terence Powderly are often as unlikable as they are visible, it is tempting to take the word of their critics as gospel. The B & B Affair suggests, however, that more attention should be focused on the institutional context in which personal vendettas take place.

The mid-1880s Knights of Labor was a complex, lumbering organization seeking to reinvent itself. It was also beset by myriad challenges from hostile employers, courts, politicians, and rival labor groups. Internally, it was riven with factions, not the least of which was the Home Club. In such a setting, it is foolhardy to saddle a man like Powderly with the blame for the Chicago stockyards strike or see him as a KOL "czar." Powderly was but one voice on a very contentious general executive board, about half of which would have gladly deposed him if they could have mustered the support.

Thomas Barry and William Bailey are often cited as well-meaning Knights who were badly mistreated by Powderly and his allies. In truth, they were as much part of the Order's problems as they were its victims. Both were undisciplined and stubborn, and neither had Powderly's gift for knowing what should be said in public versus what should be uttered only in private. Their heroic reputations aside, neither man was a particularly capable organizer. Most of their declared "victories" were little more than fragile cease-fires that rapidly disintegrated.

More seriously, Bailey and Barry were freelancers who hampered KOL centralization efforts. They seldom sought direction from superiors, they failed to inform those charged with implementing decisions that their public utterances masked hidden schemes, and they rarely followed directives. Their penchant for deflecting blame is particularly troublesome and makes them guilty of the "rule or ruin" charge that they so frequently leveled against Powderly and the Home Club.

Bailey and Barry were advocates of national trade districts, which, by their very nature, were resilient to control from the KOL's Philadelphia bureaucracy. Moreover, both knew that the KOL was more centralized on paper than in reality and that locals and districts routinely ignored executive board directives. It was self-serving to blame Powderly and the board for embarrassments like the loss of the Chicago stockyards strike since it could not have forced Barry or DA 57 to call off the strike.[73]

Still, neither man's removal from the Knights did the Order any good. Powderly's legendary pigheadedness and vanity merged with the duplicitous and deceitful will of Hayes to fan the flames of misunderstanding rather than drench them. If Bailey and Barry failed to comprehend order and discipline, Powderly and Hayes confused loyalty with blind obedience. What was lost was the opportunity to revisit the KOL's strike policy, debate some of the sensible merits of Barry's reorganization plan, define the role and scope of national trade districts within the Order, and address the serious erosion of rank-and-file membership. Instead of learning from mistakes, lost strikes, and mass desertion, both sides played the blame game. The mutual cycles of recrimination served only as a prelude to ruined organizations and shattered careers.

CHAPTER 3

In the Larger Field:
The Fate of Joseph R. Buchanan

In a popular survey of collective behavior, Ralph Turner and Lewis Killian note the normal life cycle of social movements and the types of leaders that emerge in each phase. "Prophets" who publicize injustice dominate the "preliminary stage." Movements then enter the "popular stage," in which prophets give way to "agitators" who fan discontent and create "collective excitement." In the first two stages, the movement as a whole is unfocused and loosely structured. Formal bureaucracy and directed policy emerge during the "organizational stage," which is dominated by "statesmen . . . who are masters of ceremony." If the movement survives to its "institutional stage" and becomes part of the social fabric, "administrators" rise to the top. Not all movements reach this level of articulation, of course. Both "internal and external contingencies" can disrupt, alter, fracture, or kill a movement at any of the four stages.[1]

These observations form the framework for one of the sadder studies in Knights of Labor internecine struggle, one that consumed one of the organization's brightest and best. Such was the case in 1887, when the KOL chased Joseph R. Buchanan from its ranks. By then, Buchanan had become such a thorn in Powderly's side that his name evoked the sort of contempt usually reserved for Thomas Barry and William Bailey. But though his critics often considered him the "third B" of the "B & B Affair," Joe Buchanan was too pragmatic, principled, and scrupulous to warrant such a label. As Buchanan put it in his autobiography, his concern for what was right for wage earners led him into "the larger field," one that stretched beyond the boundaries Powderly, his cronies, and his enemies wished to set.

Buchanan was precisely the sort of leader the KOL needed as it evolved as an organization. With his keen mind, golden tongue, deep commitment to working people, sense of practicality, and skills as a businessman, Buchanan could play prophet, agitator, statesman, or administrator. He was among the very few Knights who could have mollified the Order's dissident factions. Buchanan was simultaneously an ideologue, a strategist, a trade unionist, a radical, and an advocate of the "One Big Union" ideal. In fact, his career within the Knights highlights the ways in which Gilded Age political labels are highly suspect. Condemned as anarchist and often boldly proclaiming himself as such, Buchanan saw no contradiction in also advancing trade unionism or codes of conservative personal morality. He was also the single-best organizer in KOL history, a man who created scores of new local assemblies through appeals to practical agendas singularly devoid of polemics. Indeed, Buchanan was such an effective organizer and decent human being that his expulsion from the KOL was one of the few mistakes Powderly ever acknowledged publicly, writing "Labor has had many champions, [but] it has never had a more loyal or honest one than Joseph Buchanan."[2]

How a self-styled "labor agitator" was discarded despite his obvious service to his organization forms one of the more sordid chapters of KOL history. In later life, Buchanan was noted for his "good humor," wit, and "winning personality."[3] He could also be argumentative, pious, self-righteous, and stubborn; in other words, a lot like Powderly, which exacerbated his bitter clashes with the general master workman, in the context of the four issues over which they most disagreed: trade unionism, political ideology, strike policy, and support for the Haymarket anarchists.

Joseph Ray Buchanan was born in Hannibal, Missouri, on December 6, 1851, attended public schools there, and dabbled in typesetting before settling on a career in journalism. He moved to Denver in 1878, worked for the *Denver Democrat,* married Mary Ellen Holt, and joined International Typographical Union (ITU) Local 49. Shortly thereafter, Buchanan quit the *Democrat* to try his hand at an independent venture, which failed in 1880.

The Buchanans moved to Leadville, where he secured a job with *The Daily Democrat.* In Leadville, Buchanan met miners affiliated with the KOL, his first contact with the organization and his first brush with a strike. He, like most at the paper, supported miners protesting wage cuts, and he said so in print and in a short soapbox speech given on behalf of the strikers.

When he was ridiculed in a rival paper and assaulted on a Leadville street, Buchanan quickly learned that more was needed than a passel of golden words. Street clashes between strikers and police and the discovery of his name on the hit list of the Committee of 100, a local vigilante group advocating violence against striking miners, radicalized Buchanan. Rather than flee the city, he gave more speeches in support of the miners and openly carried a pistol when he appeared in public. He remained steadfast to the strike's bitter end, hastened by the importation of scab laborers, a curfew, and a passport system.[4]

Buchanan stayed in Leadville for six more months before returning to Denver for a post with the *Rocky Mountain News.* He threw himself into labor activities and was chosen to represent ITU Local 49 at its June 1882 convention in St. Louis. There, however, he witnessed infighting and parliamentary wrangling that made him feel "dissatisfied and uneasy."[5] He returned to Denver and contacted the KOL. At the time, there was a single local in the city; Buchanan helped organize its second, LA 2327, dubbed "Unity Assembly." On December 16, 1882, he and Samuel Laverty began publishing the *Labor Enquirer,* the official organ of both Denver-area Knights and of ITU Local 49.[6]

At this juncture of his life, Buchanan was struggling to articulate ideology, strategy, and tactics. He had found his voice as an orator and editorialist, but he was deeply troubled by the ease with which organized capital crushed working-class uprisings like those in Leadville. By his own admission, his fixation on work and the labor question bordered on the "fanatic."[7] At times, his enthusiasm skirted recklessness. There were calls to close the *Enquirer* when Buchanan began appending weekly reports on the cost of dynamite to his own fiery editorials.[8] By early 1883, Buchanan was a devoted reader of *Truth,* an independent paper published in San Francisco by Burnette Haskell, best known for its anti-Chinese xenophobia. Although the *Enquirer* did its share of Chinese baiting, Buchanan was far more interested in the organization Haskell represented, the International Workingmen's Association (IWA).

The IWA began as Karl Marx's attempt to create an international organization for ongoing socialist agitation. By the early 1880s, it had undergone numerous transformations, none of them particularly effective in building a mass movement. The IWA was dubbed the "Red International" and was as likely to advocate seizure of power via the ballot box as through revolutionary upheaval. To Haskell, however, the IWA's program looked more hopeful than that of the "Black International," the nickname for the International Working People's Association (IWPA). The IWPA was founded in 1881 at a Chicago conference in which members of various Social Revolutionary clubs revived the debate between Marx and Mikhail Bakunin that fractured the First International. The IWPA retained Marx's faith in trade unions but sought to make them into anarchist cells that would forcefully overthrow the state in the here and now, rather than prepare for a future socialist utopia.[9]

Haskell introduced Buchanan to the more cautious Red International. Despite his audacious printing of dynamite prices, Buchanan found the IWPA's advocacy of random violence reckless and counterproductive, though he seldom criticized the group publicly. He also retained more faith in the political process and saw the need for unions to work for short-term improvements in workers' economic circumstances. When an IWA branch opened in Denver as the Rocky Mountain Social League, Buchanan immediately joined the Reds.

But he remained open to the Blacks, should they show promise. On September 29, 1883, the *Labor Enquirer* sported a woodcut and front-page feature story on Johann Most. Other articles discussed the proper uses of dynamite and ways to commit sabotage.[10] Within weeks, the *Enquirer*'s masthead proclaimed "Who Would Be Free Himself Must Strike the First Blow," an anarchist rallying cry more associated with the Blacks than the Reds.

On the surface, Buchanan's anarchism seems soft, even amorphous. That may be true to some extent, but it was also typical of many Gilded Age radicals. Joe Buchanan was an anarchist more in word than deed. Like many, he found that anarchism provided a vocabulary through which he could vent frustration and anger, though he found it lacking in coherent tactics. Mostly, he found it a useful tool for agitating and organizing. Once aroused, workers could be channeled into pragmatic organizations, like unions. He reasoned that if all unions cooperated under the aegis of the KOL, a Marxist utopia might be attainable. Thus Buchanan entered 1884 identifying himself simultaneously as an anarchist, a trade unionist, a newspaper proprietor, and a Knight. That year was pivotal for Buchanan as it began a two-year cycle in which he led successful strikes based on solid trade-union tactics rather than rigid ideology or rash acts of violence. By 1885, only Powderly and George McNeill were better known among Knights of Labor.

Buchanan's remarkable streak of strike victories began on May 4, 1884, when Denver-area shop men from the Union Pacific Railroad asked for his help in their strike to rescind wage cuts. He enthusiastically supported them in *Labor Enquirer* editorials. More important, Buchanan helped bring Irish, German, and native-born workers into a common organization, the Union Pacific Employees Association (UPEA). From its Denver base, the UPEA spread throughout the Union Pacific system. In a mere four days, the shop men won their strike and brought their UPEA branches into the Knights as local assemblies. From this foundation, Buchanan built new assemblies. He recalled that "within thirty days we had a healthy assembly at each important point on the [Union Pacific] system. I organized assemblies in all the shops from Omaha to Cheyenne, inclusive."[11] By mid-1884, Denver alone had five operating KOL locals, one of which had thirty-seven women meeting as "Hope Assembly."[12]

Joseph Buchanan. Courtesy of the
Catholic University of America Archives.

Buchanan was a local legend by August 11, 1884, when Union Pacific (UP) machinists struck after a 10 percent wage cut and the discharge of twenty Knights involved in the May strike. In negotiations with the UP, Buchanan bluffed his way to victory by implying that all the railroad brotherhoods were united behind the machinists. In just a week, the UP backed down rather than face a long strike. In truth, it was only after the victory that coordination between railway brotherhoods took place. Through his tactical brilliance Buchanan gained enough time to build what Shelton Stromquist dubs "the best-organized road in the country."[13]

Under the aegis of Master Workman Thomas Neasham, as many as twenty-five thousand UP workers entered KOL locals affiliated with DA 82. More impressive in an age of constant railroad agitation, DA 82 and UP officials enjoyed peaceful relations into the 1890s. Even after the KOL faded elsewhere it remained powerful along the UP until 1894, when most affiliates cast their lot with the American Railway Union.[14]

Growth continued apace in Denver. By the fall of 1884, the city had eight KOL locals; by mid-1885, a dozen locals and more than four thousand dues-paying Knights. The KOL recognized Buchanan's heroic efforts when, in 1884, it elected him to the general executive board. He was its "only member . . . residing west of Ohio," but despite a constituency spread from Missouri to the Pacific, Buchanan did his best to represent them.[15] When Colorado and New Mexico coal miners got embroiled in a yearlong strike against the Canon City Coal Company and the Colorado Coal and Iron Company, he showed up to lend his personal support. When the strikes ground to an inconclusive halt, Buchanan quickly reminded them that the KOL had not authorized their strike, frank words credited with keeping most of the miners in the KOL.[16]

Buchanan was so active that he even turned his attention to matters east of the Mississippi. Few papers were as supportive of the 1884 miners' strike in Ohio's Hocking Valley as was his *Labor Enquirer*.[17] The violence he witnessed there led him to privately "despair of a peaceful solution of the labor problem," though he counseled against force in opposition to his own anarchist beliefs.[18] Once again Buchanan played the pragmatist rather than the ideologue.

Any doubt of Buchanan's ability and pragmatism was dispelled during the 1885 Southwest Railway strike. Three railroads—the Missouri Pacific; the Wabash; and the Missouri, Kansas, and Texas—made up the bulk of Jay Gould's conglomerate. In October 1884, wages for Missouri Pacific shop men were slashed by 10 percent. When asked to endure another 5 percent cut in February 1885, workers walked out. By March 9, 1885, much of the system was on strike, and Union Pacific shop men feared that Gould's wage cuts would extend to their lines. In that spirit, Denver LA 3218 dispatched Buchanan and William Morley to Sedalia, Missouri, with a $30,000 pledge of support for the Southwest Railway men. The two men began organizing KOL locals throughout the system, a Herculean task given that it sprawled over ten thousand miles. Stunned by the KOL juggernaut, Gould officials quickly rescinded the wage cuts and on March 16, 1885, workers called off their strike.[19]

Buchanan had little time to rest on his laurels. When he returned to Denver, he faced shop and track men from the Denver and Rio Grande line clamoring for a strike. He found such an action unwise and warned the men that they could not count on support from the other brotherhoods. Characteristically, though he was voted down and a walkout began on May 4, Buchanan threw his support behind the strikers. He organized rallies and parades, assisted strikers in turning aside court injunctions, and personally investigated a derailing he suspected was the act of an agent provocateur. Nonetheless, the refusal of the Brotherhood of Locomotive Engineers to honor the strike, a lack of financial support from the KOL executive board, and renewal of hostilities along the Gould lines doomed the strike. It was never officially called off, but it fizzled out by October. Thanks to Buchanan's loyalty in the face of his personal opposition, few blamed the loss on the KOL, and the Order actually increased its membership in the strike's wake.[20]

The indefatigable Buchanan was more successful in salvaging the Southwest Railway situation, where a new strike began on the Wabash line on June 16, 1885, when Gould officials failed to honor pledges made eight weeks earlier. Buchanan went to St. Louis to meet with Wabash officials, where he was joined by William Bailey, John Hayes, and Frederick Turner. According to Buchanan, his KOL colleagues were less than helpful. He claimed, "Turner simply kept the records of the meeting, [and] Hayes looked on and said nothing. Bailey put in most of the time at the window trying to get on friendly terms with the elusive zephyrs that occasionally stole through . . . while [I] . . . who had traveled a thousand miles, leaving grave responsibilities behind (the Rio Grande strike) . . . was left the task [of negotiation]."[21]

It was just as well that Buchanan was left to his own devices. Once again, he struck upon a successful, if daring, plan. When the KOL executive board vacillated on Buchanan's request to call out the entire system, infuriated Wabash men lashed out at Buchanan. He responded with a tirade of his own and told impatient leaders that if they wished to conduct their own strike they had that right, though it would be suicidal. Buchanan succeeded in calming tempers long enough for the executive board to pressure Gould more effectively. On September 3, 1885, Gould learned that no KOL line, including the Union Pacific, would handle Wabash cars. Deprived of a way to get goods to Pacific ports, Gould surrendered and the KOL claimed its greatest victory.[22]

Most historians credit the 1885 victory over Jay Gould as the major impetus behind the Order's phenomenal growth spurt during the next year. From just over 111,000 at the time of the strike, official membership mushroomed to over 729,000 by July 1, 1886, and the KOL contained untold numbers of unofficial Knights. Few observers have given Buchanan due credit in buying the needed time for strikers to position themselves for victory. Buchanan's ability to maintain discipline stands in marked contrast to Thomas Barry's inability to do so during the 1887 Chicago packinghouse strikes.

Buchanan's victory streak ended at the 1885 general assembly in Hamilton, Ontario. Despite being one of the most famous men in the Order, he was not reelected to the executive board. In his autobiography Buchanan claimed that he declined reelection because he needed rest from two years of constant travel on behalf of the Order.[23] In truth, Buchanan made an uncharacteristic but well-publicized mistake: he got drunk before the vote. That was shocking enough from a professed teetotaler, but his timing could not have been worse. As the Wabash negotiations reveal, he was already at odds with several board members, and they were not inclined to overlook his indiscretion when the KOL was in the midst of a highly public campaign to promote temperance among the working class. Buchanan tactfully withdrew his candidacy rather than face ridicule, but his brief foray into public revelry made a lasting impression; years after the incident his enemies called him a drunkard, though he had practiced total abstinence and had publicly supported prohibition candidates in Colorado.[24]

Thus Joe Buchanan was outside the corridors of KOL bureaucracy for the crucial first five months of 1886. As the KOL swelled with members—many of whom were the result of Buchanan's efforts—the Home Club consolidated a power base on the eve of the May 24 special assembly. By then, as well, six of the seven men accused of the May 4 bombing in Chicago's Haymarket Square were behind bars. (Albert Parsons surrendered in June.) Delegate Buchanan arrived in Cleveland upset that the executive board had recently authorized the very strike on the Gould lines he had counseled against the previous August, yet it had refused to endorse a May 1 general strike for the eight-hour workday. He blamed the inconsistencies and the renewed Gould strike on New York City "union haters"—the Home Club.[25] He grew restive when the special assembly took "four days to secure passage" of a simple resolution offering the "friendship of the order for all . . . organizations having the welfare of workers as their object."[26]

Buchanan blamed Home Club anti–trade union bias for sandbagging the joint Knights of Labor/Federated Trades and Labor Union (FOTLU) panel to which he was an envoy. While FOTLU was negotiating jurisdictional disputes with the KOL, the latter was busy adding six "auxiliary" members to the executive board, including Buchanan. Ominously, however, only he and Ira Aylsworth were sympathetic to FOTLU. Buchanan correctly noted that the "dove of peace turned out to be a buzzard. The war between the Knights of Labor and the trades-unions was on, and it was to be fought to a finish."[27]

Buchanan returned to the West, where he organized Denver's sixteenth local assembly and helped New Mexico miners settle a strike, but his estrangement from KOL leadership was about to become public. He was greatly troubled by the verdict in the Haymarket case and said so in the *Labor Enquirer.* His articles were so vitriolic that an ex-Knight from Denver complained to Powderly of a paper "published in the interest of socialism and anarchy as the standard bearer of the K. of L."[28] The complaint was accurate; by July 1886, the *Enquirer* was also the official journal of the Rocky Mountain Social League.

Buchanan tried his best to don the ideologue mantle and explain the differences between his socialist anarchism and that of the Black International, but this lesson was lost on Powderly. Instead, Buchanan tried a pragmatic appeal and warned Powderly of the damage to KOL organizing the Home Club's machinations exacted. In July he wrote, "I see by the papers that the fight of idiots has begun in New York and that the 'rule or ruin' policy is being put into practice with a vengeance. . . . Goodbye to organized labor if this damned idiocy is not stopped."[29] Rather than heed Buchanan's warning, Powderly focused on the very ideological issues Buchanan himself had raised. He took Buchanan to task for belonging to other organizations besides the KOL and chided, "You are pretty radical, too outspoken and give the impression you would do a dam [sic] sight worse than you really would do." In Powderly's mind, Buchanan harmed the KOL by causing the public to conflate it with anarchism.[30]

Buchanan protested that neither he nor the Rocky Mountain Social League advocated propaganda of the deed and that if violence ensued, it would be at the hands of capitalists, not workers. His ultimate goal was to "socialize industry and establish the Co-operative Commonwealth," principles in keeping with those of the Knights. He even admitted that he "looked upon Haymarket as an impediment to our progress."[31] Nonetheless, he insisted that the sentences meted out to the Haymarket men were a great injustice. He did not hesitate to accuse Chicago Knights of cowardice when DA 24 voted to condemn anarchism.[32]

By the time the Richmond general assembly convened on October 4, 1886, Buchanan was branded a troublemaker. Publicly, the convention was a model of fraternal decorum. In private, however, near chaos reigned. It took place in the shadow of the collapse of the second Gould strike, a result Buchanan had predicted.[33] Membership was already declining and debates raged over the KOL's future course. Of the subjects Buchanan most cared about, only a mild resolution requesting clemency for the Haymarket men passed, and Powderly gutted even that. Buchanan found himself amid a small but vocal minority. Among the resolutions he voted against were the abolition of the offices of insurance secretary and general auditor, investing the general assembly with "emergency" constitutional amendment power, the rejection of John Morrison's delegate credentials, the expulsion of cigarmakers affiliated with the CMIU, and the final investigation report on the Home Club. All of these passed. He also raised questions about Powderly's handling of the second Gould strike and of his initials forays into the Chicago stockyards strike.[34]

In Buchanan's mind, the issues of Morrison, the cigarmakers, and the Home Club were linked. It was Morrison who, at the June special assembly, demanded an investigation of the Home Club after blaming it for sabotaging the New York carpet weavers' strike. Morrison's credentials were challenged at Richmond over a technicality involving a transfer card, thus removing him from discussions of the Home Club report. With Morrison out of the way, a whitewashed investigation report came before the general assembly, asserting that the Home Club's only purposes were to "educate members of the order in the true polity of the labor movement and to provide homes for old and decrepit members." When Buchanan and others demanded a copy of the report before voting on it, Powderly urged members to drop the matter. Buchanan was furious and pointed out that one of the authors of the report was James Quinn, a Victor Drury confidant.[35]

Again, Buchanan was voted down and exonerated Home Club members immediately introduced a resolution to expel CMIU–affiliated cigar-makers. Buchanan denounced this as "the pet scheme of DA 49," but he lost the fight when proponents of expulsion accused him of trying to allow trade unions to dictate KOL policy. He at least made sure his comrades in Denver's DA 89 knew his heart. In his report of the convention proceedings he wrote:

> I am a Trades Unionist. Those of you who know the bitter warfare waged upon me . . . by certain representatives of Trades Unions, and the struggle I have had with the Unions . . . can say whether the insinuation that it is my wish to subordinate the order to the Trades Unions is true or not. I have for four years been an earnest, unflinching advocate through amalgamation of organized labor; and have tried to aid in bringing about a complete coalition between the Trades Unions and the K. of L. I have been of the opinion that all organized labor should be under one head, and that the Trades Unions should become National Trade Districts of the Knights of Labor.[36]

Buchanan knew, however, that his strong pledge of KOL loyalty would do little to placate his powerful enemies. To his Denver friends he also confided that his general assembly votes were "probably the last act of the kind I shall ever perform for D. A. 89."[37]

Had wiser Knights listened to Buchanan, the fate of the American labor movement might have taken a very different course. The Knights of Labor began when Uriah Stephens dissolved his Philadelphia tailors' union in 1869, but it retained a strong trade character into the early 1880s. When the FOTLU formed in 1881, sixty of the one hundred seven founding delegates were Knights of Labor. Despite the Home Club's assault on trades and its championing of mixed locals, trade assemblies predominated throughout the Order. In May 1886, the FOTLU mutated into the AFL, led by such disgruntled Knights and ex-Knights as Samuel Gompers, P. J. McGuire, Adolph Strasser, and William H. Foster.

At the time of the KOL's Richmond convention, however, the AFL was a nascent organization in which personal animosity might have been cast aside for the right kind of deal with the more powerful KOL. If serious efforts had been made to stifle Home Club attacks on trade unionism, it is conceivable that a compromise along the lines proposed by Buchanan might have stood a chance. As it was, the CMIU expulsion order led to an intense period of competition, mutual recrimination, and jurisdiction raiding. In October 1887, the KOL's general assembly rescinded many anti–trade union actions of the previous year and held out an olive branch to the AFL and unaffiliated unions, but the moment had been lost. During the next few years, trade unions and the KOL discussed ways to heal their rift, but nothing substantive came to pass. By the mid-1890s, the KOL was a paper tiger easily ignored by the AFL.

Buchanan was prophetic in his prediction that his DA 89 days were numbered, though he retained many allies in Richmond's aftermath. He urged his DA 89 colleagues to reject the CMIU expulsion order, a resolution that carried with little dissent. So too did one thanking Buchanan for his work on the district's behalf, and another condemning the "unconstitutionality" of the cigarmakers' expulsion order. According to Buchanan, "not one union man was forced out of the order in Colorado, and not one gave up his union because of the action of the General Assembly."[38] Buchanan also capitalized on widespread criticism of Powderly's handling of the Chicago stockyards strike, noting that there was "no man more unpopular with the Chicago workingmen than Mr. Powderly."[39] Such remarks caused nary a stir in Denver, where Powderly was scarcely better regarded.

Buchanan was too scrupulous to make open accusations of corruption, but his probing criticisms further sullied Powderly's reputation. Despite the presence of many Irish Catholic miners in Colorado, Buchanan struck a chord when he charged KOL leaders with kowtowing to Rome. He revived Barry's hoary charge that the stockyards strike was called off at the request of local priests, and he noted that that KOL leadership was a virtual Catholic monopoly. According to his own estimate, only 15 percent of Knights were Catholic, dubious reckoning that nonetheless won him admiration among disaffected Protestant Knights, some of whom reeled with suspicions lingering from debates over the Order's ritual. Buchanan bolstered his case by publicizing Powderly's disputes with Father Edward McGlynn, a defrocked priest involved with Henry George and the single-tax movement.[40]

Most of Buchanan's support came from trade-union Knights. They cheered his blast that Powderly "lacked the penetrative power that enabled many others to see through the thin veil behind which was hidden the selfishness and the ambition of the anti-unionists. . . . Powderly seemed entirely to lose his head immediately following the Richmond session," he charged, citing the Chicago stockyards strike and his tirades against the

Haymarket men as examples of Powderly's diminished perspective. Buchanan later admitted that he "turned the editorial page of the *Enquirer* loose against Powderly and his advisors," going so far as to lampoon favorable portraits of Powderly found in mainstream newspapers. He wryly noted that "when the daily press and the employing class begin to praise a labor 'leader,' it is time for the workingmen to keep an eye on him." In his view, Powderly was an "able agitator and leader of sentiment in a . . . general way [but] . . . almost worthless when it came to following a definite policy."[41]

Such observations won trade-union support but further isolated Buchanan from KOL leaders. So too did his scathing—and deceptive—comments on a Powderly circular urging Knights to stay out of partisan politics.[42] The *Labor Enquirer* zealously took up the 1886 elections, and it endorsed Henry George's campaign to become mayor of New York.[43] Buchanan was not alone in ignoring Powderly's political ban; Knights across the nation took up third-party banners and many were elected to state and local offices.[44] Results in Denver, however, were less sanguine. Buchanan and his Rocky Mountain Social League allies campaigned vigorously for Colorado Prohibition Party congressional candidates Joseph Murray and the Reverend Myron Reed. Both men were swamped by Republican opponents who parlayed fears of radical takeovers and saloon closings into large electoral victories.[45]

The November poll results led Buchanan to don the ideologue's mantle, and it blunted his effectiveness as a labor leader. He misread the sentiments of workers he had previously served well by taking the pragmatist's path. Buchanan's fanatical obsession with the eight Haymarket anarchists consumed him. He appointed himself as their personal savior and, on January 3, 1887, quit Denver and moved to Chicago to direct the clemency movement. He left control of the *Labor Enquirer* to his wife and to assistant editor James Callahan, and secured a post with Chicago's *Daily Star,* a job that lasted just weeks before Buchanan decided to publish a Chicago version of the *Enquirer.* The Denver paper was sold to Buchanan's onetime mentor Burnette Haskell, a man with all of Buchanan's passions but few of his virtues.

His Chicago venture was plagued with trouble from the start. The Chicago *Labor Enquirer* was even more strapped for cash than the Denver paper and Buchanan could only manage biweekly editions for most of its short existence. Nor did Chicago area Knights flock to Buchanan's paper, as they already had a journal, *The Knights of Labor.* Historian Bruce Nelson astutely notes, "From its first issue both editor and paper were out of place. Buchanan simultaneously held membership cards as an organizer for the International Workingmen's Association and as District Master Workman of the Knights' DA 89 in Denver. With a foot in both camps, he was misunderstood by both."[46] Buchanan paid numerous visits to the jailed anarchists, an exercise that deepened his radicalism without sharpening its focus. Soon, he was too tainted by anarchism for Chicago Knights who were disassociating themselves from Haymarket, yet he was too ideologically soft for the city's anarchist community. Buchanan managed to be just radical enough to engender unwanted controversy. When the paper ran a special issue to commemorate the sixteenth anniversary of the Paris Commune, the local postmaster refused Buchanan access to the U.S. mails.[47]

In an effort to mend fences with Chicago radicals, Buchanan joined the American branch of the Socialist Labor Party (SLP). Throughout the summer of 1887, he campaigned on behalf of the coalition United Labor Party (ULP), only to see his efforts backfire. When the ULP faltered at the polls, the SLP accused Buchanan of selling out to the Democratic Party, and it expelled him in early 1888. Even more troublesome was a charge leveled by prominent anarchist William Holmes. Although he felt Buchanan was a "revolutionary socialist" at heart, he charged, "the *Enquirer* could never be called a socialistic paper. It advocated radical reform in a vague way that left the reader in considerable doubt." He went on to inform *Der Sozialist* readers that Buchanan could no longer be considered a legitimate labor advocate.[48]

Holmes's comments were overly harsh, but they pointed to a reality Buchanan was slow to grasp: the pragmatic union man was out of place among dyed-in-the-wool ideologues. Although he could turn a revolutionary slogan as well as anyone, Buchanan's forte was plotting tactics and leading strikes, not debating doctrine. In July 1887, he again skewered Powderly for misunderstanding socialism, but his remarks betrayed a loose doctrinal grasp.[49] In essence, Buchanan had no base of support in Chicago. Instead of working behind the scenes within the KOL—a role more in keeping with his talents—he unwisely tried to mollify unreceptive anarchists by publicly criticizing KOL leaders, making his eventual expulsion a fait accompli.

Back in Denver, Haskell undid much of the goodwill Buchanan so carefully crafted. The situation in the city was so tense that Powderly himself made plans to visit in May 1887. By the end of April, Thomas Neasham complained that DA 89 squabbles were having an adverse effect on his own DA 82. According to Neasham, Haskell's editorials and Buchanan's rantings in Chicago made the KOL "appear ridiculous in the eyes of the Public."[50] Powderly hastily ordered Buchanan to return his organizer credentials, prompting him to remark he would gladly do so in order to dispel any notions that he was "solid with T. V. Powderly." Buchanan tartly added that his efforts on behalf of labor "are my credentials."[51]

Buchanan did not go away quietly. The Chicago *Labor Enquirer* solicited calls for Powderly's resignation from around the country and labeled General Secretary Charles Litchman "a puffed toad." When George McNeill submitted an article suggesting that Powderly might resign at the 1887 general assembly, Buchanan set it under the banner headline "Let Him Go."[52] Nor did Powderly's visit dispel turmoil in Denver. Awaiting him was a list of fifty queries drafted by Haskell, with help from Buchanan. Powderly was forced to defend a series of controversial actions, dating back to his handling of the 1882 Duryea Starch boycott and Theodore Cuno's expulsion.

Powderly was also called upon to explain why he called off the Chicago stockyards strike, why he refused to defend fellow Knight Albert Parsons, why he opposed both Henry George and Father McGlynn, why he sabotaged efforts at forming independent labor parties, why he allowed the expulsion of CMIU cigarmakers, why he supported the Home Club in its dispute with Brooklyn's Montauk Assembly, and why he denounced socialism when he was once a card-carrying member of the SLP. There was also a long list of indictments masquerading as questions including allegations that Litchman squandered KOL resources, that executive board members were involved in graft, and that Powderly cleared all KOL decisions through the Pope and that he revealed the Order's secret work to Cardinal Gibbons.[53]

Powderly was never one to allow character aspersions to go unanswered. He foolishly gave long written answers to each question, an act that gained him official DA 89 exoneration but assured his words would be scrutinized for inconsistencies for months to come. DA 89 dutifully condemned both Haskell and the Denver *Labor Enquirer,* but the city pulsed with charges and countercharges all summer, especially after Buchanan and Haskell drafted a report titled "Concerning the Visit of G.M.W. Powderly to Denver." DA 89 was rent in half, with one faction siding with Powderly and the other inclined to embrace the Buchanan-Haskell report. Matters were complicated when Neasham's DA 82 blasted the report as a "tissue of lies . . . [put forth by] a coterie of adventurers, Anarchists and cranks, and their disreputable organ the *Labor Enquirer*."[54] The Rocky Mountain regional unity Buchanan had forged through four years of laborious toil lay in tatters. In the immediate aftermath of Powderly's visit, local assemblies began requesting transfers between DA 82 and DA 89, on the basis of whether they sided with Powderly or DA 89 malcontents. Even Neasham admitted things had not gone as well as he had hoped.[55] While the rank and file chose sides, Haskell hammered away at Powderly from the KOL's left wing.[56]

Powderly largely blamed Buchanan for the troubles, even when Haskell was the culprit. Buchanan, who saw himself as a plainspoken man whose reputation was his bond and whose words were public record, furiously lashed out against the "cowardly, sneaking, lying curs" who besmirched his reputation. He turned the tables on his accusers, insisting that rumor, innuendo, and clandestine activity were the style of the Home Club, not himself. He proclaimed himself "an indefatigable fighter against rings and conspiracies" and pledged to fight them "until [they] are broken or I am dead." He denied responsibility for Haskell's outbursts and told Powderly he thought some of them were erroneous, though he added, "You can rest assured that I have not endorsed all your actions."[57]

When John Hayes revived charges that Buchanan was a drunkard, an incensed Buchanan suspected Powderly of using Hayes as his hatchet man in the manner in which he stood accused of using Haskell. He responded by carefully analyzing Powderly's every action and using the Chicago *Labor Enquirer* to catalog his errors. When Powderly told a journalist that European "paupers" should not be allowed to immigrate to the United States, Buchanan charged him with hypocrisy. He sarcastically added that Powderly's suggestion was "a little bit inconsistent, to say the least," given that he was the son of Irish immigrants. One week later he picked apart Powderly's grasp of semantics when he tried to define "socialism."[58]

Such petty backstabbing was unworthy of Buchanan, but it contributed mightily to a rising anti-Powderly tide within the KOL. Powderly was besieged on all sides. By late summer, the reorganized Home Club with which he aligned was once again in turmoil, and executive board members Thomas Barry and William Bailey were in open revolt. Craft unionists were increasingly restless, while numerous Knights gravitated toward the reform-minded Provisional Committee of the KOL. When the *Labor Enquirer* began to print news of the committee's progress, Powderly charged that Buchanan was a member.[59]

Powderly was premature; Buchanan was not yet involved with the Provisionals, though his Chicago friend Charles Seib was. Just before the general assembly convened in Minneapolis on October 4, Buchanan wrote the editorial that "sealed my fate." In it, Buchanan lampooned recent Powderly circulars advising Knights not to strike or engage in partisan political activity. Buchanan raised the poignant question, "What are we organized for?" He went on to identify Powderly with labor's past and suggest his replacement was necessary for it to have a future.[60] Although Buchanan was steeled for a floor fight, he was "totally unprepared for the unknightly, unmanly and cowardly treatment" that befell him in Minneapolis.[61]

Buchanan came to the convention armed with a traveling card from his local assembly and organizer credentials issued by DA 89. In addition, he was an elected delegate from DA 89. All three documents were rejected, and Buchanan was refused a seat at the assembly on the pretext that his local assembly had been suspended for nonpayment of dues. Buchanan wired DA 89 headquarters and produced a cable assuring him that his local was "in good standing." Nonetheless, the Credentials Committee refused to accept either the cable or Buchanan's pledge to pay the alleged arrears out of his own pocket "ten times over."[62]

The battle over Buchanan's credentials consumed two entire days of the assembly agenda. Powderly's "string of charges . . . that embraced everything from trades-unionism to revolutionary Anarchism" went on for over an hour. When Buchanan begged for time to address the charges, Powderly screamed, "Sit down! Sit down!" and "shook his gavel" at Buchanan. In a moment of what was likely calculated drama, Powderly threw down that gavel and stormed off the floor, crying out, "I can stand this no more; take your Master Workmanship!" Threatening to resign was a familiar Powderly ploy, but it worked once again. In the end, Buchanan was denied an assembly seat, and that body later expelled him.[63]

Once out of the KOL's official graces, Buchanan naturally gravitated to the Provisional Committee. In print, he called its leaders "intelligent Knights of Labor . . . representing the honest sentiment of the general assembly." He avowed that the "general office has become a luxurious haunt for men whose chief aim is to benefit self," charging that the KOL was run by an "organized conspiracy" that monopolized salaried positions, stymied dissent, and squandered funds on an illegal "war . . . against trade unions and trade districts." Haskell's Denver *Enquirer* added that the KOL was disintegrating and suggested that disgruntled members consider the AFL.[64]

The general assembly adjourned on October 19, 1887; by November, Buchanan headed the Chicago chapter of the Provisional Committee of the KOL, a full-fledged breakaway movement. At least six Chicago locals quit DA 24 for the committee and several other districts, including John Morrison's DA 126 and powerful Philadelphia DA 1, the KOL's parent assembly, favored the Provisionals. Each affiliate announced it would discontinue paying assessments to the central office, a solid blow given the overall drop in revenue in 1887. Rumors abounded that Brooklyn and New York City Knights fed up with the Home Club and DA 49 would soon join the Provisionals. This was hardly idle speculation; Home Club foe George Murray openly embraced the splinter movement.[65]

Buchanan, however, was consumed by a more immediate cause: the fate of the Haymarket anarchists.[66] The same assembly that ousted Buchanan also rejected a clemency resolution, an act that drove numerous Knights from the Order.[67] For nine months, Buchanan made repeated visits to the cell blocks to visit the eight convicted men, and he often served as a go-between for the prisoners and Illinois governor Richard Oglesby. Buchanan hand-delivered August Spies's letter withdrawing an earlier request for clemency and offering his own life to spare the other seven. Buchanan also delivered a clemency petition signed by fifty Knights present at the Minneapolis assembly who defied the anticlemency resolution adopted by the convention. He also handed Oglesby a letter from Albert Parsons requesting that the state also execute his wife and two children as they were equally culpable under Illinois law.

On the very eve of the execution date, Buchanan and a legal team sped to Springfield with evidence that they had unearthed the identity of the true Haymarket bomber. Oglesby rejected their plea for a stay of execution and, on November 11, 1887, George Engel, Adolph Fischer, Albert Parsons, and August Spies were hanged.[68] Buchanan's final service was to appear as one of Parsons's pallbearers.

At about the time Buchanan helped lay the four martyrs to rest, the ULP expired at the polls. It took Buchanan some time to recover from the twin shocks and when he did, he was in no mood to exchange foolish barbs with Powderly. In December, he jumped on Powderly's assertion that the general master workman had made "sacrifices" in the cause of labor. Buchanan thundered, "It's all rot, the rottenest rot," and pointed out that when Powderly was a mechanic he had earned $3 per day but currently commanded a $5,000 yearly salary while being "patted on the back by newspapers and lauded by the aristocrats of mart and church." He acidly concluded, "But hold on. Mr. Powderly has lost something in the past eighteen months. He is becoming the tool of a ring of boodlers in the general assembly, [and] has sacrificed the respect and support of the honest men who fought with him in the other days to build up the labor movement. Yes, he has 'sacrificed.' "[69]

One week later he printed a string of Powderly remarks to the daily press, including a passionate defense of private property and a vitriolic denunciation of those who opposed him. Buchanan remarked, "Powderly has a habit of calling names at long distance, and those who know him will not be influenced or frightened by the bluff he is making with the assistance of his friends of the associated and capitalistic daily press." In the same issue, he ran George Murray's attack on Powderly under the headline "Nailing a Liar."[70]

Throughout 1888, Buchanan chronicled Powderly's faults and the Provisional Committee's virtues. In February, he noted that many KOL districts were in the throes of collapse and estimated that there were no more than two hundred fifty thousand Knights remaining in the Order. He also accused Powderly of mismanaging the recently lost Reading Railroad strike.[71] Over the next few months he unleashed his most bitter attacks on Powderly. Buchanan charged, correctly, that Powderly helped the Home Club reorganize and took him to task for using his long service as master workman as a cover for numerous dishonorable deeds. He went on to say:

> Here is the key to the man's character. He cares only to be in the majority— right or wrong—no matter what deception he stoops to. He has not the breadth of character to be right at all times regardless of how many or how few are with him. It was his moral cowardice that seduced him and made him the victim of the wiles of the conspirators at Richmond and Minneapolis. The men of New York who have fought him for years, and who have supported him at Richmond that they might assassinate him later, recognized the man's weakness years ago. They hate the man; the Provisional hates his methods . . . and cares nothing for T. V. Powderly as an individual.

Buchanan gave no quarter as he painted Powderly to be vain, pompous, and utterly rigid: "Mr. Powderly's definition of a 'true Knight' is one who believes in the infallibility of Terence V. Powderly." Several weeks later he offered a simple solution for the KOL's woes. In an article titled "They Must Go," Buchanan suggested that only a clean sweep of KOL office-holders could save the Order. Powderly, he remarked, "might make a good Sunday school superintendent, but he is too light for his present job."[72]

Once again, though, Joe Buchanan the rhetorician got the better of Joe Buchanan the tactician. By the spring of 1888, the Provisional revolt had nearly run its course as workers discovered its literary bark was considerably sharper than its organizational bite. Incendiary circulars and editorials did not alone create an alternative to the Powderly-led Knights. As Buchanan later admitted in his autobiography, "[T]he principal effect of this open warfare was to hasten the withdrawal of the dissatisfied rank and file from the order—a result not desired by the Provisionals."[73]

Buchanan was at his best when he chose practical action over union politics. In 1888, he once again demonstrated organizational and tactical mettle superior to that of many other Gilded Age labor leaders. Shortly after the Knights of Labor lost the Reading strike, another involving engineers and firemen broke out on the Chicago, Burlington, and Quincy (C, B, & Q) line. Many Knights welcomed the strike as a payback opportunity; during the Reading troubles several brotherhoods scabbed on the Knights and the Brotherhood of Locomotive Engineers (BLE) refused to honor it. Indeed, among many KOL rail workers only Jay Gould was more hated than BLE chief Peter Arthur. When the Burlington strike erupted at the end of February, numerous Knights ignored the call to boycott C, B, & Q cars and a few took the places of BLE engineers.

Along Union Pacific lines, however, Buchanan still commanded respect. He worked feverishly with Eugene Debs of the Brotherhood of Locomotive Firemen to keep scabbing at a minimum. Buchanan even tried to convince Knights that Arthur had learned his lesson and should be supported, an argument he later admitted cost him influence in Denver where the BLE chief was despised. For the most part, however, Buchanan's lobbying paid off; both DA 89 and DA 82 honored the strike, though several members of the latter replaced BLE engineers.[74] Nonetheless, the strike ended in failure at precisely the time Debs was making his initial plea for a federation of railroad brotherhoods. Buchanan's involvement with the Union Pacific men ended and influence passed to Thomas Neasham, a more cautious and less able man. Neasham gloated over Arthur's loss and the collapse of Debs's federation dreams. It would be another six years before Union Pacific workers considered federation.[75]

The collapse of the Burlington strike and the declining fortunes of the Provisionals led Buchanan back to formats in which he was less capable: public speaking and party politics. In April and May 1888, he took part in the Chicago Ethical Society's Sunday evening opinion forum devoted to economic issues. Speeches filled the air on topics including the banking system, the greenback cause, socialism, trade unionism, and the principles of the KOL. Buchanan's offering, "A View from the Labor Movement," was laced with clichés, incendiary remarks, and stirring calls to action, but was vague and shallow. His words and tone were appropriate for a picket line but wholly out of place for a lecture hall. In predictable fashion, the daily press ridiculed his comments.[76]

He fared no better as a political agitator. He concluded that the fragmentation of independent votes into scores of small parties was responsible for the ULP's electoral flop. To correct this, Buchanan advocated that all the groups—including the ULP, the American Reform Party, single-tax advocates, Greenbackers, Grangers, and the Progressive Labor Party—combine under a single banner. As he was sometimes prone to do, Buchanan gave the right message in the wrong tone. Instead of appealing to solidarity, he blasted past movements as controlled by elites who were "crotchety and bigoted." Rank-and-file voters felt alienated from erstwhile leaders and "left the cranks to fight it out" while they sat out elections. Blanket criticisms—with which he frequently took Powderly to task—won him few admirers. By his own admission, only his call for government ownership of railroads and telegraphs attracted much enthusiasm.[77]

By mid-1888, Buchanan was a frustrated agitator without an audience. In June, he had to borrow money in a vain attempt to keep the *Enquirer* afloat. Distrusted by both Chicago-area Knights and radicals, the paper continued to slump, and on August 18, 1888, the *Enquirer* ceased operations and sent its small subscription list to Henry George. Buchanan tried to resign from the SLP a few days later, only to discover he had already been expelled. A dispirited Buchanan moved his family to Montclair, New Jersey.

On balance, Buchanan's entire Chicago venture was a mistake. He was a pragmatic westerner more at home with trade unionists than ideologues. By allowing his passion for the Haymarket eight to cloud his judgment, Buchanan removed himself from his Denver power base and thrust himself into doctrinal battles for which he was ill suited. He tried to fit in, but his rhetorical excesses exceeded his tact and he made more enemies than allies. Further, his relocation to Chicago allowed him to be removed from the 1887 KOL general assembly via maneuvers that would have been unthinkable had he remained in Denver. Moreover, he was unable to direct Denver affairs from afar, thus leaving much of the KOL's future in that city to the fractious Burnette Haskell, who alienated local Knights, split the Rocky Mountain Social League, and bankrupted the *Labor Enquirer*. As 1888 drew to a close, powerful DA 82—which Joe Buchanan had helped create—was controlled by forces hostile to him. In this light, Buchanan's move to New Jersey made sense; there was little left for him in Denver.

His first few years in Montclair were quiet ones. Buchanan resurfaced in 1892, when he again immersed himself in political and KOL affairs. He was attracted to People's Party campaigns in New Jersey and New York, and in June, he attended the Omaha, Nebraska, convention in which those dubbed "Populists" hammered out a platform and nominated James Weaver for president. Buchanan was elected to a national strategy committee, a post to which he was reappointed in 1896 and 1900.[78] His links to the Populists also renewed ties to the truncated KOL; enthusiasm for the party was high among rural Knights.

In September 1892, Buchanan received a letter from Powderly that stated, "I am desirous of re-establishing our old friendly relations . . . and nothing will give me more pleasure than to cement anew the ties that were once linked in sentiment and action." He even admitted, "I owe you an apology."[79] Years of quiet reflection had cooled Buchanan's anger. Further, the Home Club was dead, with New York City now in the firm control of a Marxist anti-Powderly faction headed by Daniel DeLeon. Powderly was doubtless seeking allies for his upcoming battles against the DeLeonites, but for once he was tactful and politic. In December, Powderly informed Buchanan, "I am going to ask you to return to the Order again, for no matter what others have said or done, there has always been a warm spot in my heart for you. You never resorted to underhand work or unmanly actions and whatever you had to say or do was done openly."[80] When Buchanan succumbed to such flattery, Powderly personally issued and delivered Buchanan's new membership card.

Throughout 1893, Powderly apprised Buchanan of brewing plots against the administration within KOL ranks. Buchanan did little more than offer sympathy. He did, however, once again demonstrate his tactical prowess. On the eve of the Knights' general assembly, Buchanan issued a call for what he dubbed a "Labor Unity Conference" to be held in Philadelphia in April 1894. Since it bore Buchanan's imprimatur, not Powderly's, numerous representatives from trade unions agreed to attend. Some Knights held out the hope that the conference would revive the sagging Order, and the general assembly heaped effusive praise on the project. Powderly pronounced Buchanan the "Knightliest Knight of us all" and confessed publicly that his biggest mistake as general master workman had been allowing himself "to be deceived into doing Buchanan a great wrong." Buchanan was impressed and wrote, "Could anything have been more manly, more Knightly than that? Good men do such things sometimes; bad men never."[81]

Convention delegates, however, were less inclined to view Powderly as a good man and finally ousted him as general master workman. Nonetheless, Buchanan held the April unity conference, and he, Powderly, and Baltimore's J. G. Schonfarber represented the Knights. Also attending were representatives from trade unions, several railroad brotherhoods, and the AFL. Typical for such labor congresses, effusive rhetoric flowed, impressive-sounding resolutions passed, and the assembled organizations pledged mutual cooperation, peaceful coexistence, and class solidarity. Buchanan was less sanguine, however, and fretted over the lack of specificity embedded in the conference's various documents. His fears quickly materialized when the Pullman strike collapsed from lack of cross-organizational labor support.[82]

Buchanan embraced railway federation modeled by the American Railway Union (ARU), even though it threatened absorption of the KOL's District 82. Unlike so many of his contemporaries, Buchanan separated self-interest from class interest. However, such noble sentiments again placed Buchanan beyond the pale. The betrayal of the ARU by the AFL and the BLE, Gompers's denunciation of Populism, and the AFL's exclusivity forced Buchanan to conclude that the Labor Unity Conference had been a failure. Further, he suspected that the post-Powderly KOL administration was incompetent.

With the labor movement sputtering, Buchanan turned anew to politics and again discovered it was not his forte. He was nominated for Congress in New Jersey's sixth district. As a People's Party candidate, he did not expect to win, but he did have high hopes of finishing second given that Debs, Powderly, and Gompers all campaigned on his behalf. When the results were tallied, however, Buchanan received fewer than a thousand votes. He consoled himself with charges of fraud but, in truth, he was simply a lackluster candidate.[83]

He attended the KOL's 1895 convention and came away thoroughly convinced that the new KOL leadership was inept. When Powderly and two other former officers sued the Order for back pay and were expelled, Buchanan simply drifted away from the Knights. He and Powderly briefly flirted with still another splinter group, the Independent Order of the Knights of Labor, spearheaded by Pittsburgh's James Campbell. Buchanan agreed with its cardinal principle that the Order should contain both trade and mixed assemblies, but he held out little hope for it or the official KOL.[84] He allowed his KOL membership to lapse and was, at long last, free from the Order. Buchanan kicked about for several years as a freelance labor agitator and as an organizer for the People's Party. He was even persuaded to make another futile bid for Congress, but his most notable action before the century closed was to add his voice to those opposing the Spanish-American War.[85]

In 1904, Buchanan came full circle and returned to the mainstream press. For the next eleven years, he was the labor editor for the *New York Evening Journal*. During World War I, he worked for the National War Labor Board, and afterward for the Department of Labor.[86] The self-proclaimed "labor agitator" died at his Montclair home on September 13, 1924.

In his autobiography, Joseph Buchanan titled a chapter describing his move to Chicago "In the Larger Field." An earlier chapter was called "Disappointing My Friends." These chapter headings encapsulate what motivated Buchanan, what made him successful, and what caused him to lack allies at key moments in his career. Unlike many of his contemporaries, Buchanan insisted on seeing the "larger field" rather than confining himself to parochial objectives. The KOL was filled with individuals with broad vision, but few could match Buchanan's scope. As Gregory Kealey and Bryan Palmer observe, he was among those Gilded Age reformers who rode "the wave of class militancy and consensus without a forceful sense of organizational direction or ideological clarity" and were thrown into "a radical milieu that contained Marxist, Lassallean, Anarchist, Greenback, Georgite, Freethinking, and Irish Nationalist influences."[87] His ability to see the interconnectedness of diffuse ideas ought to have made Buchanan an indispensable leader in an organization as diverse as the Knights of Labor.

In some regards, Joe Buchanan was an improved amalgam of key KOL leaders. Like William Horan, he played the prophet whose clarion calls to justice forced workers to evaluate their own circumstances. For Horan, ritual fraternalism was a bulwark against oppression; for Buchanan, more concrete forms of organization were necessary. As an agitator, Buchanan was a more honest and likable version of Powderly. His picket-line speeches and hard-hitting editorials packed an effective wallop he lacked when on the political stump, as the latter demanded he pull his punches. In the role of the gruff westerner, Buchanan's plain speech and fiery demeanor played well. He was also a fine tactician and strategist because, unlike Thomas Barry, Buchanan could play the statesman. Whereas Barry resorted to double-dealing, deception, and secrecy, Joe Buchanan negotiated in public and with the full authorization of both rank and file and his superiors. One need only contrast the manner in which Buchanan kept men in the Order after a lost strike with the mass exodus that resulted from Barry's losing efforts. Even Buchanan's capitalist foes praised his honesty and forthrightness. As an ideologue, Buchanan represented a more promising version of Victor Drury because he could also be an administrator when need be. Whereas Drury insisted on dismantling trade unions as a prerequisite for ushering in a cooperative commonwealth, Buchanan's view was what I would dub "incremental amalgamation." Both men believed that the trades should organize under a common banner in which class interests took precedence over craft concerns, but Buchanan tempered his hopes for the future with concrete actions in the present. If the road to the One Big Union necessitated formation of trade unions, so be it. He handled strike logistics with aplomb, routed contracts and paperwork through the proper channels, administered strike funds, and left permanent organizations in his wake before moving on.

Unfortunately, the KOL was led by men whose vision was more narrow than Buchanan's, whose temperaments made them less willing to compromise, and whose concern for public opinion made them less able to see beyond labels. Buchanan variously labeled himself a trade unionist, an anarchist, a socialist, and a populist. His favorite role was that which he titled his memoirs, the "labor agitator." As we have seen, Buchanan's least effective role was that of the ideologue. However, because he used labels so indiscriminately, he experienced difficulties with those to whom they mattered. He was too much a trade unionist for the Home Club, too much of an anarchist for cautious Knights, too ideologically imprecise for Chicago radicals, and too much of a labor man to attract cross-class voters to the People's Party. On occasion, even his views on trade unionism isolated him. By simultaneously promoting trade districts within the KOL while championing the ultimate amalgamation of all trades, Buchanan alienated half of the KOL and all of the AFL. He insisted that trade-union sovereignty did not require affiliated organizations to authorize every ill-conceived job action just because it was decided democratically. This was in keeping with AFL volunteerism, but it was alien to KOL principles. The price of being in the larger field was that Joe Buchanan made enemies and disappointed his friends.

The AFL survived without Buchanan's services, but the KOL did not. In 1887, the KOL ostracized the best organizer in its history. When Buchanan was in the fold, new western-based locals entered the KOL in greater numbers than existing locals folded; after 1887, the reverse was true. If Buchanan had remained in good standing, would he have led a movement to reform the Order? Could he have staved off involvement in hopeless strikes that crippled the KOL? Might he have negotiated a concrete unity treaty with trade unions when the KOL was still strong enough to make a difference? Could he have led the Order away from bureaucratic wrangling and into a reexamination of tactics and principles? Such speculation is a risky venture for a historian, but it is sobering to contemplate what might have happened had the Knights of Labor kept Joe Buchanan and rid itself of Terence Powderly and Victor Drury.

CHAPTER 4

Portrait of a Difficult Man: Charles Litchman and the Problem of Personality

The name Charles Litchman has surfaced in each of the controversies discussed thus far, usually in an unflattering context. This is telling, given that Litchman struggled for over a decade to be a popular functionary within the KOL's ever-expanding bureaucracy.

The Knights of Labor conforms badly to most sociological models of bureaucracy. As Max Weber argued in his classic study, bureaucracies are hierarchical, rational structures whose professionally trained staff is assigned clearly delineated roles and responsibilities. Rigid procedures are overseen by a ladder of command whose various rungs must be ascended one at a time.[1] In the KOL, the actual working of bureaucracy—even when the rules were obeyed—more resembled the nightmare scenarios noted by C. Northcote Parkinson and Laurence J. Peter than the well-oiled machine of Weber's imagination.

Parkinson warned that bureaucrats often create work for each other instead of accomplishing tasks of real merit.[2] The flood of mail to Powderly's office confirms that within the KOL, insignificant administrative wrangling consumed much of the Order's time, energy, and money. Laurence Peter—whose critique is dubbed the Peter Principle—warned that bureaucracies often promote individuals to their levels of incompetence.[3] This happened often in the KOL, where a substantial number of Knights were quite young when they assumed power. (Powderly was a mere twenty-nine when he became grand master workman in 1879.) Few leaders were trained for the offices they held. KOL meetings, courts, and conventions were often only one ill-advised statement away from chaos. Once it broke out, nonprofessional leaders faced an overabundance of ambiguous procedures and rules through which to right matters. Improvisation often short-circuited bureaucratic process.

William Birdsall argued that the KOL's structure was flawed. The diffusion of power over so many levels—national, district, state, local, and national trade districts—blurred procedural lines.[4] Messy structures allowed personality to circumvent official channels and placed organizational pressures on leaders.

As Weber saw it, leadership derived from traditional, charismatic, or bureaucratic sources. That is, positions could be customary and inherited; they might be conferred because of one's personality; or they could be attained through promotion based on merit and service. Once a person assumed power, he exercised power in one of three ways. The authoritarian leader centralizes authority and allows no decisions to be made without his knowledge. By contrast, a laissez-faire leader abrogates decision making to his line staff and is mostly distant from bureaucratic process, while the democratic leader makes decisions based on the input and suggestions of staff.[5]

In the KOL, the line between a charismatic and a bureaucratic leader was razor thin, with personality determining one's position as much as merit. Nor did leaders always exercise authority the same way. The Order's most effective leaders allowed contingencies to determine which of the three strategies they adopted at a given moment. Nonetheless, labor historian Warren Van Tine largely adapted Weberian models for his study of union bureaucracy. In his analysis, American labor leaders of the late nineteenth and early twentieth centuries tended to be "traditionals," whose power derived from charisma and crony networks that distributed discretionary spoils. Van Tine accepted Birdsall's structural critique and criticized the Knights for failing to develop professionals capable of administering intricate bureaucracies.[6]

Charles Litchman's experience in the KOL reveals some of the weaknesses of Van Tine's analysis of the KOL and of Weber's assumptions that a well-defined bureaucracy could operate independently of personality. If Van Tine is correct, a man like Litchman should never have risen very far in the Knights, as he was singularly devoid of charm. Yet Litchman held several of the Order's highest offices, edited its national newspaper, and had access to vast power, even though much of the membership actively loathed him. Similarly, if Weber's models are applicable, once Litchman achieved his posts—whether by merit or deception—he should have been able to exercise bureaucratic power by funneling it through proper channels. This did not happen, though few men were ever so faithful to KOL procedure as was Litchman.

More is at stake than quibbles over how bureaucracy works. Ralph Turner and Lewis Killian persuasively argue that a social movement seeking to become permanent must evolve into an "institutional" stage, in which capable "administrators" keep the organization running. Turner and Killian recognize the inadequacy of Weberian formulations and argue that effective leaders combine "charismatic" and "decision-making" roles. Those who are merely charismatic, they assert, are often either martyrs or fools, while those who seek merely to exercise power are prone to procedural rigidity and authoritarianism and are thus easy targets for both democrats and ideologues.[7]

The travails of Charles Litchman demonstrate many themes touched upon thus far: the link between charisma and procedure, the structural muddiness of the KOL, the Order's inchoate bureaucracy, and the ineptitude of some KOL leaders. Although it may be overly harsh to label Litchman a fool, he certainly embodied some of the KOL's less admirable leadership qualities. Litchman made many and powerful enemies and his actions provided them with myriad opportunities to subvert official chains of command and marginalize him.

Charles Henry Litchman was born in Marblehead, Massachusetts, on April 8, 1849, the son of William and Sarah (Bartlett) Litchman. His father owned a shoe factory, one of the hundreds of small-time operations that dotted the New England countryside by mid-century. Charles attended Marblehead public schools until the age of fifteen and then worked as a traveling sales agent for his father from 1864 through 1870. He married Annie Shirley on February 2, 1868, and she soon bore him a son. In 1870, Litchman simultaneously opened his own shoe company and took up law studies. Both ventures were halted by the Panic of 1873, which bankrupted him. In order to support his family, Litchman was forced to labor as a journeyman shoemaker.

The shoemakers' Knights of St. Crispin was one of the nation's strongest trade unions and Litchman joined as soon as he took up the trade. He especially enjoyed the Crispins' elaborate quasi-Masonic ritual. In 1876, he was elected grand scribe of the Order, a position akin to union secretary, and the next year became a salaried lecturer on behalf of the Crispins. After 1876, Litchman never cobbled another pair of shoes, spending the rest of his life in journalistic and bureaucratic pursuits.

As Litchman rose in prominence within the community, he began to demonstrate a talent for making enemies that dogged his career. He was active in Marblehead politics, serving on the school committee from 1873 to 1878. He often used that post as a bully pulpit for making pro-labor speeches that gained admiration from a few, but that most felt were inappropriate for that forum.

Though Litchman's star rose, the Knights of St. Crispin were in severe decline. Even before the Panic of 1873, their strength was sapped from so many lost strikes that the organization tried to abandon a strike policy in favor of arbitration. Litchman represented a new breed of leaders hoping to revive the union, but by 1878, the Crispins were a spent force. Some time in 1877, Litchman joined New York Local 221 of the KOL and quickly obtained an organizer's commission.

The decline of the Crispins serendipitously coincided with the KOL's first national convention. Litchman was one of four shoemakers to attend the KOL's grand assembly held in Reading, Pennsylvania, January 1–3, 1878. He ingratiated himself with KOL founder and Grand Master Workman Uriah Stephens, the pair sharing a fondness for Greenback Labor politics and ritual fraternalism. Like Stephens, Litchman was an inveterate joiner who held membership in the Freemasons, the Odd Fellows, the Order of Red Men, the Royal Arcanum, the Massachusetts Legion of Honor, and the Order of the Holy Cross.[8]

The 1878 convention was a crystallizing moment for the Noble and Holy Order of the Knights of Labor. For the first time, delegates representing most of the Order's nearly ten thousand members gathered in one place to discuss a common agenda. Litchman served as convention secretary as delegates fashioned the KOL's preamble, platform, and constitution. Moreover, the Knights of St. Crispin were absorbed en masse into the KOL, ensuring that shoemakers would play a key role in the emergent organization. Litchman was elected grand secretary of the KOL, and another ex-Crispin, Ralph Beaumont of Elmira, New York, became grand worthy foreman. As the Order expanded, Massachusetts DA 30 became the Knights' largest, with a sizable part of its membership made up of shoemakers.[9]

Litchman also helped revise KOL ritual, as codified in the *Adelphon Kruptos,* and offered insights on the Greenback Labor movement. Like many early KOL leaders, Litchman was active in the movement in the 1870s, though he was an ardent Republican both before 1877 and after 1880. He failed in a bid for the Massachusetts Senate in 1877, but was elected to the General Court (the commonwealth's lower house) in 1878 and served a single two-year term. Litchman was one of several KOL national leaders briefly involved with the Greenbacks. In 1879, Stephens resigned as grand master workman, ostensibly due to exhaustion but in truth to devote energy to a Greenback Labor run for the U.S. Congress. He was replaced by Terence V. Powderly, the sitting Greenback mayor of Scranton, Pennsylvania.

Powderly's elevation proved fateful for Litchman. The two men developed a complex relationship that rocketed between mutual respect and mutual contempt, with Litchman often groveling in an effort to curry favor. Both men shared a belief in Roman Catholicism, and each had a prickly personality and a penchant for deals, double crosses, and intrigue. But Powderly emphatically rejected many of the ritualistic fraternal practices

Litchman cherished, and the two clashed over pending changes to the *Adelphon Kruptos* at the very convention that chose Powderly as grand master workman. Powderly often found Litchman meddlesome and obsequious.

Litchman's first two years as KOL grand secretary went smoothly enough, his main duties being to answer correspondence and to pass on to members Powderly's rulings on various matters of constitutional minutiae. His first major crisis came with the Order's decision to launch a monthly national journal, the *Journal of United Labor*. To capitalize this venture, the 1880 grand assembly voted to divert 10 percent of the Order's defense fund for "educational" purposes. This decision raised hackles, given that the fund was designed to support workers displaced by strikes and lockouts. Litchman exacerbated the situation by treating the money as a discretionary fund for what was essentially a personal enterprise centered in his Marblehead home.

Litchman understood the high start-up costs of a publishing venture, but he paid the price for dubious accounting practices. He spent $4,600 to begin the *Journal*, although the actual funds allotted to him by the assembly totaled a mere $788. As secretary, he was in charge of maintaining membership lists, and he simply cooked the books. Litchman appropriated funds based on a "projection" of expected membership by the next assembly and by incorrectly assuming that all members would dutifully pay their assessments. When membership shrank from 28,136 in October 1880 to 19,422 one year later (many of whom withheld voluntary donations to the defense fund), Litchman was in hot water.

Even worse, Litchman experienced difficulty getting the *Journal* into print. The paper debuted on May 15, 1880, but missed its June deadline. July and August issues came off as planned, but September's *Journal* was late, as was November's. The next year was no better. Several issues were tardy and September's never appeared. Instead, the *Journal* published a "double issue" in October, but by the time it made its way to members, Litchman was out as secretary.

In September 1881, Knights assembled in Detroit for their fifth grand assembly. A battle raged over whether to make the KOL a public organization, with some feeling that the *Journal* had already exposed the Order more than they wished. Litchman was a convenient whipping boy for malcontents. As early as April 1881, complaints resonated that Chicago Knights were quitting the Order over the defense fund debacle.[10] Several convention delegates demanded to know how Litchman spent the money and who authorized it. He was accused of squandering funds on needlessly fancy paper, ink, and printing presses, and the assembly debated whether he illegally used defense funds. There was even talk of ordering Litchman to reimburse the KOL from his own pocket.[11]

Had Powderly not intervened, Litchman probably would have been expelled from the Knights. A series of frantic letters from Litchman convinced Powderly that his error was one of oversight, not malice or greed.[12] Serious charges against Litchman were dropped, but not before he endured withering sarcasm and a torrent of charges from assembly delegates. It is not surprising that he lost his secretary job (to Robert Layton).

Layton kept Litchman on at the *Journal* for a time, though he disliked him and wished him gone. In December 1881, Layton complained to Powderly that he was "forced" to take over the printing of the revised *Adelphon Kruptos* from Litchman and that the latter was still "not on top" of the defense fund situation. Layton thundered, "Litchman has done nothing yet but print a single number of the *Journal* under the promise of a double one. How long! O Lord! how long must this be endured?" One week later he charged that Litchman was ruining the *Journal.*[13]

As he and Layton battled, Litchman tried to manipulate Powderly through a series of "Dear Terry" letters. In a pattern too often repeated, he blamed enemies for his troubles.[14] Litchman even began to copy Powderly's mannerisms in an effort to curry his favor. A photo from this time period reveals that Litchman adopted Powderly's style of dress, right down to the use of a pince-nez instead of eyeglasses.[15] In truth, however, it was Litchman who was being manipulated.

Shortly after Litchman lost his secretary post, the KOL suffered its first major internal crisis. As the Order expanded into New York City, it absorbed many of the ideological radicals who would dog Powderly throughout the 1880s. Doctrinaire Marxist Theodore Cuno launched the Duryea Starch boycott, which degenerated into a power play among New York City Knights and led to attacks on Powderly's leadership.

Privately, Powderly was furious with Layton's handling of the Duryea matter and suspected him of being sympathetic to Cuno.[16] He was also displeased with Layton's slowness in clamping down on secrecy advocates in Brooklyn Local 1562. By early 1882, Powderly dropped hints that he would resign at the next grand assembly, a ploy designed to weaken his opponents and assure his reelection. One of the first to fall for it was Litchman. In March, he wrote to Powderly and urged him to stay on as master workman but added that he would be willing to serve a term as grand master workman if Powderly decided to step down.[17]

Powderly played a cat-and-mouse game throughout the spring and summer. In June, Litchman reiterated his willingness to replace Powderly and bitterly attacked Layton, whom he accused of being more interested in politics than in KOL affairs.[18] Litchman began to belittle Layton in his own newspaper. This was precisely what Powderly wanted, as it allowed others to attack his opponents while he posed as the voice of moderation and

Terence Powderly (left) and Charles Litchman (right). Courtesy of the Catholic
University of America Archives.

reason. In August, Powderly flattered Litchman by berating Layton's handling of New York matters and told him that had he remained in office,
"this whole trouble would have been smoothed over in a different way."[19]

The September grand assembly reelected Powderly, Griffiths, and a
chastened Layton. To Litchman's detractors, his pre- and postconvention
actions confirmed that he was little more than a self-seeker. Litchman spent
the next several years actively seeking, but failing to secure, patronage jobs
within the KOL and the Republican Party. In all his efforts Litchman's
vanity far exceeded his reason. That he felt he could win election to head

the Knights a scant year after being unceremoniously booted from office is incredible. He lacked popularity even within his own district.

Litchman chartered Marblehead LA 500 in 1878 and became its master workman. He and Uriah Stephens created DA 30 in 1879, with Litchman serving as its second district master workman when A. C. Robinson resigned in mid-1881. Like many Litchman pursuits, his DA 30 reign was a short one. At the January 1882 convention, Litchman announced his "retirement" as district master workman and was replaced by Albert A. Carlton. The convention praised him for introducing the KOL into Massachusetts "at a time when it was exceedingly unpopular and even dangerous" to do so, but there is little doubt that Litchman stood down because he doubted his ability to get elected.[20] The DA 30 convention met just months after his ouster as grand secretary, and stalwarts like Carlton and George McNeill disliked Litchman.

By 1882, Litchman's power base was reduced to his post in Marblehead and his DA 30 organizer's commission. With hopes of a national office disintegrating, Litchman tried to resurrect his image through publishing. Beginning in 1882, Litchman edited *The American Statesman* from his Marblehead home. Ostensibly the official KOL journal of the region as well as a general reform paper, the *Statesman* looked very much like the *Journal of United Labor,* aside from the addition of a women's page and its full-size format. He even appropriated the *Journal* motto "Agitate, Educate, Organize!" and reported on some of the same issues covered in that paper.[21]

Again, Litchman's endeavors won him more enemies than friends. Some speculated that the venture was funded by embezzled KOL funds, while others complained that he paid salaries below prevailing scale. Worst were the charges of nepotism. With Litchman traveling often on behalf of the KOL, or in pursuit of political appointment, he habitually turned over the paper's operation to his son, a lad of only seventeen. The *Statesman* died a quick death, but ill will lingered for years.[22]

Litchman also made enemies by abandoning the Greenback Party. He attended the 1880 Greenback Labor convention and served as its secretary, but charged "treachery" when the party in Massachusetts failed to nominate him to run for reelection to the General Court. The party no doubt found his record undistinguished. He dutifully voted for failed bills on currency reform and abolishing convict labor but made no mark of his own, serving on the relatively unimportant Committee on Engrossed Bills.[23] Litchman returned to the Republican Party, and he tried to wrangle numerous patronage jobs from it. In 1883, he sought—and failed to secure—appointment to the Massachusetts Bureau of Labor Statistics when Carroll Wright resigned to head the National Bureau of Labor Statistics.[24]

Dramatic change provided Litchman with another brief moment in the KOL limelight. When the Home Club rose within New York City, Layton became a marked man. He barely weathered reelection as grand secretary in 1882 and was ousted by Frederick Turner the following year. At the 1884 and 1885 conventions, now dubbed "general assemblies," Turner was reelected to a combined secretary-treasurer's post.

A dual responsibility position made sense in 1883, when the Order contained just over fifty thousand members, but Turner was soon swamped by his duties. Meteoric expansion in the aftermath of the Knights' unexpected strike victory over Jay Gould nearly collapsed the KOL's bureaucracy. A June 1886 special assembly elected six auxiliary members to the general executive board to alleviate the burden. As noted earlier, four of these individuals were sympathetic to the Home Club, as were sitting board members Turner, John Caville, Homer McGraw, and John Hayes.

By 1886, the Knights of Labor was a juggernaut lacking a clear vision of where it was heading. Further, factions surfaced for and against the Home Club, brutal disputes emerged with several trade unions (especially the cigarmakers), and debates raged over political ideology (including third-party politics). These transformed the Order into a den of intrigue at precisely the moment it was outwardly prospering. The KOL hardly needed the meddlesome Litchman in the midst of such troubled waters, but it got him nonetheless. As in the past, his stubbornness, persecution complex, and lack of charm made him an easy pawn for would-be manipulators.

In April, Powderly complained to Litchman that "not only is capital opposing us, but the trade union element of the country have determined to wipe us out of existence." He alleged that a conspiracy between typographers and cigarmakers—led by Strasser and Gompers—sought to pack and disrupt the fall convention.[25] Powderly was once again fishing for allies when he shared this information, and once again Litchman took the bait.

His first loyal act took place within DA 30. The KOL's battles with trade unions resonated deeply within DA 30, the bulk of whose locals and seventy-five thousand members were craft unionists. District Master Workman John Howes defended the administration line that the KOL alone could solve labor's problems, while Albert Carlton, Frank Foster, and George McNeill argued that although Howes was correct in principle, cooperation with trade unions was essential until all workers were brought into the KOL fold. Debate was so intense that a splintering of DA 30 seemed imminent. Litchman supported Howes and when the latter abruptly resigned, Litchman took over his post.

Litchman advised Powderly that he and Howes were "stronger than ever before in the hearts of the members" and predicted a quick healing of district wounds.[26] Behind the scenes, John Hayes advised Powderly to encourage Litchman and Howes. He suggested commissioning Howes as a state organizer for Massachusetts to "give him a better chance to watch the ring there," a reference to Carlton, Foster, and McNeill.[27]

Litchman's forecasts were naive and he was hardly the man to put salve on wounds. Haverhill and Brockton shoemakers were still reeling from bitter strikes in 1885, and they were in no mood to dismantle hard-won organizations to satisfy a debate over which type of structure would best usher in a coming utopia. Litchman woefully underestimated the power and discontent of Foster and McNeill who, as editors of Boston's *Labor Leader,* had a loud forum from which to criticize both the Home Club and the KOL's trade-union policy. McNeill blasted everything from the Order's flirtations with socialism to its policy of allowing employers to take out membership. In an unsigned editorial, he even suggested that Powderly should resign.[28] When Hayes visited Gardner, Massachusetts, a furniture- and cabinet-making center, he discovered that Foster had pre-viously canvassed the region seeking support for his pro–trade union, anti-Litchman views.[29]

Litchman temporarily escaped the DA 30 fires when, in October 1886, he fulfilled a five-year dream and was reelected to the general secre-tary post, lengthened by the convention to a two-year term. However, Fred-erick Turner—who despised Litchman—was returned to the treasurer's post, a position once again separated from the secretary's office. Nor did Litchman's new job isolate him from troubles within DA 30 for very long. Within two months of the general assembly, George McNeill renewed an old complaint of allowing employers to join the Knights, and in December, he and Powderly began what would become a year-long petty dispute over McNeill's book, *The Labor Movement: The Problem of To-Day.*

McNeill listed Powderly as an "associate editor" of his book, but the latter claimed he never saw the work until it came on the market. (Vanity played a role as Powderly was busy at work on his own *Thirty Years of Labor,* and he resented McNeill's beating him to the bookstores.) As gen-eral secretary in charge of all correspondence, Litchman was thrust into the middle of these disputes.[30] Given his past history of supporting Powderly's every action, Litchman's opposition to McNeill was presumed and his DA 30 opponents struck a preemptive blow. McNeill and Foster so thoroughly besmirched Litchman's reputation that when he attended the 1887 district convention, he took his seat "without a breath of recognition." He listened impassively as delegates blasted Powderly for trampling "upon the most sacred sections of the [KOL] constitution" by upholding the expulsion of the cigarmakers at the 1886 general assembly and for supporting the Home Club.[31]

Powderly placed Litchman in a difficult position. Privately, Powderly claimed that the decision to cast out the cigarmakers was unconstitutional and that he might resign over it, but publicly he and Litchman were obliged to support the decisions of the executive board.[32] Litchman predictably both urged Powderly to stay and offered his own services should he step down. He also shared his suspicion that a spy at KOL headquarters was leaking news of executive board discussions.[33] He was correct on that score, and the culprit was Hayes. But Litchman was unaware that Hayes was doing Powderly's bidding. Powderly sought to strengthen his power base by either cooperating with or opposing the Home Club, depending on the situation. The ambitious Hayes played along when promised he would replace Turner as treasurer. Ultimately, Hayes hoped to also topple Litchman and recombine the secretary and treasurer offices.[34]

Powderly further confounded Litchman by suggesting they both resign at the 1887 convention and "take with them the right kind of Knight."[35] Several weeks later he listed Joe Buchanan, Tom Barry, John Morrison, and George McNeill as those who had put on "WAR paint," no doubt confident that Litchman would promptly make them his enemies as well.[36]

Powderly used the pliant Litchman at will. When a reporter queried Powderly about a controversial editorial in the *Journal of United Labor,* Powderly replied that he was not responsible for anything that appeared in print unless it bore his signature. A red-faced Litchman wrote to Powderly, "If there is anything unsatisfactory to you in the management of the *Journal* or its editorial utterances I think you could speak to me just as well as to a newspaper reporter and thus spare me the inference which will certainly be drawn." Powderly duly apologized and blamed William Bailey for his impolitic remarks.[37]

Powderly correctly gauged the depth of Litchman's unpopularity among members. Boston Knights accused Litchman of hiring nonunion workers in his print shop and of billing the KOL for plates forwarded to Marblehead for personal use. Chicago Knights repeated the charges and threatened to withhold their dues.[38] As we have seen, Powderly got much of his way at the 1887 assembly: Bailey and Barry were expelled, Buchanan was denied a seat, and a clemency resolution for the Haymarket anarchists was voted down. Powderly emerged with his power intact, thanks to Home Club support, but Litchman fared poorly. The assembly authorized an investigation into his affairs based on the Boston and Chicago allegations. The sole reason Litchman continued in office was that he was not up for reelection.

Serious organizational problems loomed that mingled with petty personal quarrels. Disastrous strikes rocked the Order in 1887, including one of DA 30 shoemakers and lasters that the KOL executive board refused to sanction. As job actions failed, workers fled the Knights. In November, Litchman advised Powderly that only three hundred fifty thousand members had paid their per capita tax, a falloff of over one hundred fifty thousand since July. He noted, "It will be impossible to keep this fact secret and when known it will be seized upon as evidence of decay and be used to drive away still more of the timid and wavering." He suggested that Powderly settle differences with LA 1, many of whose members supported the Provisional Committee revolt. Litchman warned Powderly "out of friendship" that dissent was gathering and that "many who voted with us [at the convention] were only lukewarm in their fidelity. These may be nursed into open opponents." He also recklessly named Hayes as the ringleader of plots against Powderly.[39]

Taking on Hayes marked the end for Litchman, as he no doubt realized several weeks later when he told Powderly that he had learned that Powderly and Hayes "confide in one another."[40] Powderly's real feelings toward Litchman were made clear in a letter to Tom O'Reilly, a printer on the *Journal* staff who frequently complained of Litchman's editorial decisions:

> I believe that Litchman is doing more to kill the Order today than all the other causes combined. He does not mean to do harm, but . . . no matter who goes into his office he quarrels with them over the veriest trifle and then after turns away insulted. This trait in Litchman has traveled far and wide until it is a well-known matter. Men withdraw and write to me saying when we get rid of our "pet" they will come back again.[41]

By December 1887, Litchman's relationship with Powderly had cooled, and his familiar "My Dear Terry" salutation had given way to "Dear Sir and Brother" on all official correspondence. He implored Powderly to ignore "scandalmongers" who maligned his character but added, "If it is necessary that the friendship of ten years standing be shattered, tell me so man fashion and I will not trouble you."[42] Powderly tried to ignore Litchman, but Hayes's interference in *Journal* editorial policy exacerbated tensions. In February 1888, Litchman complained:

> Hayes has brought over a couple of articles lately and not only *ordered* them in but has also *ordered* where they should be put and that the style of the "make up" should've changed to suit his idea, regardless of the fact that the looks of the paper would thereby be marred. . . . If I am to continue as Editor I must and will be supreme. If you and Hayes and Turner prefer someone else, let me know it and you will take that much labor off my shoulders. I will not *nominally* exercise functions that require *absolute* authority.[43]

Litchman remained blind to the fact that Powderly, Hayes, and Layton had long ago decided to scapegoat Litchman for the KOL's decline.[44] Powderly informed Gilbert Rockwood that he planned to depose Litchman at the next convention. He thundered, "I would never serve with him again for a million . . . he makes enemies all around him and he is so babyish that he expects of us to stand by him in everything. I have grown tired of it."[45]

Powderly's aspersion on Litchman's manhood was deliberately provocative and was probably uttered in the expectation that Rockwood would repeat it. Powderly knew that Litchman and Rockwood were longtime colleagues. Rockwood served as DA 30's recording secretary under Litchman's tenure as district master workman and was his assistant during Litchman's first tenure as grand secretary. By July, Litchman and Powderly were exchanging sophomoric insults by mail. When Litchman published one of Powderly's off-the-cuff remarks, Powderly rebuked him. He and Layton complained about delays in printing assembly proceedings, prompting Litchman's acid retort that anyone who thought that a 624-page report could be issued in sixty days was "not only a fool but a hog as well."[46]

Powderly's reply stung Litchman. His seven-page letter accused Litchman of paranoia: "If your mind didn't run so much to treachery you would not have so much unmasking to do. You will want to curb that propensity of yours while holding in on your temper." Advice soon gave way to rancor. He repeated another Knights' charge that Litchman was a "joke" and maliciously rambled:

> He was right, you are not only a joke but a whole arsenal of humor; a fellow only has to express an opinion of his own that differs from one of your constructions and at once your mirthfulness knows no bounds and bubbling over with fun you paralyze a fellow. . . .
>
> When I look back over the past ten years and contrast the twelve months now coming to a close I am led to the conclusion that you were woefully deceived in me. You are of the opinion now that I have long held something against you, and looking over your letters of the past months I judge you hold me accountable for your misfortunes in some way or another. I may in some degree be responsible for your misfortunes but I can go to sleep with an easy conscience knowing that I am not responsible for you.[47]

Litchman tried to salvage pride by justifying his actions but, true to form, the dignified tone of page one of his reply yielded to rancor in the next three. He told Powderly, "I really think that you are more successful in analyzing and cornering coffee than you are in understanding about the time necessary to do a job in printing." He added, "No, you are not responsible for me. The time may come when being responsible for yourself will be all the burden one mortal ought bear." In closing he implored, "When in the future it is necessary for you to be vulgar and obscene . . . at least mark the envelope 'personal' and no eyes but mine will see to what base uses an intelligent mind can sometimes be put."[48]

Litchman finally realized his predicament and on August 25, 1888, resigned as KOL general secretary. In his press statement, Litchman claimed that he was quitting to work on Benjamin Harrison's presidential campaign.[49] But Litchman's woes were far from over. Still unresolved was the investigation ordered by the 1887 general assembly, and Knights across the Order delighted in excoriating their departing secretary.

Hayes advised that even William Bailey wanted to shake Powderly's hand for getting rid of Litchman, and Tom O'Reilly remarked upon seeing Litchman and his wife depart, "May the Devil and bad luck go with them. He is unworthy of any regret. He was not your friend—he could not be any man's friend, because he is a scoundrel." Both men accused Litchman of stealing KOL property, an allegation made more tangible by their admission that they had broken open several of the bundles "he had prepared to ship home." Hayes counseled placing an attachment on Litchman's boardinghouse until matters were resolved. On September 12, Powderly authorized Hayes to search Litchman's remaining parcels.[50]

As secret intrigue unfolded, Litchman's public pillorying continued. A Buffalo paper commented, "Truth never held Litchman in high esteem. He was a friend of labor for what he could get out if it." A Baltimore KOL journal called him a "bump of egregious vanity," with similar scorn raining forth from Boston, Detroit, Louisville, New Orleans, and Philadelphia.[51] It did not help that his boxes contained numerous official documents, multiple copies of the *Adelphon Kruptos,* code books, and "hand stamps, several gross of lead pencils of all kinds, boxes of erasers, boxes of pens, several long sticks of sealing wax, bundles of lances, postage stamps," and other items Hayes assumed were KOL property. He gloated to Powderly, "If you were so inclined you have it in your power to send this fellow to state prison."[52]

By October, Litchman feared he would be denied a seat at the upcoming general assembly. Once again he resorted to cajolery and flattery in an effort to get Powderly to protect him. This time Powderly would have none of it. He chided Litchman, "Whenever you have occasion to write me again do not fall into the fish wife style of taunting in one sentence and complaining in another." He told Litchman in no uncertain terms that "You have charged me with too many things for me to believe that you are sincere in wishing to retain my friendship, or that you care a pin for it." Powderly ended his scorching letter by cataloging both the contents of the boxes Hayes had opened and his own past attempts to rescue Litchman's reputation. Litchman bit his tongue with a "My Dear Terry" reply and stated his readiness to address all charges.[53] His obsequiousness paid a small dividend: neither Hayes nor Powderly brought his name before the assembly.

Election day brought a brief respite from Litchman. When Harrison defeated Grover Cleveland, the new president rewarded Litchman with a minor post in the Treasury Department. But Harrison was scarcely in office before Litchman's ambition sent him trawling for bigger fish. When the labor commissioner's post came up for renewal, Litchman sought the position. His quest was complicated, however, by a *Journal of United Labor* editorial promoting Powderly for the job. As he had done in 1884, Litchman sought to finesse Powderly into declaring his intentions by pledging he would support him. True to form, he also implied that Powderly was damaging Litchman's chances by not declaring or withdrawing. Powderly curtly informed Litchman that he was not responsible for editorial remarks in the *Journal* and that he found no fault in the current commissioner, Carroll Wright. He also inferred that Litchman was a "political camp follower" seeking self-aggrandizement. This provided an avenue to close with a holier-than-thou sermon, in which he claimed to be above partisan politics.[54]

Frustrated in his attempt to replace Wright at the BLS, Litchman tried to content himself with his Treasury post. He did not, however, avoid controversy within the KOL. By 1889, the Order was hemorrhaging members rapidly. DA 30 members seethed over the expulsions of Bailey, Barry, and Buchanan, interpreting each man's fall as further proof of a Powderly/Home Club–led conspiracy to destroy trade unions. Many soon-to-be ex-Knights also blamed lost strikes in 1887 and 1888 on Home Club perfidy. In February 1889, Henry Skeffington was expelled for saying as much. He took many Massachusetts shoemakers with him and into the AFL. Frank Foster also quit the KOL and transformed the *Labor Leader* into an AFL paper.

Litchman continued to hold an organizer's commission and to serve as master workman of Marblehead LA 500. Ironically, his dwindling influence eroded further when allegations arose that he was still a Powderly flunky. Philadelphia's T. J. Wallace, a former clerk in the general office, unleashed a rambling attack on Powderly's leadership that also indicted Litchman. Wallace charged Litchman with being involved in everything from the Home Club conspiracy to a cover-up of Hayes's faulty record keeping and the plot to expel Bailey and Barry from the Knights.[55]

DA 30 dwindled to a shell of its former self, which is the only reason Litchman was able to become state master workman in 1890. He set about the task of reorganizing the sagging district and at least one observer, P. F.

Derby of North Easton, Massachusetts, thought his efforts good ones. But Derby noted that Litchman also made "enemies by the score who have not and will not stop at anything short of his utter annihilation as a member of the Order."[56]

Litchman's fiercest enemy was Maurice Bishop, DA 30's secretary-treasurer and an outspoken critic of Powderly's leadership. Bishop provided anti-Litchman forces with the ammunition they needed to get rid of him when he discovered that Marblehead LA 500 had fewer than ten paying members, thus making it ineligible to retain a charter. Bishop charged that LA 500 was a "vest pocket assembly," a mere paper organization existing only for Litchman's convenience. In choosing this tack, Bishop revived a charge that Henry Skeffington, Frank Foster, and George McNeill had leveled years earlier. Bishop, however, made it stick.

DA 30 quietly dissolved LA 500 and declared that Litchman was no longer a member of the KOL. Litchman did not even know he was ousted until he was contacted by a reporter from the *Boston Globe*.[57] He wrote numerous letters requesting that Powderly either authorize LA 500's reorganization or a transfer card to another assembly. Powderly ignored his inquiries, as he was too busy fending off a challenge to his leadership at the upcoming general assembly. Predictably, Litchman responded with several huffy missives demanding an answer "even if it must be unfavorable," but these too were ignored.[58]

Maurice Bishop used bureaucratic technicalities to effect what some had labored over a decade to accomplish: getting rid of Charles Litchman once and for all. To add insult to injury, Litchman also lost his patronage post when Cleveland defeated Harrison in the 1892 presidential election. For the next few years he eked out a modest living as a printer. In 1893, he edited a project that was probably special to him, *The Official History of the Order of Red Men.* When Republican William McKinley won the presidency in 1896, Litchman received another minor bureaucratic post and, in 1900, he was appointed to the U.S. Industrial Commission. He held that post until early 1902, when Theodore Roosevelt dissolved the commission. Litchman went to Washington, D.C., in May 1902 to visit friends and to lobby for another posting. He arrived in the midst of a typhoid epidemic, contracted the disease, and died on May 20.

Litchman's life ended as ingloriously as had his KOL career. The man-who-would-be-master-workman died in a boardinghouse while on a mission to grovel for a bureaucratic post. Embedded within the tragedy are irony and metaphor. Temperamentally, Litchman was simply not suited to be a leader. He was, however, the stuff of which line personnel are made.

If Litchman had been able to curb his ambitions and content himself with proximity to power rather than access to it, he might have been successful.

Although Litchman was petulant and difficult, he was also loyal. As vitriolic and childish as his feuds with Powderly and others were, they took place within the confines of KOL correspondence and on the floor of closed gatherings. Unlike Barry, Bailey, or Buchanan, Litchman kept his battles private. He certainly had motive to rebuke the Order publicly and, as a printer, he had the means. Instead, Litchman internalized problems. His very egotism made him a loyal KOL foot solider to the bitter end.

Litchman's career reveals problems with adopting bureaucratic models to labor organizations. In Weberian terms, the machine should have run itself. A clear chain of command posits specific responsibilities within discrete offices and a top-down power structure. Those above a particular level formulate policy; those below implement it. Among KOL leaders, however, it often seemed that Litchman was the only one who believed this. In an ideal bureaucracy, once Litchman became the editor of the *Journal of United Labor,* he should have formulated editorial policy. It should not have been possible, for example, for Hayes to subvert or countermand Litchman's decisions. Litchman's complaints, though inappropriate in tone, would have been correct in content had the KOL been an ideal bureaucracy.

But it was not. KOL command could be circumvented because charisma still mattered within the Order, and Litchman had none. Herein lies one of several flaws within Weber's formulation. Individuals are supposed to rise within an administrative structure because of skill and service; as Laurence Peter reveals, in practice, connections frequently matter more than skill. Within the KOL, reputation and name recognition were prerequisites for getting elected. Litchman was first chosen as a KOL officer because of his Knights of St. Crispin connections. His second stint as general secretary was due to Powderly's patronage. One could rise through cronyism, but charisma was necessary to retain power.

Terence Powderly was every bit as difficult as Litchman, but he maintained his position from 1879 through 1893 because he was careful to cultivate personality. For every member who hated Powderly, there were several others who championed him. He was labor's first media star. Outside the Order, Powderly was perceived as a respectable, cautious labor leader and temperance advocate. Litchman knew how to fawn, beg, and bluster, but Powderly was more skilled at coalition building, strategic flattery, quick quips, fiery speech-making, moralizing, and stroking potential enemies. He saw the big picture, whereas Litchman seldom saw beyond himself.

Litchman's difficult personality made him an easy target for those willing to pit their stature against his. Robert Layton used his reputation for incorruptibility to unseat Litchman in 1881, just as opponents piggy-backed off the charm of Bailey, Barry, and Buchanan to force him out in 1887. Hayes, as devious a leader as the KOL ever produced, carefully maintained a positive public profile that belied his deep involvement with the Home Club and other conspiracies. Instead, Litchman was assailed for Home Club machinations in which he had no part whatsoever.

In theory, Litchman's lack of charisma ought not to have mattered. In a well-defined bureaucracy, the post, not its holder, confers powers and duties. Turner and Killian note, however, that charisma and bureaucracy are usually symbiotic. Few leaders gain power without charisma, and few hold onto authority unless they cultivate it. Litchman's penchant for making enemies translated into a dearth of allies. Attempts to wield constitutional power were constantly thwarted because he had no means to enforce de facto power.

Nor was there a consistent pattern of authority within the KOL. Litchman got into trouble in 1881 when laissez-faire leadership failed to offer guidance or provide oversight in setting up the *Journal of United Labor.* Litchman correctly complained that it would have been impossible to start the *Journal* with the allotted resources. When he improvised, he was accused of usurping authority.

Nor were there many Weberian "democratic" leaders within the KOL. General assembly delegates essentially invested the KOL's executive board with autocratic power except for the few weeks a year in which the convention was actually in session. They were accountable only to each other, which is why the executive board was such a den of intrigue. Outside the boardroom, most national officers exercised some degree of authoritarian leadership, which they disguised by rhetorically appealing to the Order's best interests or, if it suited, citing conveniently culled sections of the Order's constitution.

Skillful leaders like Powderly knew how to adapt their leadership styles to meet the contingency at hand. When he was not able to get his way immediately, Powderly could artfully keep an issue alive for months and bring it before the convention for what appeared to be a democratic vote. Or he could take a laissez-faire approach and ignore matters when he deemed it too risky or too trivial to involve himself. Charles Litchman simply did not possess such skills.

All of this would seem to confirm Warren Van Tine's assertion that the KOL was a premodern labor organization whose "traditional" leaders and cumbersome structure were a transitional phase in the evolution of business unionism. Van Tine's nuanced view of bureaucracy is more realistic and flexible than that in Weber's classic study, and he recognizes that there are great similarities between labor leaders past and present. Nonetheless, he overstates when he claims that the KOL lacked "bureaucratic values."[59] According to Van Tine, in a business union, one gains entry through the protégé system, rises by blunting one's radical proclivities, cultivates an air of public and personal respectability, and relentlessly pursues promotion. This describes KOL leaders fairly well.

This was precisely the path followed by stalwarts like Powderly, Hayes, Thomas McGuire, and a host of others. Powderly was a Greenbacker and socialist in 1880; by 1890, he was a public model of cautious decorum. Hayes began his KOL career as a Home Club sympathizer; by the mid-1880s he posed as a small businessman who would bring fiscal responsibility to the Knights. By the time he died in 1916, the one-time anarchist Thomas McGuire was noted for his Civil War service and volunteer work.[60]

Of the characteristics Van Tine lists as necessary for business unions—centralization, an oligarchic clique of high-salaried leaders, trained line staff, and detailed administrative procedure—only centralization is in question. The KOL's executive board met infrequently, and even Powderly spent more time at his home in Scranton than at KOL headquarters. Moreover, to evoke William Birdsall again, the KOL's ambiguous structure diffused power along national, district, local, and trade district lines. Still, the KOL executive board did meet in Philadelphia, whence decisions flowed, and a paid staff worked there and administered the day-to-day operations of the KOL. Although *elected* leaders were often incompetent and argumentative, line staff often did a very fine job. Powderly's personal secretary, Emma Fickenscher, for instance, was a model of efficiency.[61]

The KOL neatly fits all of Van Tine's other criteria. Powderly's $5,000 yearly salary was enormous by nineteenth-century labor standards, and executive board wages were far in excess of what most laborers commanded. As for detailed administrative procedure, the thousands of rulings and ever-evolving constitution illustrate that KOL modus operandi was dense by any standard.

More often that not, leaders—not flawed structures—undermined KOL bureaucracy. When it suited, KOL leaders took advantage of bureaucratic minutiae. Procedural technicalities felled both Joe Buchanan and Charles Litchman. But this sort of bureaucratic manipulation is not what Weber had in mind. Litchman was undone through official channels on several levels. It was not possible to expel a Knight simply for being obnoxious. Even a charge as vague as "conduct unbecoming a Knight" had to meet certain guidelines. In the end, Litchman's tantrums, insults, and financial ineptitude did not do him in; a potently administered technicality did.

It was the capricious application of procedure that proved so troubling within the Knights of Labor. Charisma allowed some to sidestep technicalities, while those devoid of it were skewered on them. Internal conflict was so rancorous partly because so much of it turned on personality rather than cold administrative logic. Detailed procedure aside, real-life practice inside the Knights too often resembled a culture of contentiousness.

Laurence Peter suggests that modern bureaucracies are plagued by the same charisma versus structure dilemma that bedeviled Gilded Age organizations. Whether he is correct, one can say definitively that within the Knights of Labor bureaucratic power and charisma were two sides of the same coin. Successful KOL leaders functioned as charismatic bureaucrats. Outside the complex KOL, one might retain one's reputation—as did Tom Barry and Joe Buchanan—or opt for a quiet administrative post, as Frank Foster eventually did. But if one was endowed with neither the charm to attract followers nor the humility to administer, the Gilded Age could be tough on aspiring leaders. Such was the fate of Charles Litchman.

CHAPTER 5

The View from Below:
The Trials and Tribulations of
Obscure Knights

The cases discussed thus far mostly involve Knights with high profiles who held offices on the general executive board. Of the three protagonists in this chapter—Henry Sharpe, John Brophy, and Daniel Hines—only Sharpe held a national office and not even he was well known across the Order. None had much of a career in the labor movement before or after his involvement with the KOL. Why bother with three obscure individuals?

We will do so because, as Jonathan Garlock writes, "the pulse of the organization [KOL] beat most strongly at the local level."[1] Garlock estimates that the Knights founded twelve thousand local assemblies in five thousand communities. That alone is an important reminder for scholars too quick to identify the Knights as some sort of Powderly machine. As with all organizations, what happens on the local level is often a better guide to how that organization works than official pronouncements or the rhetorical flourishes of high-profile leaders. One gets a skewed view by looking only at famous leaders.

Taking the local "pulse" often reveals institutional illness within the Knights of Labor. There is the matter of KOL courts, for example. Garlock argues that KOL courts were an "important experiment in popular justice" when compared to official Gilded Age courts.[2] The latter made no attempt to disguise their bias toward elites or their contempt for labor organizations. Garlock concedes, however, that "the quality of judicial performances was necessarily dependent on the competence of court officers." Melton McLaurin is more blunt, charging that local KOL leaders were often "incompetent" and "ignorant of the Knights' structure, procedures, and principles."[3]

The truth of McLaurin's assertion is seen in the expulsions of Sharpe, Brophy, and Hines. Although separated in place and time, all ended up as victims of the same twisted legalisms that rid the Order of Charles Litchman. In each case, legalistic machination ran roughshod over justice, evidence, and common sense, thus allowing acrimony, personality clashes, and desire for revenge to dominate local agendas.

Still another reason to turn to more obscure individuals is that they embody larger trends within the KOL. Henry Sharpe symbolizes unresolved disputes over cooperative enterprises, John Brophy the KOL's battles with trade unions, and Daniel Hines disputes over the decision to allow businessmen to become Knights. Legalism also sharpened internal battles with competing "isms": the utopianism of Sharpe, Brophy's pragmatism, and the universalism championed by Hines.

For one tumultuous year, 1883, Henry E. Sharpe was president of the KOL's Co-operative Board. His departure from that post in late 1884 altered the KOL's approach to cooperation, and his expulsion from the Order the next year signaled the triumph of those who favored decentralized cooperative efforts. The way Sharpe was deposed illustrates the ways in which local KOL leaders misapplied well-intentioned policies, in this case, codes of personal morality.

Sharpe was a logical choice to head the Co-operative Board. In the early 1880s, he split his time between New York City and Eglinton, Missouri, where he founded a cooperative community based on the productive and associationist principles of Albert Brisbane, Charles Fourier, and Robert Owen.[4] Like many Knights, Sharpe saw cooperative production as a panacea for labor's ills. As Norman Ware noted, "Before the Civil War the wage system was a fact, but not necessarily an irrevocable one, and attempts to escape from it or replace it by something else were not so obviously hopeless as they later became."[5] Cooperative dreams emerged from the belief on both sides of the Atlantic that the existence of a permanent wage-earning class was an unjust condition fraught with the potential for revolution. Even before Marx and Engels prescribed violent upheaval as the antidote to capitalism, many Americans denounced capitalism's individual-profit ethos and experimented with alternatives. Many of these were rooted in romantic agrarian ideals stemming from Thomas Jefferson's famed debates with Alexander Hamilton over the wisdom of allowing industrial production to grow in the United States.

By the end of the Civil War, American industrialization was well into its takeoff phase of development. Nonetheless, the United States remained an agrarian nation through the nineteenth century, and ideals of agricultural production, self-sufficiency, and rural community life were viewed as normative. Rare was a worker willing to defend the virtues of industrial, wage-based, impersonal cities, or a Gilded Age reformer who failed to champion land-reform programs that would enable laborers to flee factories for rural tracts reserved for settlers.

American history is replete with utopian socialist experiments, the most famous being Robert Owen's New Harmony, Indiana, a transplant of

Scottish experiments in profit-sharing and self-contained village life. The most successful collective attempts were those of religious communitarians like the Moravians, the Shakers, and the Mormons. Most secular, heterogeneous communities, including New Harmony, were short-lived but they inspired workers more than religious efforts. The four decades before the Civil War spawned efforts including various Owenite communities, Frances Wright's Nashoba, Tennessee, commune, the Fourierest Brook Farm settlements, and John Humphrey Noyes's Oneida community. Even newspaper editors like Albert Brisbane and Horace Greeley sang the praises of rural life. By the time of the Civil War, the land theories of Brisbane, Fourier, Owen, George Henry Evans, and Thomas Skidmore were widely discussed. After 1876, Victor Drury's writings were popular.

For a time, agrarian utopianism coexisted with urban cooperative experiments. The first known American attempt at cooperative production was that of Baltimore shoemakers in 1794; by the early 1800s, several other shoemaking concerns operated cooperatively. Other ventures opened in Pittsburgh and in Massachusetts, with a group in Boston establishing the first network of cooperative stores in 1831.[6] By the 1840s, numerous trade unions maintained small cooperative stores and a few managed to operate factories, many of which were modeled on the Rochdale movement, a British import that sold workers shares in a wholesale buying club. Investors hoped eventually to fund factories and communities from profits. That proved elusive, but several Rochdale stores did well.[7]

Most nineteenth-century American labor movements jumped on the cooperative bandwagon and the Knights of Labor was no exception. But by the time Sharpe sought to direct KOL efforts, there were competing and contradictory strains within the cooperative movement. Romantic agrarianism was largely incompatible with factory production which, by nature, tended to locate in cities where labor, power, and transportation needs were more easily met. Further, yeoman individualism did not mesh well with the collective practices of factory work, labor unions, and fraternal orders.[8] Nor did agrarians remain the isolated and self-sufficient individuals of romance. Long before Sharpe set up his Eglinton, Missouri, community, most farmers realized they were part of an expanding business network and that their livelihood depended on getting products to urban markets. The United States grew less agrarian with each passing year. Romantics could wax poetic, but industrialization was a fait accompli. The unresolved issues were how that production would be managed and to whom its benefits would accrue.

In Terence Powderly's words, the KOL intended "to supersede the wage-system by a system of industrial co-operation, productive and distributive."[9] The goal was clear enough, but the means to achieving it were not.

KOL founder Uriah Stephens hoped that a combination of wage concessions won by KOL trade unionists and the social pressures applied by
mixed-assembly members would collapse capitalism.[10] The Order's 1878
constitution called for the creation of cooperatives, but little attention was
given to them until the 1880 grand assembly. In his first address as grand
master workman, Powderly lambasted capitalism and called cooperation
"the lever of labor's emancipation."[11] At that convention, the Order's resistance fund, which supported strikes, was converted to a "defense fund,"
30 percent of which was set aside to develop cooperative enterprises.[12]

In 1881, the formula was changed to reserve 60 percent of the defense fund for cooperation, and to require each member to pay ten cents
per month into a special fund for which shares would be distributed for
every thirty cents an individual contributed. Controversy ensued, however,
when KOL trade unionists insisted the defense fund ought to fund strikes,
not idealistic cooperatives.[13] Grand Secretary Litchman rendered the point
moot by bankrupting the defense fund in setting up the *Journal of United
Labor*. In 1882, cooperation contributions were made voluntary.

By 1883, however, only nineteen locals reported cooperative experiments.[14] This prompted the 1883 convention to establish a Co-operative
Board. Chosen to serve on it were Henry Sharpe; Ralph Beaumont of Addison, New York; Oliver Boyer of Louisville, Kentucky; George Holcombe
of Trenton, New Jersey; and William Vale of Hamilton, Ontario. Sharpe
was the logical choice to head the board given that he was already engaged
in a cooperative experiment. He promptly unveiled a plan to establish a
guild-like network of productive and distributive enterprises across KOL
districts, the coordination of which would be directed by the Co-operative
Board. To whip up enthusiasm, Sharpe launched a *Journal of United Labor*
column devoted to the history and current practice of cooperation. He also
made a direct appeal for funds, though in that effort he generated more
enthusiasm than cash. By September, the Co-operative Fund had only $970
in its coffers.[15]

Sharpe did succeed, however, in popularizing cooperation. An 1884
survey of over one thousand local assemblies yielded 212 responses; of
these, 132 locals reported experiments.[16] These numbers indicate that at
least one of every ten KOL assemblies was engaged in some sort of cooperative activity, a nearly 700 percent increase in a single year. Several ventures were spectacularly successful, including a cooperative shoe factory
in Lynn, Massachusetts, where share prices were raised to $100 each in
order to limit the number of those clamoring for a piece of the action.[17]
In early 1884, the KOL took up Sharpe's suggestion and intervened in a
Cannelburg, Indiana, coal strike. The KOL leased and operated the mine
as a KOL cooperative concern.[18]

Sharpe's hopes were dashed when the 1884 general assembly rejected a motion to make contributions to the Co-Operative Board manda-
tory, deemed his guild plan too risky, and resolved that cooperative efforts
should be decentralized. Sharpe angrily resigned his post and a new Cooperative Board was created, the guiding spirits of which were decentralization champions from urban America: John McCartney of Baltimore and
John Samuel of St. Louis.[19]

Why reject Sharpe's plan when it seemed to be making progress?
Some leaders felt it would be impossible to raise the funds necessary to
implement Sharpe's vision. Still another reason lay in the reluctance of the
Order's Philadelphia bureaucracy to impose another centralized program
on locals and districts already clamoring for more control over their own
affairs. But the real problem was ideological.

Gary Marx and Douglas McAdam note that ideology serves a variety
of organizational and individual purposes, ranging from identifying social
injustice and generating possible solutions to helping individuals "redefine
their identity and to see themselves in a new way."[20] But as Marx and
McAdam also note, "ideology seldom rests on logic or science so much as
its rhetorical force"; thus there is little guarantee that even those attuned to
ideology "will agree on its interpretation."[21] Sharpe believed so intensely
in the power of cooperation that he came to see it as a panacea for all of
labor's ills and presumed that all Knights would embrace his vision, once
it was explained. When that proved false, Sharpe became outspoken and
troublesome, thereby opening the door for opponents to use legal chicanery
to rid themselves of him.

Sharpe was an irascible man who never established a network of
friends or allies. In fact, under his tenure the Co-operative Board never
convened. In 1883, however, his Eglinton community was a full-fledged
cooperative colony for which Sharpe applied and received a KOL charter
as LA 2776. By late 1884, however, Eglinton was faltering and several
Knights challenged the validity of its charter. Sharpe lashed out against
the general executive board with such fervor that he was threatened with
suspension. In the bargain, Sharpe angered several Home Club members.

Though Sharpe spent most of his time in Missouri, he was a legal
resident of New York City, where he was also a member of mixed assembly
2022a, an affiliate of DA 49. In September 1884, Sharpe complained to
Powderly that "anarchists" made it "unsafe . . . to remain" in the district,
singling out Victor Drury for scorn. Drury was among those who ques-
tioned the legitimacy of LA 2776's charter and opined that the Eglinton
cooperative existed only in Sharpe's imagination. Perhaps anticipating
2776's collapse, Sharpe applied for a transfer to Scranton, Pennsylvania,
LA 222. Drury blocked that move on the procedurally correct grounds that

Sharpe was neither a resident of that area nor a locomotive tradesman like the rest of the assembly members.[22]

Instead of mending fences, Sharpe went on the offensive. He attacked Frederick Turner for being "subservient" to "anarchists" and complained that Turner refused to print news of his guild plans in the *Journal of United Labor,* though there was "no end of Drury's rubbish" therein. When he received no satisfaction from Powderly, Sharpe introduced a resolution to impeach him at the 1884 general assembly.[23]

Sharpe entered 1885 feuding with Powderly, Drury, Turner, and John Caville, the latter also deeply involved in Home Club activity. Moreover, Sharpe's cavalier reign as Co-operative Board chair alienated Ralph Beaumont and William Vale, and his criticisms of the new board made John Samuel an enemy. All three were sympathetic to the Home Club. If Sharpe thought he would prevail against such powerful foes he was badly mistaken. By the end of 1885, Sharpe was out of the Knights, his reputation and honor in tatters. Ironically, the weapon used to destroy the pietistic Sharpe was morality itself.

Turner wasted no time in casting aspersions on Sharpe. Turner told Powderly that Sharpe's letters were mere advertisements for the guild plan rejected by the assembly or personal attacks on members "he styled anarchists." Turner insisted that the "*Journal* while I am in charge must be used for educational purposes and not for villifying."[24] Sharpe responded by citing two incidents in which efforts of the Co-operative Board were thwarted "by the active hostility of the Knights of Labor." He threatened to publish his own journal and "commence open war upon the anarchists" he felt controlled the KOL.[25] When the easily riled Turner responded indignantly, Sharpe whined to Powderly of the "trashy letter" he got from Turner.[26]

Sharpe received no succor from Powderly, who was still smarting from Sharpe's attempt to dislodge him in 1884. Powderly ignored an offer from Gilbert Rockwood to mediate the dispute between the KOL and Sharpe.[27] This left Turner and the Home Club to tighten the screws on Sharpe.

Sharpe's Achilles' heel was a mentally unstable wife who was in and out of sanitariums. When she charged that Sharpe abandoned her for another woman, DA 49 offered her aid. Local 2022a expelled Sharpe for "conduct unbecoming a Knight," arguing that his abandonment of his wife constituted a grossly immoral act. This placed Sharpe in the unenviable position of appealing the decision to a DA 49 court. Since he had little hope of winning in such a venue, Sharpe appealed to Powderly, though he did so by threatening to bring suit against the Order if he was not satisfied. In an even more foolish action, Sharpe tried to apply tort law to the matter:

This affair is purely a domestic quarrel in which the woman is wealthy and able to take her own part and not being able to get vengeance through the Law Court is having recourse to a court which she had reason to believe was prejudiced against me and which I have little doubt offered its services and fomented the discord. But all that apart, the fact remains that this is a family squabble which the Law Courts will not permit the K of L to interfere in.[28]

Sharpe's logic was flawed. Knights made little distinction between workplace and hearth and routinely expelled workers for offenses such as spousal abuse, drunkenness, failure to pay rent, or use of abusive language. Thus when Mrs. Sharpe swore an affidavit that her estranged husband used violence and coarse language against her, his fate was sealed. The *Journal of United Labor* duly recorded Sharpe's expulsion from the Order.[29] Sharpe's only recourse was to make himself a nuisance and he did so with vigor.

Sharpe turned the tables and brought a countersuit against LA 2022a member Harding Weston, whom he charged had been intimate with his wife. KOL officials had no choice but to grant Sharpe's request for a formal trial. Powderly even allowed the matter to be moved from New York to Scranton for a hearing. Privately, he admitted, "I wish I never knew the Sharpes."[30]

Only Gilbert Rockwood offered much sympathy for Sharpe; he advised Powderly that he thought that the "attack on Brother Sharpe is the work of a few individuals" and that his wife truly was unsound.[31] But Powderly was ill disposed to listen to Rockwood. He reversed his own decision to move the hearing to Scranton and granted DA 49 full jurisdiction in the case.[32] Sharpe vehemently defended himself at his trial and charged several LA 2022a officials with violating their oaths, but to no avail.[33]

Sharpe no doubt figured he had little to lose once DA 49 had jurisdiction over his suit and a final appeal to Powderly failed. On the eve of his hearing he sent several nasty letters to Powderly in which he complained of Powderly's decision to allow DA 49 to hear the case and again threatened a lawsuit. In one letter he arrogantly sneered, "I am out of the Order and do not care to re-enter it." He claimed interest in pursuing the matter only because he had been "publickly [sic] branded . . . as 'BRUTAL' and 'INHUMAN' and as 'GROSSLY IMMORAL.' "[34]

With procedural technicalities out of the way, Powderly washed his hands of the affair and informed Sharpe that the decision lay with DA 49, and it did him little good to flood Powderly's office with letters. By July, Powderly was even able to convince Rockwood that Sharpe was guilty as charged.[35] Powderly then sat back and waited for DA 49 to issue a decision.

At the behest of William Horan, DA 49 withheld the verdict and waited for Sharpe to self-destruct. They knew their enemy well. In September 1885, Sharpe resigned from the Co-operative Board hoping, he claimed, that his absence would convince the assembly either to charter it as a local or attach it to the executive board. Neither occurred; LA 2276 lapsed before the year closed. In October Sharpe resigned from the KOL, thereby saving the Order the trouble of determining whether his expulsion was legal.[36] After this date, little more was heard from Henry Sharpe, though he did join the National Protective Tariff League for a time.

Too many pieces of the record are missing to determine whether Sharpe actually abandoned his wife. It is clear, however, that ideology, not morality, was the real issue. Sharpe held utopian views of cooperation with which he was so enamored that he became uncompromising and impolitic. His centralized cooperative plans clashed with decentralizers within the Order, but the two need not have been mutually exclusive had Sharpe been willing to scale back his grandiose schemes. He chose his enemies un-wisely, as the decentralizers had the ear of the Home Club at a critical juncture in KOL history.

Sharpe's fall cleared the way for John Samuel, a man who, Selig Perlman noted, saw decentralization as "nothing short of a religion."[37] Samuel may have been as zealous as Sharpe, but his political instincts were sharper and he knew how to sublimate his ultimate dreams to what was realistically possible.

After Sharpe's departure, little attention was given to a national co-operative plan. The much ballyhooed Cannelburg coal mine never made money and in 1886, it was leased to the Mutual Mining Company. Small rents trickled in until 1897, when the mine was sold for $4,000.[38] After 1885, the Co-operative Board was chronically short of money. An 1886 attempt to make board contributions mandatory failed, and in 1890, it offi-cially disbanded. It was reconstituted in 1893 but accomplished little.

The KOL hardly ignored cooperation. The decision to allow local assemblies to set up their own projects bore more fruit in the short term. The pinnacle of KOL cooperative activity was in late 1886, a year *after* Sharpe was out of the Order and two years after his removal as head of the Co-operative Board. By then, some two hundred KOL cooperatives oper-ated across North America.[39]

Cooperative stores were the most common enterprise; they were es-tablished in locales as scattered as Brainerd and St. Paul, Minnesota; New Iberia, Louisiana; Northampton, Massachusetts; Pulaski City, Virginia; and Toronto, Ontario.[40] The KOL also operated production cooperatives, sev-eral banks, and a number of innovative building and loan schemes. African Americans in Stewart's Station, Alabama, operated a cooperative cotton gin, while Knights in Birmingham formed an entire village dubbed "Pow-derly," complete with cooperatively built homes, a store, and a factory.[41] The province of Ontario was crisscrossed with projects involving such trades as cigarmaking, biscuit baking, and horse-stay manufacturing.[42] Knights in Menominee, Wisconsin, operated an ice company, those in Spencer, Massachusetts, a boot and shoe factory, and those in Blooming-ton, Illinois, a stove manufactory.[43] Fannie Allyn, a respected well-known leader, helped Cincinnati LA 4457 bring KOL cooperators from around the country together for a fair. More than a dozen exhibited, with representa-tives coming from as far away as Minneapolis and Connecticut.[44] DA 49 did more than criticize Sharpe's plans; it created a network of a half dozen "Solidarity" cooperative companies operating according to principles laid down by Victor Drury. New York Knights had two cooperative leather goods factories, as well as a co-op printer, cigarmaker, plumbing concern, and store.[45]

Most KOL cooperatives were short-lived, but few failed for lack of zeal. Several collapsed because of internal squabbles or poor management, but most failed for a simple reason: lack of adequate capital. As Powderly noted, many cooperative factories were begun in reaction to strikes, a situa-tion not conducive to accumulating reserve capital.[46] Like ventures later founded by the Populists and Farmers' Alliance groups, Knights found commercial banks loath to lend money for projects designed to supplant capitalism. The life of KOL cooperatives was almost always tied to the vitality of local assemblies. Hard times, capitalist backlash, and shrinking membership ultimately doomed both. Capitalism proved more resilient than Sharpe's utopianism and the perverse legalism that derailed his KOL career.

Sharpe fell from grace because he tried to foist utopian plans upon unreceptive leaders, refused to modify his views, and made himself obnox-ious. John Donnelly Brophy was even more unfortunate. He held the wrong views at the wrong time in front of the wrong people. Brophy hailed from Troy, New York, where he was an iron worker, the recording secretary for KOL Local Assembly 3275, and an occasional correspondent to the *Jour-nal of United Labor.*

Brophy also enjoyed minor renown as an author of songs, short sto-ries, and novels. One song, the satirical "Mike McChanic's Relatives," appeared in *John Swinton's Paper* shortly after a committee upon which Brophy sat failed to mediate an agreement between stove mounters and the Fuller and Warren Company. Brophy set new words to "Yankee Doodle" to rally workers.[47] He is credited with at least three stories: "The Ironworker's

Dream," "Tom Strang Killed," and "Bowery Lou." Several circulated beyond the Troy area, though Brophy was little known within the Order.

Of all Brophy's writings, the one that attracted the most notoriety was an address he wrote when he was rebuffed by the 1886 general assembly: "Equality among Men: As She Works North of the Mason-Dixon Line, Not Far from District 49." It is a rambling seventeen-page pamphlet in which Brophy pleads for justice and denounces the hypocrisy of fellow Knights, especially those of Home Club–controlled DA 49.[48]

Brophy toiled as a stove mounter for the Fuller and Warren Company, a Cleveland-based corporation with foundries in Troy. An economic downturn in 1883 led to wage cuts, but Brophy led a KOL boycott of Fuller and Warren stoves that temporarily softened reductions. The job market remained glutted, however, and production slowed further. By April 1884, some mounters had been out of work for more than three months. When Fuller and Warren finally resumed full production, it demanded another 20 percent wage reduction, that mounters pay their own apprentices, and that all employees quit their unions. Workers holding dual membership in a national stove mounters trade union and in LA 3275 agreed to all conditions but the last. Their defiance landed them on a blacklist honored by firms belonging to the Stove Manufacturers Association.[49]

In response, LA 3275 went on strike and called for a new boycott of Fuller and Warren. In both efforts, Brophy played a key role. Because he was skilled with the pen, he was chosen to write articles and letters for *John Swinton's Paper* that kept workers elsewhere apprised of events in Troy. He also served on the negotiating committee. By June, 300 of Fuller and Warren's 379 stove mounters were on strike, but they were dogged by hunger and physical attacks from a local Law and Order League. Brophy and fellow committee members did a good job of appealing to solidarity, and strike funds were partly replenished by revenues from a benefit boxing match. By July, only three stove mounters remained off the picket lines. But unity proved no match for the resources of the association; in August 1884, the mounters conceded defeat.[50]

Business conditions remained depressed, and in January 1885, Brophy reported of workers in Troy who "have not worked in fourteen months." In February, he described Troy in Dickensian terms:

> Here are the homes of the overworked, underpaid ironworkers—long rows of dingy, straggling, smoke-begrimed tenements, with their 7×9 panes to let out the gloom. And here are some of free America's child-prisoners, with their pale, wistful faces pressed against the windowpanes, each pair of humid eyes wearing the same mournful, longing expression—the pitiful, yearning look of captivity—each childish mouth ready to quiver with childish grief for joys denied by forced confinement.[51]

Brophy appealed to the KOL executive board to reissue the boycott against Fuller and Warren, and on April 10, 1885, the board complied.[52]

Eighteen eighty-five was a tough year for Troy iron mounters and for Brophy. His articles for *John Swinton's Paper* and the *Journal of United Labor* assuring readers that Fuller and Warren was near capitulation proved more cheering than prophetic. The company made C. W. Jones its point man in the troubles. Jones was a wholesale manager based in Cleveland, a city located a comfortable distance west of the quarrelsome iron mounters of Troy. Jones leaked internal company reports to the press claiming that only the company's Troy works was bothered by labor strife and that the KOL there was nearly defunct.[53]

The KOL took the bait and expended precious energy refuting Jones's charges. Jones insisted that Fuller and Warren would not negotiate with the KOL which, he claimed, represented only "fifteen or twenty men." He dismissed the KOL's boycott as an Irish import that would never work "in a free and enlightened country" like the United States.[54] Despite Brophy's protests, most newspapers accepted Jones's views as gospel.

Brophy was also troubled by KOL internal developments. His Troy local was part of DA 68, for which he had been recording secretary. By 1885, power had shifted to newer Knights. F. W. Price, a man who disliked Brophy and thought he mishandled the Fuller and Warren troubles, filled Brophy's old post. Those views were shared by the new district master workman, Peter Cattanooch, and by DA 68 power broker J. R. Mansion, the master workman of Troy LA 3275.

Mansion was an early booster of the Home Club who rallied DA 68 to back the Club in its 1886 executive board coup. Although he is a shadowy figure, it appears that he held Lassallean beliefs about the unsuitability of trade unionism, sentiments that clashed with Brophy's pragmatic views. Moreover, the stove mounters were a dual union at a time in which KOL leaders were suspicious of trade unionism.

In August 1885, Brophy lampooned delegate choices for the KOL's upcoming general assembly: "As [a] humble member who has declined to go . . . I hope that the 'popular man' will be laid on the shelf as a delegate this year, while the 'able' man is trotted out just once and put into the harness." He complained of the expense involved in holding the convention in Hamilton, Ontario, and warned against giving power to "street corner and fireside agitators."[55] Several comments were directed at DA 68 delegates.

Brophy's stature was bolstered by strike victories that predated the June 1886 special assembly. Brophy skillfully positioned Fuller and Warren stove mounters by linking their job actions to other disputes in the region. It was a bold gamble, but it paid off. Rising worker militany led corporate heads to settle with Troy workers lest a general strike engulf the city.

In addition to the stove mounters, iron molders and horse railroad operators were on strike, and boycotts crippled a local dry goods merchant, a clothing store, and a Troy newspaper. The March 10, 1886, headline of *John Swinton's Paper* proclaimed: "A Great Day for Troy: Six Memorable Victories All Won at Once." Fuller and Warren agreed to rehire 110 black-listed Knights and to issue wage increases. In Troy, March 10 was an impromptu workers' holiday marked by joyous parades and celebrations. It was also marked by the KOL's removal of the Fuller and Warren boycott.[56]

Agreement proved harder to achieve on the shop floor than on paper. Brophy's clout within DA 68 evaporated when Fuller and Warren broke its promises. Brophy's Home Club foes interpreted the breakdown as more evidence of trade unionism's flaws and of Brophy's lack of judgment. At least five men with this point of view were elected to serve as DA 68 delegates to the fall general assembly.[57] In September, the KOL renewed the boycott of Fuller and Warren after the firm reinstated only twenty of 110 Knights and demanded ironclad contracts of them.[58]

Strikes and boycotts against Fuller and Warren were well under way when the assembly convened on October 4, 1886. By then, however, Brophy could not legally attend the convention as he was under suspension. He showed up, nonetheless, hoping to plead his case. He left a frustrated and angry man; "Equality among Men" tells his side of the story. Unlike his poems and short stories, the pamphlet is so rambling and inelegantly written that it only would have confused anyone unfamiliar with his complaints and innuendoes. He raises concerns about blacklisting, ideology, the election of assembly delegates, and violations of KOL procedure. Brophy blamed his own troubles on "the ghoul of conservative despotism, which aims to perpetuate itself and its opinions by the force of organized combinations." Only at the end of the pamphlet does one learn that he equates "despotism" with the Home Club. Brophy charged that Mansion and others rigged DA 68 elections to assure that all ten delegates to the 1886 assembly were Home Club sympathizers.[59]

According to Brophy, the Home Club assured rank-and-file discipline through expulsion and side agreements with employers. He charged that Mansion and his cronies reopened the March 10 Fuller and Warren agreement in hopes of convincing the firm not to rehire several men DA 68 deemed troublesome. If Brophy is correct, Mansion undermined the Fuller and Warren agreement much as the KOL executive board had done to John Morrison during the 1885 carpet weavers' strike.

Brophy hailed himself a "champion of the spirit of independent freedom in the field of labor reform" who defied the compliance demanded by

DA 68 leaders. But as Brophy asserted his independence, he encountered what he called "the most heartless, the most relentless, and the most brutal of all oppressors, the workingman's worst enemy—the workingman."[60] Brophy and his allies found themselves under suspension from the KOL and blacklisted from those shops in which the KOL controlled hiring decisions. By late summer, Brophy claimed only the title of secretary of the Stovemounters' Defence Association (SDA).

Brophy demanded justice and sought it in KOL courts. Like Henry Sharpe, Brophy found no solace there. In fact, Brophy could not even get a hearing. One local assembly ignored his request, while another passed a resolution asking the district to investigate the matter. When Brophy's formal charges reached the district level, its courts ruled the resolution out of order and refused further mediation.[61]

Attempts to circumvent the chain of command and put the matter before Powderly or the executive board proved equally futile. A judge advocate representing Brophy and the SDA traveled to Philadelphia, where they were denied the courtesy of an interview. Brophy charged his enemies with "extorting money . . . at mock trials held in the name of your organization, and driving men crazy by persecution and mummeries practised [*sic*] in a darkened room."[62] He begged for a chance to address the general assembly and appealed to rudimentary justice, "If any of our side is found guilty of anything wrong, we are willing to suffer the severest of penalty your laws can inflict, and if, on the contrary, it is found that we are right and justice is done, our association will immediately disband and, with the exception of myself, will join yours, and let the controversy end without further redress."[63]

Brophy's enemies countered with rumors that he was an anarchist and a supporter of Morrison, currently under suspension for his direction of the New York carpet weavers' strike. Brophy's tepid response did little to help him. He wrote, "[I]f I am an anarchist *that's my business,* and if I were the devil, what is the difference? Our *cause* is the question for you to consider and *my* anarchism has nothing to do with the case."[64]

Brophy mocked DA 68 district court as a "Star Chamber" and labeled the practice of blacklisting one's own members "a new kind of cannibalism." He added, "For when the members of an organization like the Knights of Labor, enlisted in the service of suffering humanity and pledged to uphold the noblest of principles, when they attempt to trample these glorious principles in the dust . . . then, indeed, the hell-born offspring of the associated dictum, 'the fiend of Inconsistency,' laughs triumphantly in the saddened face of the God of Justice, while brutal Capital is driving another rivet into the shackles of blind, selfish labor."[65]

Brophy met only with more frustration. In his words, "I came here expecting to meet 'representatives' . . . meeting on a plane of perfect equality, each man the acknowledged peer of his associates, the master of his own actions, and the keeper of his own actions." What he found instead so infuriated him that he peppered his descriptions with asterisks, a common author's device used in lieu of obscenities. He ended his pamphlet on a disturbing and divisive racial note. Brophy called DA 49 delegates "hypocrites . . . who have almost caused the streets of Richmond to run with blood in upholding the citizen right of a colored brother to live at a public hotel," while neglecting "to uphold the inalienable God-given right of white brothers . . . to live on the face of the earth."[66]

Brophy's impolitic remarks offended some who might otherwise have been allies. His attack on "mummeries practised in a darkened room" was an insult to KOL ritual at a time in which long battles were fought over it. He unwisely dodged the charge of anarchism at a moment in which the term was used to discredit instantly any person or cause. (Indeed, it was even used by real anarchists in the Home Club to discredit their enemies.) Moreover, Brophy cited Powderly, Thomas Barry, and William Bailey for failing to consider SDA complaints when all three would have been useful in countering the Home Club's reach into DA 68. No doubt other Knights were put off by the overly passionate rhetoric with which Brophy made his case. His is a polemic in which details are mere incidentals. To "consider both sides" and then judge, as Brophy requested, would not be possible based on the sketchy account he offered.[67]

Brophy never got his day in court and disappeared from KOL view after 1886. The SDA was a small group whose blacklisted members quickly scattered. Some who remained in Troy probably later joined the AFL, but this is sheer speculation as we know the name of only one member: Brophy. Were it not for his surviving pamphlet, few historians would have heard of J. Donnelly Brophy.

But more is indicated than the misfortunes of a relatively obscure Knight. Brophy's case has distressing parallels to that of Joseph Buchanan. Both tirelessly toiled on behalf of the KOL, both proved skillful tacticians, neither sought to aggrandize himself, and each was unceremoniously bounced from the Order by men less able than they via questionable means. Moreover, devotion to trade unions proved problematic for both Buchanan and Brophy. Brophy's travails demonstrate that the issue was as contentious on the local level as it was on the national level.

Brophy's pamphlet also represents organizational chaos. By rights, such a work should have been the final recourse, not the first. Of all Brophy's allegations, the one that rings most true is the claim that the new men of DA 68 ran roughshod over KOL procedures. Any Knight who was suspended or charged with a violation had the right to a hearing, but Brophy was denied one. It is doubtful he would have won, but he was entitled to try. In the chaotic days of rapid growth, KOL procedure grew lax and was too easily manipulated by the unworthy, the unscrupulous, and the incompetent.

DA 68 violated KOL law by simply ignoring Brophy, hoping that he and the SDA would just go away. It was easy to deny them; it was harder to silence them. None of this counted for much in mid-1886, when the KOL was at the height of its power, but a year later it mattered a great deal as workers began to leave the Order in droves. There is no way of knowing how many workers read Brophy's pamphlet, but every bit of bad publicity hurt the Knights. When Brophy began his battles with the KOL, there were thirty-two KOL locals in the city of Troy. By the end of 1887, that number was down to twelve; in 1888, there were only four.[68] The Fuller and Warren boycott lingered for the rest of the decade, but the company took increasingly less notice of the declining Knights of Labor.

Having one's day in court was no guarantee of justice, nor was upholding the KOL principle of universal brotherhood. Daniel Hines of South Abington, Massachusetts, found himself embroiled in Dickensian cycles of hearings, appeals, and constitutional minutiae that were a veritable American version of *Bleak House*. The Hines affair illustrates what Gregory Kealey and Bryan Palmer call the "underside" of the Knights of Labor, and is the flip side to the small-town "fraternal voluntarism" historian Faye Dudden notes between modest employers and Knights.[69]

Critics from Samuel Gompers to the present have condemned the KOL's practice of admitting employers into its ranks. As the logic runs, employers sitting in KOL locals blunted the development of class (or craft) consciousness and cast a bourgeois pall over the Order. Employers in the ranks supposedly reinforced the KOL's reluctance to sanction strikes, thus depriving workers of a valuable tool in combating capitalist power.

Such assessments are problematic. The KOL's antistrike policy predated the admission of employers and more strikes occurred after they entered. More balanced studies reveal that large employers and corporate heads rarely joined KOL locals and that the non–wage earners who entered were mostly men of modest means: shopkeepers, proprietors of small factories, low-level bureaucrats, and service-sector employees.[70] There were local assemblies in which conservative members held sway, but the majority of Knights were wage earners. Nor should one assume that Knights gleefully welcomed employers into their ranks. Class bias was a factor in the Daniel Hines case. When combined with gross procedural violations, the two made a mockery of the KOL's universalistic rhetoric.

Hines was a member of KOL Local 3770 in South Abington, a small town located south of Boston and east of Brockton that is now called Whitman. LA 3770—like Charles Litchman's local—was under the aegis of DA 30, the KOL's largest for much of the 1880s. Geography and jurisdiction were important factors. Nearby Brockton was a shoe town, LA 3770 consisted primarily of shoemakers, and DA 30 was among the most craft-conscious of all KOL districts. From the beginning, Hines was a man out of place in LA 3770. He was not a shoemaker but a furniture dealer who regularly sold goods to area Knights. His business dealings got him into trouble with the KOL, a story his brother Thomas related in a hundred-page booklet titled "The Anarchist's Conspiracy, or, The Blight of 3770."

Though Hines's account is self-serving, its details reveal a black comedy whose central themes were envy, personality conflict, and revenge. What ought to have been a minor, personal matter snowballed into a major conflict involving KOL local and district courts, as well as the Massachusetts legal system. Petty bickering persisted for nearly two years.

The bare outlines of the case are simple enough. In 1887, Daniel Hines was expelled from the Knights after pressing for payment on a bed lounge sold to local Knight J. D. Plummer. Hines claimed he held a legal lease on the furniture and Plummer countered that Hines was a rapacious capitalist who had barged into his home and bullied Plummer's wife into signing said lease. Most KOL courts found in favor of Plummer; nearly all were illegally constituted.

As noted in the Sharpe case, personal morality was of utmost importance to Knights. A person who would defraud another, let alone a fellow Knight, was deemed unworthy of membership. Indeed, had Hines been upheld, LA 3770 would have been compelled to suspend Plummer. Knights stood ready to shun individuals with the same force with which they boycotted huge firms like Fuller and Warren. But the Hines case had less to do with ethics than with a desire to excise an employer from KOL ranks. By his own admission, Hines was a shrewd merchant who separated sentiment from sound business practices. Among shoemakers, a notoriously underpaid craft, this alone made Hines suspect.

Hines's version of the events is as convoluted as Brophy's account. In addition, much of Hines's "evidence" is attributed to a mysterious interloper, "Perley Denton." Hines claimed this pseudonym was chosen to protect the identity of a prominent Knight, but Denton may well have been fictitious. Denton allegedly recruited Hines to the KOL in 1885, after Hines was convinced that the KOL would affect a "great change in the condition of the workingman" and bring down "his proud oppressor, the capitalist." If he is to be believed, Hines initially was blackballed when one Knight charged that he made "a business of cheating everybody."[71]

One wonders why Hines persisted in seeking KOL membership, but he does not explain his motives or how he overcame blackballing. His account telescopes to the moment when Denton informed him that his billings were being scrutinized. Hines struck first and on December 19, 1885, he asked a local KOL judge advocate to help him recover money (or the goods) owed by KOL member William Tubon.

Hines's aggressive business practices led to conflict with J. D. Plummer, who had obtained a lounge from Hines on a lease-to-buy option. Many of his customers were in arrears, prompting Hines to renegotiate all of his leases. All was well until he reached the Plummer home. J. D. Plummer was out, but Hines convinced Mrs. Plummer to sign a new lease. Upon his return, Mr. Plummer was furious as he had just made a $2.16 payment on the furniture, leaving a balance of just $1.85.

The trifling amount involved suggests that what ensued was premeditated. On February 9, 1886, Hines was summoned before LA 3770 to answer a charge of "conduct unbecoming a Knight." Hines laid out the facts and produced both the original and new leases before a tribunal in which Henry Powers served as judge and John F. Murphy was the judge advocate. Hines was satisfied with the proceedings, though he was troubled when both Powers and Murphy discussed the case with him as he walked home. He grew quite alarmed when Denton told him the next day that his conviction was "a foregone conclusion" and that new issues would surface at the next hearing.

One week later, Hines was pronounced guilty in the Plummer case. He was then asked if he had loaned money to Henry Ward. Hines confessed that he advanced a small sum to enable Ward to pay a cruelty-to-animals fine. When he volunteered that he asked for neither security nor interest, Judge Advocate Murphy asked why he then charged interest on furniture leases. Hines was dumbfounded and blurted out, "Mr. Murphy, have you any right to ask such questions? Do you intend to say that you can dictate my business?" The answer floored him: "Yes sir, the Knights of Labor have the right . . . and you will soon find out." Hines was promptly lambasted for shady business practices. Plummer interrupted the denunciation to shout his own accusations of fraud and swindle. When Hines protested the insult, he was told that Plummer "is only telling the truth."[72]

Six weeks passed before the next hearing. In the interim, Hines walked into another trap. His business had been increasing dramatically, though most of his customers were Knights leasing goods secured by minuscule down payments. Why the otherwise shrewd Hines did not suspect something is unclear, but he claimed astonishment when Denton alerted him that his customers had no intention of paying.

Still another problem emerged. In 1884, Mr. and Mrs. Edward E. Brown leased furniture from Hines. Very little was paid before the Browns' marriage failed, with Edward Brown taking some of the leased furniture with him to the nearby town of Lakeville. On March 3, 1886, Hines, a deputy sheriff, and a deputy's assistant went there to reclaim the leased furniture. No one was home, but Hines proceeded to remove the goods in question. Before he could complete his task, Brown's mother and brother returned and tried to stop the process. Hines produced the lease and removed the rest of the goods. Six days later, Hines was arrested for theft and had to appear before a court of law. Unlike the KOL court, the local magistrate scrutinized the leases and found him not guilty.[73]

On April 8, Hines appeared for a third time before the local KOL court. He declined to defend himself and appealed his case to a KOL district court. He nonetheless took vigorous part in silly sidebar semantics debates, including whether dividends collected from KOL cooperative investments were a form of interest-taking, the likes of which Hines stood accused of abusing. Hines was convicted of conduct unbecoming a Knight and returned the next day for sentencing, armed with the KOL constitution and prepared to demonstrate how LA 3770's court deviated from procedures. A Kafkaesque debate ensued concerning the exact charges against Hines, who was responsible for hearing them, and whether an actual hearing had taken place.

Hines was forced to go to Boston to lay his case before District Master Workman John Howes, who opined that the local's violations of procedure rendered its decisions invalid. At the May 12 district court hearing, more farce emerged. John Murphy neglected to bring the hearing documents to court as he had loaned them to J. D. Plummer, the plaintiff in the case. The District 30 court properly judged the matter a personal one and returned it to LA 3770 with an offer from Judge Henry Powers to mediate a friendly settlement.

Before that effort could be made, Powers was replaced by Everett Perry, a man even less likely to favor Hines. Hines appealed for Perry's removal, though he was warned that several district judges were part of the "ring" against him. Matters went badly at the new trial. When Hines protested that the hearing was illegal because no friendly settlement had been attempted per district court order, Perry declared Hines in contempt of court. Hines pleaded not guilty to the contempt charge, Perry rejected the plea, ordered Hines to leave, and threatened to call a law officer if he refused. A local constable was present: I. T. Churchill, the master workman of LA 3770.

New appeals to DA 30 led to a temporary stay of sentence, though the local suspended Hines at its very next meeting. Hines's protest led to a debate as to whether a district communication came to Perry as a "personal" or "official" document. Master Workman Churchill ordered Hines to leave the assembly room, but Hines lost his temper and refused, and was cited for contempt. According to Hines, this rash act turned sympathetic Knights against him and into the arms of "the anarchists."[74]

Hines appealed his contempt conviction, a procedure not permitted under the KOL constitution, but to which the district court acceded. A hearing in Boston was set for June 11. Once again the presiding judge recommended arbitration, but Hines refused it and claimed that the legality of his leases was a matter for the commonwealth to determine. Knights on both sides clamored to speak and the court nearly dissolved in chaos. When calm was restored the court decided to hear only the contempt charge, a matter whose decision was foregone as Hines was indeed guilty. The district court ruled thus on June 15.

While Hines continued his futile search for justice, he received two more blows. First, Edward Brown's mother charged Hines with assaulting her while removing goods from her house, and a Plymouth jury agreed. Second, the Knights sprung their financial trap and defaulted on their leases. On June 16, 1886, Hines published notice that he was abandoning his business and that accounts needed to be settled.[75] He defiantly showed up for a local assembly meeting and was allowed to sit on the grounds that since he had not yet been sentenced he was still a KOL member. The next night, however, the local court convened and asked the town constable to bar Hines's future entry.

More absurdities followed. Perry abruptly resigned as judge, thus delaying Hines's sentencing.[76] Then, as if Hines had not offended enough Knights, he misrepresented the KOL during a strike called by the Lasters' Protective Union. Many lasters held dual membership in the KOL, but relations between trade unions and the KOL were tense. Hines repeated derogatory remarks about the lasters, which he claimed came from a key KOL official. Allegedly the official told him, "[I]f we give [the lasters] a chance they will soon have a division in this town, and that will never do, for the Knights of Labor must crush out of existence every other labor organization."[77]

Hines's comments were nonsense. The KOL supported the lasters' strike and even helped them raise money to replenish strike funds. Hines's remark was meant to embarrass the KOL and expose its universalistic rhetoric as hypocritical. In October, James Bates, the worthy foreman for LA 3770, issued a report detailing the Hines investigation. Numerous members expressed a desire to drop all future discussion of the case. When that sagacious advice was ignored, the way was paved for still another round of Hines appeals.[78]

The matter ended up on Powderly's desk. Much to the detriment of all involved, he ruled *all* previous decisions invalid and offered the opinion that the Plummer-Hines case was strictly one for the legal system. Hines's sorry affair dragged into 1887. By then, Henry Waugh was LA 3770 judge, and he tried one last time to smooth things over. Buoyed by Powderly's opinion, Hines "indignantly rejected" a Waugh compromise that would have quashed the Plummer case and suspended the contempt case if Hines agreed to apologize to Master Workman Churchill for his outbursts. Instead, Hines demanded a new trial and threatened to sue Waugh if not granted one.

An exasperated Waugh convened court on January 25, 1887, and even indulged a rambling letter from Hines outlining all the supposed illegalities and injustices he had suffered. This was Hines's sole line of defense before he abruptly accused the current court of being illegally constituted. Once again the assembly dissolved into chaos. Hines resolutely refused to give up or shut up. After taking as much shouting as he could tolerate, Waugh ordered Hines to leave. When he refused, William Gaffney and Patrick Smith shed their KOL personae for those of town constables and arrested Hines for disturbing the peace. Hines left the assembly in handcuffs and was hustled off to jail, where he stayed until his brother Thomas posted his bail. The next morning he pleaded nolo contendere and was fined one dollar.[79]

Still Hines refused to quit. The Reverend Jesse Jones, District 30's new judge, was no more successful in his arbitration attempts than were his predecessors. In a personal meeting with Jones, Hines refused to apologize to Churchill and demanded reimbursement for monetary losses resulting from time spent in KOL courts. Jones washed his hands of the matter and sent it back to Waugh. He declared Hines guilty of contempt and of behavior unbecoming a Knight. At long last LA 3770 voted to expel Hines.

It is doubtful that many locals allowed their troubles to linger as long as the Hines affair, though many had equally messy cases.[80] This detailed and rare look inside a small KOL local shows what could go wrong when inept leaders, petulant personalities, ideological differences, and procedural ignorance collided. The Hines appeal process lingered because, technically, Hines was correct in claiming that one KOL court after another violated KOL law.

The KOL court system was an odd jumble of practices incompletely spelled out in the Order's constitution. It was supplemented by general assembly resolutions, rulings from the executive board, and unilateral decisions from Powderly. To master KOL legal minutiae would have required the services of lawyers, a profession barred from KOL membership. Anyone as skillful and persistent as Hines could find grounds to appeal nearly any ruling. The KOL's court system was too complex to render justice quickly or efficiently.[81]

Very few KOL locals contained members with more than a working knowledge of basic court procedure. Workers periodically wrote to non-KOL newspapers to bemoan unfair treatment from the Knights. Many of those letters likely contain legitimate complaints, but the KOL usually suffered more damage from prolonging disputes than from persecuting the innocent. It is nearly impossible to reconstruct the truth of the Hines-Plummer suit and one should certainly not trust Hines's self-serving account, and there is no evidence that "anarchists" were out to get him. Knights in the South Abington area suffered more from the time they wasted on Hines than from negative fallout from his expulsion.

Ideology helps explain the Hines debacle. In the eyes of some Knights, Hines's position as an independent furniture dealer marked him as an oppressor unworthy of KOL membership. Hines saw himself as a humble shopkeeper, but in a village dominated by shoemakers, such a post was perceived as solidly bourgeois. Trial remarks indicate that many Knights felt Hines's lease rates were usurious; still others felt he ought to be operating his shop according to cooperative principles. All of this suggests that caution is in order before asserting that the presence of employers in KOL locals bathed them in a bourgeois light. In some instances, employer Knights intensified class conflict instead of ameliorating it. To be sure, Daniel Hines was the victim of a personal vendetta. But some of the Knights who leased furniture they had no intention of buying did so in the name of driving out a capricious capitalist tyrant from their midst.

Hines was hardly an innocent victim. His brother's account clearly shows him to have been argumentative, rash, rude, and stubborn. Further, his insistence that his business practices were above KOL scrutiny showed a thorough misunderstanding of KOL principles and implied exactly the sort of middle-class arrogance some Knights suspected. Given what he went through, he was also a glutton for punishment. Why he bothered with the KOL is as baffling as why the Order trifled with him.

Daniel Hines, an insignificant member of a small local, managed to redirect the energies and resources of the KOL's largest district assembly. KOL courts were not courts of law. Why didn't someone somewhere along the line simply toss Hines out of the Knights and let him complain from the outside? Given his disruption of several hearings and his refusal to obey his master workman, there was cause to do so, even if he was wronged in the Plummer affair. Again, the complexity of KOL structure may be the culprit. LA 3770 consistently ruled against Hines only to be reversed by DA 30 officials seeking amicable compromise. Hines was finally removed when he exhausted the patience of DA 30. Perhaps district officials were more anxious to foster cooperation between capital and labor than Knights

in South Abington who defined "cooperation" a bit differently. Whatever
the reason, what timid leaders lacked in decisiveness they paid for in chaos.

The experiences of the three men highlighted in this chapter paint an
ugly picture of what could happen in the day-to-day operations of the
Knights of Labor. The cases of Henry Sharpe, John Brophy, and Daniel
Hines show what could and did go wrong on the national, district, and local
levels. The Hines case seductively suggests that the KOL was often little
more than a collection of bickering backstabbers. Of all the conclusions to
draw, however, that would be the most erroneous.

Each man's fate caused ripple effects more profound than their personal dramas. Sharpe's removal altered how the KOL approached cooperation, while Brophy's removal shows how Home Club intrigue resonated
beyond the New York City metropolitan area. It had the effect of placing
control of an important district into less capable leaders' hands. The Hines
case threw an entire local and much of the KOL's largest district into
chaos, and it also raises important questions about the class makeup of
local assemblies. Moreover, each case raises interpretive questions about
ideology, authority, and structure within social movements.

Elsewhere I have written about the problems inherent in the KOL's
move from a ritual-based fraternal organization to a more bureaucratic,
political labor advocacy group.[82] Such a shift invariably involves ideology,
a set of ideas generally more divisive than the shared bonds of ritual fraternalism. As Charles Tilly notes, social movements employ a variety of tactics, ranging from private rituals and public parades to expulsions of unpopular leaders and political action.[83] However, some behaviors bind
members whereas others divide them. Moreover, as Gary Marx and Douglas McAdam observe about ideology, it is usually better at "identifying
the problem and legitimizing the need for action than . . . on the precise
specification of how the problem is to be solved."[84]

Regrettably, Sharpe, Brophy, and Hines illustrate the exclusionary
tendencies of ideology. Sharpe upheld a widely shared belief in the need
for cooperative productive and distributive enterprises as the antidote to
competitive capitalism and the wage system. But when Sharpe's abstrac-
tions became a concrete centralization scheme, he ran afoul of decentralizers. Because he was ideological rather than pragmatic or politic, Sharpe
was unable to compromise or scale back his vision.

Much the opposite was the case for John Brophy: he was a pragmatist
adrift in a sea of ideologues. Brophy championed both trade unions and
individual advocates of them "like John Morrison" who were under official
sanction. This made him a target for Lassalleans and anarchists associated
with the Home Club for whom anti–trade unionism was an article of faith.

Much as with Joseph Buchanan, Brophy's past service and tactical competence was deemed less important than the principles he held.

Though he did not practice what he preached, Daniel Hines challenged the KOL to live up to its rhetoric of universal brotherhood. During the days in which Knights shared common mysteries and rituals and the Order was a relatively small band of laborers, universal brotherhood sounded suitably high-toned and moralistic. For some, however, the principle broke down in real-life contexts in which Knights were called upon to share the assembly room with shopkeepers and employers.

None of the three was officially tossed from the KOL for his beliefs. The legalistic maneuvers employed shifts the focus to authority and structure within the KOL.

I have already refuted the charge that the KOL was a Powderly machine; he never controlled the Order to the degree that critics charge. In a peculiar way, this chapter suggests that the KOL might have been a healthier organization if a despot had ruled it. What is most striking about all three affairs is how small disputes mushroomed into gigantic ones. No one was capable of making a quick, firm decision; instead, petty intrigue and legalistic mumbo jumbo caused minor sores to fester and erupt. Appeals were made to Powderly in all three instances, but he did not resolve them because he *could not* do so.

Knights of Labor courts may well have been, as Jonathan Garlock suggests, an experiment in popular justice, but they were equally emblematic of structural weaknesses within the Order. Neither lines of authority nor dispute resolution procedures were clear. Garlock analyzed KOL expulsions from 1880 through 1886. In all, he identifies eighty-one offenses leading to removal. However, 70 percent of the total came from just two charges: conduct unbecoming a Knight and violation of obligations.[85] From a long list covering everything from divulging secrets, forgery, scabbing, embezzlement, and murder, Knights were most likely to be removed for the Order's two most ambiguous charges.

The Knights of Labor too often engaged in legalistic equivocation because concrete guidelines were missing. In an organization with clear standards, someone like Sharpe, whose policies failed to secure a mandate, would have either accepted the will of the majority or resigned. As an outside critic, he could cause temporary embarrassment, but the internal bureaucracy would proceed anon. Likewise, a smooth-running Order would not allow legalism to be used for blatantly ideological ends, as in the case of John Brophy. Nor is it likely such an organization would waste time on a matter so trivial on behalf of a man so obnoxious as Daniel Hines.

It is too much to expect that an organization like the KOL should have worked out all its structural details during the crucial years between

1884 and 1887, when Sharpe, Brophy, and Hines challenged the Order. During that period the KOL increased its membership a thousandfold. New members begat new leaders, some of whom relied on old leaders for guidance, while still others took on duties for which their temperaments, intellect, or lack of experience ought to have disqualified them. Whether good, bad, or indifferent, KOL leaders worked within a structure designed for a much smaller organization.

These three tales suggest that a successful social movement needs to manage carefully its ideological disputes. One way of reducing the chances of allowing disagreement to disrupt an organization is to have clear procedures for addressing disputes. Legal channels should be reserved for concrete charges that affect the organization, not serve as a forum for personal dispute, innuendo, or clashing ideas. Ultimately, the KOL illustrates for the nineteenth century the same problems of uncontrolled growth that have plagued some twentieth-century social movements.[86] In times of great stress organizations, like individuals, sometimes make bad decisions.

CHAPTER 6

A Dubious Equality:
Leonora Barry and Women
in the KOL

In 1891, Alzina Stevens of Toledo, Ohio, was offered the recently vacated post of director of women's work for the Knights of Labor. Stevens declined and opined that there was "no need for the maintenance of a women's department, for the reason that women [have] equal rights with the men in the organization and it would be a needless expense to keep up the department."[1]

Charlotte Smith disagreed, and said so on the pages of *The Woman's Journal.* She pointed out that women paid the same assessment fees as men did, but that there was "altogether too much man legislation in the labor movements, with the mottoes pay your dues, do as we Knights tell you, be modest, remain in the background."[2]

Encapsulated in this minor tiff are underlying questions and assumptions about the proper role of women within the KOL. Stevens dutifully echoed the words of Leonora Barry, who had been director of women's work since 1886, but who had just tendered her resignation. Publicly, Barry announced that her recent marriage after years of widowhood required her to devote her energies to her new household. Besides, Barry argued, there was no longer a need for the women's department.

Charlotte Smith smelled a rat and much of the evidence justifies her suspicions. Barry's resignation and the pending reorganization of the women's department involved darker forces and secrets. In truth, Barry was hounded out of the KOL, thus robbing the organization of another of its brightest and best.

Leonora Barry's saga reveals dimensions of the ongoing debate within KOL ranks regarding women's proper relationship to the labor movement and of the existence of separate women-centered organizing models. On a broader level, it demonstrates how sexism damages social movements. Nearly eighty years after Barry resigned her post, Marge Piercy mused on how male activists within the New Left viewed women. Piercy complained:

> The Movement is supposed to be for human liberation: how come the condi-
> tion of women inside it is no better than outside? . . . The typical Movement
> institution consists of one or more men who act as charismatic spokesmen,
> and negotiate and represent that body . . . and who manipulate the relation-
> ships inside to maintain his or their position, and the people who do the
> actual work of the institution, much of the time women.[3]

In the interval between Smith's protests and those of Piercy gender
bias became entrenched so deeply that it polluted labor and social reform
organizations as profoundly as it did mainstream American society. Both
Emma Goldman and Elizabeth Gurley Flynn criticized the sexism of erstwhile male comrades, while the AFL made no bones about its disapproval
of working women.[4] In 1897, Edward O'Donnell of Boston's Central Labor
Union called women wage earners "the error of the age" and "an evolu-
tionary backslide."[5] Within those few trades that did allow women to join,
Alice Henry complained that "men, mostly older men, run the meeting and
often are the meeting."[6] Women within the Congress of Industrial Organizations were hardly immune from sexism, nor were those in more progressive trade unions such as the United Auto Workers.[7]

Within this litany of gender blindness it is sobering to realize that the
KOL was historically precocious in its views on gender. It took the late
1960s' women's movement to elevate most unions to the paltry levels
achieved by the Knights in the 1880s. In 1878, the KOL's first statement
of principles included a plank dedicating the Order "To secure for both
sexes equal pay for equal work."[8] Convention delegates also discussed the
possibility of admitting women as members. This marked a change in the
KOL's official view on women, and Uriah Stephens was not favorably
disposed to the idea. Stephens held to a fraternal vision of the KOL involving elaborate secret rituals, and he fell prey to the popular stereotype that
women were gossips. By his logic, women were incapable of keeping secrets and thus were poor candidates for assembly room camaraderie. Moreover, most Gilded Age fraternal groups were aggressively male, with the
assembly hall serving as a refuge from the feminized Victorian home.[9]

But an organization with such strong universalist pretensions as the
Knights could ill afford to ignore the very real presence of women in the
workplace. From 1880 to 1890, the number of women working rose from
more than 2.6 million to over 4 million. Large numbers of women workers
were concentrated in clothing and textiles, eastern-centered industries located in areas of KOL strength.[10] Not coincidentally, the rapid increase of
women wage earners occurred in areas where women could be utilized as
a secondary labor market to suppress wages across the board.

Despite Stephens's objections, Phillip Van Patten of the Socialist Labor Party introduced a resolution at the 1879 grand assembly to admit women to the Knights. It was tabled, but it was revived the next year and passed. Henry Skeffington, a Philadelphia shoemaker and advocate of women's rights, seized the initiative and organized Garfield Assembly #1684, an organization of female shoemakers headed by Mary Hanafin and Mary Stirling. The KOL voted to became an open, public organization at its 1881 convention. The same convention wrestled with the mechanics of absorbing women into the Order with an ensuing debate over what kind of ritual women would use. The convention adopted Powderly's compromise: women would use the established *Adelphon Kruptos* and simply exchange gender pronouns when appropriate.[11]

But this compromise did little to alleviate the fears of some men, and women's organization proceeded slowly. According to Philip Foner, only three new women's locals were founded in 1882, nine in 1883, and thirteen in 1884. It was not until 1886 that more than one hundred new female locals appeared.[12] But as late as 1887, George Bennie wrote to complain that he would sooner "leave the Knights a thousand times over and bear the brand of scab" than sit at a local assembly meeting with women.[13]

Even individuals more accepting than Bennie held views that could scarcely be labeled progressive. As Susan Levine convincingly demonstrates, much of the nineteenth-century labor movement was torn between conflicting views about working women. On the one hand, an "egalitarian principle" suggested that women could "carve a sphere of action outside the limits of contemporary womanhood"; on the other, Victorian notions of "hearth and home" held the domestic ideal of home as a woman's proper sphere.[14] As most Knights saw it, women in the workplace were evidence of capitalist abuse. From a male perspective, a just society was one in which work accorded males a "living wage" that allowed wives to be at home and children in school. Thus, even as the KOL championed such causes as suffrage and equal pay for equal work, women in the workplace were viewed as aberrations that future progress would correct.

Despite inherent contradictions, the KOL organized between fifty thousand and sixty-five thousand women, many into the very mixed-gender assemblies George Bennie so feared. Further, important women leaders like Susan B. Anthony, Mary Jones, Mary Lease, Leonora O'Reilly, Charlotte Smith, and Frances Willard not only sang the Order's praises; they took out KOL membership.

Reconciling this seeming contradiction requires abandoning the temptation to deconstruct nineteenth-century labor from a modern (or postmodern) feminist perspective. Though the women's movement had a vocal feminist wing, the Gilded Age majority—regardless of class, ethnicity, or gender—was at least mildly essentialist when it came to gender. It was assumed that women were by nature different from men and that they possessed special feminine qualities that made them morally superior, physically inferior, and temperamentally unique. Many reformers argued that women's spheres should be broadened, but few felt they should be eliminated. Leonora Barry, for example, argued fervently for the equality of women textile and shoe workers, but she drew the line at women iron workers. She wrote that "every woman who went to work in the iron industry threw a man out of employment . . . [probably] compelling some other woman to leave her home and with one of two of her little ones seek employment to support the home the man should have supported." Hers was no economic argument. She went on to write that iron work was "not conducive to culture or refinement in women, nor are its duties such as to insure good physical conditions."[15]

Although there were numerous individual exceptions, the Victorian hearth-and-home ideal was hegemonic, even within working-class families where it made little economic sense to embrace it. This did not mean, however, that actions with feminist implications, women's consciousness, or women's culture were unknown in the Gilded Age.[16] Indeed, the advances made by the "New Woman" of the Progressive Era were built upon Gilded Age foundations. Nonetheless, the scholar who encounters prototypes of contemporary feminism within late Victorian society generally unearths the exception, not the rule.

This grounding is necessary to appreciate fully both the remarkable achievements and the wasted potential embodied in the KOL career of Leonora Barry. She was born Leonora Marie Kearney in County Cork, Ireland, on August 13, 1849, the daughter of John and Honor (Brown) Kearney. She came into the world at the height of the potato famine. More than 1 million Irish had starved in the previous four years, and another 1.5 million emigrated. Leonora's family was among the next wave of 1.2 million Irish who came to the United States between 1847 and 1854, the Kearneys arriving in 1851.

They settled in St. Lawrence County in upstate New York. Leonora's mother died in 1864, and John Kearney remarried. Leonora did not get on well with her stepmother and left home at the age of sixteen. She pursued her education at a girls' school in Colton, New York, and obtained a teaching certificate in a mere six weeks. Before she was seventeen, she was a teacher in upstate New York.

Leonora taught until 1871, when she married William E. Barry, a painter, and moved to Potsdam, New York. In 1873, Barry gave birth to a daughter, Marion Frances. Moves to Haydenville, Massachusetts, and Amsterdam, New York, were accompanied by the birth of two more children, William Standish in 1875, and Charles Joseph in 1880. Whatever domestic bliss Leonora Barry enjoyed ended abruptly in 1881, when her husband and daughter both died of lung disease.

In Barry's words, "I was left without knowledge of business, without knowledge of work, without knowledge of what the world was, and with . . . fatherless children looking to me for bread."[17] To support herself and two sons under the age of seven, Barry took work as a seamstress, but it proved too strenuous for her eyes, and she quit for a machine hand's position in an Amsterdam hosiery mill.

Barry toiled long days for low wages, an experience that made her consider the labor question. In 1884, she joined the KOL's Victory Assembly and rose to the rank of local master workman the next year, heading an assembly of over nine hundred women. Before 1885 closed, she led Victory Assembly through a short, successful strike and became a key DA 65 leader. Her efforts caught Powderly's attention and in June 1886, he made her part of a team negotiating with retail magnate John Wannamaker.[18] As a DA 65 representative to the KOL's general assembly, Barry was one of only sixteen women among the 658 delegates. Powderly personally pushed her candidacy for the newly created position of general investigator for women's work.

Barry's official task as head of the Department of Women's Work was "to investigate the abuses to which [women are] subjected by unscrupulous employers [and] to agitate the principles which our Order teaches of equal pay for equal work and the abolition of child labor."[19] But her position's high-sounding rhetorical charges offered little insight into how to do her job. It was also different from original proposals developed by Barry, Mary Hanafin, Nellie Hardison, and Mary O'Reilly, which had included duties to "instruct and educate" women, to "organize female locals," to give lectures, and to speak out against "the remorseless grasp of tyranny . . . greed . . . the pangs of hunger . . . [and] the yawning chasm of immorality."[20]

Barry complained that her new job description was vague. At times, she was expected to conduct investigative work that was a gendered equivalent to the Bureau of Labor Statistics, but she was also a member of the executive board charged with formulating policy for the entire Order. She also served as an organizer, lecturer, political lobbyist, researcher, and as Powderly's personal spy. All the while Barry tried to convince male Knights that female members had different work, home, and assembly experiences from those of men.[21]

Male Knights would have done well to heed Barry's admonitions on the last score. By 1886, one of every seven Knights in Massachusetts—home to District 30, the KOL's largest district assembly—was a woman, and C. Fannie Allyn was quickly becoming nationally known. But here, as elsewhere, women were largely segregated vocationally. Female Knights could be found toiling as laundresses, cloak makers, collar makers, carpet weavers, knitters, boardinghouse keepers, and feather curlers, but they were seldom found in traditionally male-dominated jobs.[22]

Occupational segregation led Canadian Knight Katie McVicar to argue that male-centered organizing techniques did not work for women, especially appeals to the rituals men found so moving.[23] Women in St. Louis featured an assembly life with more singing than men's assemblies, and women everywhere were disproportionately involved in activities like running cooperatives, organizing craft fairs, participating in reading circles, holding fund-raisers, socializing at tea parties, and agitating for suffrage and child labor law reform.[24] Barry also assured Powderly that female Knights found assembly-room smoking and chewing tobacco repellent.[25] Susan Levine argues that many KOL women longed for all-female locals as they saw male-dominated assembly behavior as akin to saloon culture.[26]

If all of this justified the KOL's decision to establish a separate Department of Women's Work, it did little to disentangle working women's knotty dual burden of gender bias and class discrimination. One of Barry's first investigative tasks was to determine how much of women's oppression was due to sexism and how much resulted from capitalist oppression. It was a question she never fully resolved, though not from lack of effort.

Barry placed her children in boarding schools and, for the next four years, traipsed the countryside lecturing, organizing, and investigating. She gave at least five hundred KOL lectures and organized men as well as women into new and existing local assemblies. She also helped establish several cooperative shirt factories.[27] Given that she had little training or previous experience to guide her, Barry's correspondence exhibits equal parts insight and naiveté. An example of the latter is a section of her 1887 report to the general assembly in which she confesses it had not occurred to her that women speaking to her during factory inspections might be jeopardizing their jobs.[28]

Despite occasional blunders, Barry provided comprehensive statistics and firsthand reports of the actual conditions of American working women. In 1886 and 1887, Barry traveled through New England and the mid-Atlantic states. What she found shocked her to the core. In most locales, men's wages averaged $9 to $15 per week, while those of women were a mere $2.50 to $3. In Newark, New Jersey, one factory owner fined women ten cents each time they were caught eating, laughing, singing, or talking on the job. The same employer locked the factory gates precisely at 7 A.M., and a late-arriving employee had to wait until 7:30 to enter and forfeited two hours' pay. In Auburn, New York, she observed a sweatshop that forced women to buy their own machines on a fifty-cent per week installment plan. Most workers were dismissed shortly before they paid their balances, thereby freeing the employer to resell the machines to their replacements. Women also had to buy their own thread and were assessed fines for spoiled work. According to Barry, some workers were lucky to clear seventy-five cents a week for their labors. In Paterson, New Jersey, women linen thread workers operated machines that sprayed cool water on their bodies and onto the concrete floor upon which they stood barefooted. And all of these incidents, she claimed, paled in comparison to New York City's conditions, where sewing women endured "more injustice, trickery, and frauds of all kinds . . . than . . . any other class of wage-earners on the American continent."[29]

Barry spared little vitriol in denouncing the conditions she witnessed, or in chastising Knights who were slow to agree with her. She threatened to publish the names of recalcitrant employers "if I can find no other measure to reach their callused hearts," though such an action was far beyond her prescribed powers.[30] She blasted the "selfishness" of KOL men for failing to show zeal in effecting the KOL's goal of securing equal pay for equal work. Barry chided, "Thus far in the history of our Order that part of our platform has been but a mockery of the principles intended."[31]

All of this won her both praise and condemnation. Phily Sallon called Barry "the first woman that ever came among us that was able to explain the condition of the women worker." She spoke of the "great impression" Barry made in her visit, as did those in Washington, D.C., District Assembly 97 who heard her speak at a Fourth of July picnic.[32] But Barry also had an impatient side that led some to consider her difficult. In a *Journal of United Labor* article she expressed discomfort with women who "complained that they are working for nearly nothing" but would not give the KOL the "opportunity to do something for them."[33] She reiterated those charges at the 1887 assembly and claimed a "majority of [women] are entirely ignorant of the economic and industrial question."[34]

Barry suggested "more thorough educational measures" to correct these problems, but implementation of such measures was clouded by murky conceptions of women's proper place within the KOL. Barry was besieged by so many requests that she establish and lead an all-women's branch of the KOL that she was forced to repudiate such views publicly. In a *Journal* article, Barry defended mixed-skill/mixed-gender assemblies and insisted that women had to "organize as a part of the industrial hive, rather than because they are women."[35] This was an oddly inconsistent position from one who routinely defended female assembly life and lectured men that women had different lodge etiquette, social concerns, and political styles.

Barry's altered rhetoric was consonant with the mixed-assembly defenses of the Home Club conspirators from whom she may have felt pressure. It also signals Barry's descent into KOL intrigues, which diverted her from the issues regarding women in the KOL. By mid-1887, New York City was riven by plots and counterplots. Barry naively trusted Powderly as her champion and thus thrust herself into situations she ought to have avoided.

In July, she informed Powderly that the Home Club intended to concoct a bribery charge against him. Powderly replied, "I don't want to involve you in this matter, but will you find out from [George] Dunn[e] (and all of 49) everything?"[36] Such an assignment was fraught with peril. Not only was Dunne the master workman of Barry's own local, he was still a Home Club insider, though he later turned against it.

Barry did not realize the depth of Powderly's own double-dealing with the Home Club. Nor did Barry have the political acumen or powers of deception to hide her role for long, and she utterly failed to do so. Her fervent trade unionism made her suspect among New York City Lassalleans whose vigilance made them well aware of her inept spying efforts long before she perceived their suspicions. She also made an enemy of John Hayes, who became her personal nemesis. At the 1887 convention, Hayes toppled Charles Litchman and came away with the newly expanded post of general secretary-treasurer. This gave Hayes more power than even Powderly could command.

Barry had little idea of how thoroughly Home Club machinations dictated the KOL agenda, nor did she have an inkling of Hayes's might. As 1888 opened, she attempted to redefine her role in the Order and to use Powderly as a shield from Hayes. Neither gambit was successful. In her 1888 report to the assembly, Barry claimed to have visited nearly 100 different cities, distributed 1,900 leaflets, answered 97 telegrams, responded to 537 requests to organize women's assemblies, and delivered 100 lectures.[37] The last point was problematic, as her critics felt that public lecturing was both beyond her charge and a needless expense in an organization that funded official general lecturer positions.

Barry was unapologetic and insisted on addressing women's injustices publicly. She told *Journal of United Labor* readers, "as long as I am engaged in an endeavor to promote the welfare and comfort of my sister toilers . . . I will do all in my power to see that justice is done for her."[38] Hayes grew so annoyed with Barry's public posturing that he began to zealously scrutinize her department's expenses. In May, he denied her funds to purchase a typewriter. Powderly assuaged Barry's anger by disingenuously claiming that the executive board was too strapped for cash to honor her request. He also advised her to give up the podium and thus "deprive your enemies of the opportunity which they will have at the next G.A. to say that you took to the lecturer's platform instead of the field of investigation." He acknowledged that there were factions that wished to abolish the women's department and cautioned, "Unless the Board will pay for lecturers as freely as the Board paid for strikes in the days of '86 we can not send out" many lecturers.[39]

Barry utterly ignored Powderly's advice. In September, Frances Willard requested that Powderly send Barry to a Women's Christian Temperance Union rally, as an earlier Barry speech "roused the convention more than any other person."[40] Barry arrived at the KOL general assembly in a feisty mood. To those who demanded she confine her activities to "investigative work," she replied,

I did not feel justified in spending the time and money of my constituents playing the spy or detective, as since we have set the ball of exposing the wrongs and injustices done workingwomen, rolling others have entered the field in this line. . . . Neither did I feel justified in going among industries and gathering from employers such information as they would give, knowing that such knowledge could be gleaned from the reports of our Labor Bureaus and State Factory Inspectors.

My understanding of the duties implied in my office was that I was to do everything in my power . . . that would have a tendency to educate and elevate the workingwomen of America and ameliorate their condition. Therefore, when I spoke to a public audience of American citizens, exposing existing evils and showing how, through the demands of Knighthood, they could be remedied, I felt I was fulfilling the duties of my office. When I found a body of workingmen who were so blind to what justice demanded of them on behalf of women . . . I felt I was performing a sacred duty toward women by trying to enlighten those men. . . . When I found an opportunity of laying before other organizations of women the cause of less fortunate sisters and mold a favorable sentiment, I felt I was doing that which is an actual necessity.[41]

Barry's report took the wind out of the sails of critics by reciting a litany of towns and factories she visited, giving information on assemblies to which she traveled, and naming the locales in which she organized local assemblies. She even provided detailed statistics on working women that belied her own claim that she could rely on others to supply such figures. She advised, for example, that Albany, New York, shirtmakers were paid forty cents per dozen shirts, but had to buy their own thread. Likewise she

Leonora Barry. Courtesy of the Catholic
University of America Archives.

gave painstaking accounts of abuses by pants manufacturers in Cincinnati
and of the horrors of child labor in Chicago and Philadelphia. Barry also
complained that Canadian wages were superior to those in the United
States, regaled delegates with the successes of cooperative factories she
visited (or organized), and accounted for every penny of the $2,561.88
spent by her department since its inception. As Barry neared the end of her
report, she added a note ringing with pride and veiled defiance. She said:

> It has been intimated that the Woman's [*sic*] Department was started on
> sentiment. Well, if so, it has turned out to be one of the most thoroughly
> practical departments in the Order. Without egoism I can safely say it has
> done as much effective work in cheering, encouraging, educating and in-
> structing the women of this Order in the short year of its existence as was
> done by the organization in the whole time of women's connection with it
> previous to its establishment. Ten thousand organized women today look to
> the Woman's Department for counsel, advice and assistance. It is their hope,
> their guiding star; and the free and full outpouring of sorrow stricken and
> heavy-laden hearts . . . that comes to the Woman's Department for consola-
> tion and comfort cannot be recorded here because that would be a breach of
> sacred confidence.[42]

Questions linger, however. Why did Barry discount Powderly's advice? Why did she risk Hayes's ire? The answer lies partly in Barry's faulty assumption that Powderly would support her decisions out of respect for her talents and in gratitude for special services rendered. Despite her October protest that she felt no calling to "play the spy," Barry once again sleuthed for Powderly. In the ongoing campaign to discredit William Bailey, Powderly caught whiff of a sexual scandal. Barry provided information that the married Bailey contemplated elopement with a much younger woman from Amsterdam, New York. Powderly encouraged Barry to have the woman involved compose a "written statement of the transaction." What came of this is unknown, as Powderly instructed Barry to keep the matter confidential and to burn or return all correspondence relating to it. But it is known that Barry went as far as Ohio to visit Bailey's parish priest.[43]

Barry perhaps overestimated Powderly's patronage because he had earlier defended her so arduously from the attacks of Father Peter McEnroe. Barry incurred the rabidly anti-union Catholic prelate's ire during a visit to the mining hamlet of Mahoney City, Pennsylvania. McEnroe was especially incensed that the Knights would send a woman into the field and allow her to give public addresses. He slandered Barry as a "Lady Tramp" and charged that her labor activities masked "immoral purposes," implying prostitution. Barry was outraged. Powderly first suggested that she get a character reference from her own parish priest and confront McEnroe "in a courteous yet firm" manner. When this failed to move the intransigent McEnroe, Powderly remembered his own youthful run-ins with antilabor priests and rushed to Barry's defense. Powderly asked Archbishop Patrick John Ryan to silence McEnroe and encouraged Barry to denounce McEnroe publicly. Barry's forceful speech was widely reported and applauded by Pennsylvania newspapers.[44]

Barry's confidence was shattered at the 1888 assembly. Weeks earlier Powderly informed her of impending motions to eliminate the women's department but promised that he would personally support a motion to expand her department to include lecturing.[45] At the convention, however, Powderly sided with the majority that stripped the women's department of its independence and transferred it to the secretary-treasurer's administrative care. This meant that Barry's immediate supervisor was now her arch rival, John Hayes.

Hayes immediately demanded that Barry keep a complete record of all her expenses and steadily complained about her in correspondence with Powderly. It is difficult to tell whether Hayes's comments took their toll or Powderly merely decided defending Barry was too risky, but by the end of 1888, Powderly had abandoned her. In a letter to trusted confidant Tom

O'Reilly, Powderly accused Barry of leaking news of impending changes
to the *Adelphon Kruptos*. He groused:

> Mrs. B. is entirely too loose to place any confidence in. She should have not
> lisped a word about the change in the secret work; all the enemies in the
> world will be on the lookout for the changes from now until they give them
> to the world. I shall write to her next week in a way that will not be mistaken.
> To write her is dangerous unless one writes a full and complete sermon, for
> she would twist your letter to suit herself.[46]

Several weeks latter, Powderly composed a "full and complete sermon" to Barry, a condescending five-page letter masquerading as advice.
Among other things, he charged there were only five thousand women in
the KOL, not the ten thousand to fifteen thousand she claimed, and he
challenged her to increase the count fivefold before the next general assembly. He also chastised her for gossiping instead of working at the general
office, for not disciplining her staff, of having a negative attitude, and of
squabbling with Hayes.[47] Powderly sent a copy of the letter to Hayes with
the attached suggestion that he try to win Barry's "confidence as much as
you can and do not . . . allow her to go away with the impression that you
are angry with her." He also cautioned Hayes to monitor Barry's actions
carefully.[48]

Barry tried to make the best of her situation and wrote a rosy New
Year's letter to the *Journal of United Labor*.[49] Nonetheless, 1889 proved to
be one of the most trying years of Barry's life. In an effort to keep Barry
away from the KOL's Philadelphia headquarters, Powderly and Hayes sent
her on an investigative tour of the South. Her years in the labor movement
and experiences with northern factory abuses did not prepare her for the
horrors she witnessed there. Her letters to the *Journal* are bleak and pessi-
mistic. They speak of children being worked to death, of debilitating dis-
eases, of intense racial hatred, of paternalistic textile towns that held workers in thralldom, and of the crudest and rawest poverty imaginable.[50] Barry
remained in the South from February 6 through April 26, 1889. By then,
she was exhausted physically, depressed, and plagued by professional
doubt. To compound her miseries, in June, she was felled by malaria.

Frustrations continued to mount. Later in June, a dispute with Tom
Barry turned heated and violent. Leonora Barry grabbed a tin water bucket
and crashed it on Tom Barry's skull with such force that he needed hospital
care to patch his bloodied scalp. Although reports that Tom Barry "almost
died" are greatly exaggerated, it was clear that his namesake (no relation)
was in a black state of mind.[51]

In her darkest moments, Barry agreed that the women's department was a failure that ought to be abolished. She foolishly shared those thoughts with Hayes, who feigned sympathy and fiendishly advised her not to reveal these thoughts to the fall assembly. Privately, he wrote to Powderly to advance a devious course of action:

> After I have thought the matter over, I think it would be much better if she would recommend its [the women's department's] abolishment, and let her continue in the field as a Lecturer. . . . By that means we can get rid of the department first and the woman afterwards. She does good work as a Lecturer, but we do not have sufficient control over her. . . . If you write to her (and I think you should), and want to give her this Idea, don't mention receiving any word from me. . . . It would be a good plan to tell her that she has got the right Idea.

Hayes made light of Barry's emotional state. He told Powderly that he had suffered through her "tale of woe during [which] . . . a big tear of woe was dropped on the table." He warned Powderly to prepare himself "to see her *cry*" when he next met her.[52]

Powderly played his part well. The next day he wrote Barry a tender letter absolving her of any blame for the collapse of the women's department. He told her that she had done as much as anyone could do to "infuse, and enthuse, life into the women of the land" and said, "I feel proud of you anyway." He advised her to take no action on a proposal to abolish her department until they spoke, although his tone made it clear he would recommend said course.[53]

In the meantime, Hayes's position hardened. On the eve of the assembly he bluntly advised Powderly, "If there is an opportunity for the abolishment of her department . . . do it and let her go into the lecturer's field. That will only give the Order one more year of *her*!!"[54]

At the 1889 assembly, Leonora Barry played the part Hayes and Powderly had scripted, and added a scene they had not anticipated, but which no doubt delighted Hayes. She told the delegates,

> When I took the position as . . . head [of the women's department] I fondly hoped to weld together in an organization such a number of women as would be a power for good in the present, and a monument to their honor in the relief it would establish for women in the future. I was too sanguine, and I am forced to acknowledge that to fulfill my best hopes is a matter of impossibility; and I believe now we should, instead of supporting a Woman's Department, put more women in the field as Lecturers to tell women why they should organize as part of an industrial hive, rather than because they are women. There can be no separation or distinction of wage-earners on account of sex, and separate departments for their interests is a direct contradiction of

this. . . . Therefore, I recommend the abolition of the Woman's Department, believing, as I do now, that women should be Knights of Labor without distinction, and should have all the benefits that can be given to men—no more, no less—thereby making it incumbent upon all to work more earnestly for the general good, rather for sex, assembly, or trade.[55]

These remarks came near the end of Barry's report to the assembly and they shocked and confused many. A massive contradiction lay in her spirited rejections of gender essentialism and separate women's assembly culture, and the remarks that preceded them. Earlier in the speech, she spoke of a woman's "natural pride and timidity, coupled with the restrictions of social customs [that] deter her from making that struggle that can be made by men." Later, she decried the "foolish pride, prudish modesty, and religious scruples" that prevented women from joining the KOL. And although she defended the right of women "to become proficient in whatever vocation they choose or find themselves," she prefaced that remark by saying, "If it were possible, I wish it were not necessary for women to learn any trade but that of domestic duties, as I believe it was intended that man should be the bread-winner."[56]

The bulk of Barry's report addressed the special challenges facing women. Her litany of abuses she had witnessed in the South suggested that women were treated more harshly than men, and that tactics necessary to organize them were different from those used to bring men into the fold of organized labor. Southern men, in particular, she found "earnest and enthusiastic" concerning unionism, a contrast to the reluctance and reticence of Southern women.[57]

Given Barry's contradictory report, it is hardly surprising that the assembly rendered equally ambiguous decisions. It accepted Barry's resignation as head of the women's department but did not abolish it. Mary O'Reilly was appointed as the new head of the department and Barry was commissioned as a general lecturer on behalf of the Order. Hayes no doubt relished the fact that Barry proposed herself for a lecturer's post as it removed his stain from the sordid plot that ensued.

With Barry off the executive board, Hayes intensified his personal campaign against her. In late November, Hayes charged that a precipitous drop in revenues required a cutback in lecturer salaries. It was left to Powderly to inform Barry that she might not be able to lecture; he encouraged her to rebuild locals in the Philadelphia area until matters were resolved. On February 26, 1890, Hayes pleaded with Powderly not to send Barry on the road. "If you start her in again it will be impossible to stop her," he wrote.[58]

Barry made matters easy for both of them when she abruptly resigned her lecturer's post in April, stating that a woman's proper place was in the home. Those sentiments were sparked by her quiet marriage to Obadiah Read Lake, a printer and editor with the *St. Louis Globe-Democrat* and a respected leader among Missouri Knights. Powderly dutifully sent a congratulatory letter to Lake that read, in part, "I don't know whether to congratulate you or to abuse you, for you have taken one of the best women in the Order from among the staff of general officers and that place will never be filled by another as she filled it."[59]

With her remarriage, Leonora Barry-Lake ceased her active involvement with the KOL. But did she believe her remarks concerning women's spheres or were they loyally disguised comments designed to mask internal turmoil within KOL leadership ranks? A letter sent to the 1890 general assembly suggests the latter interpretation. It opens, "As a child longs for its mother, as the wanderer longs for his home, so do I long to be with you on this occasion." But she also defended the women's department in terms far more vigorous than those she delivered a year earlier.

> [The women's department's] value cannot be determined by the number of women in our Order, so much as by the sentiment its establishment aroused in the minds of the public in favor of ameliorating working women and securing for them justice and equity. Four years ago at Richmond we were the pioneers in advocating working women's rights and exposing their wrongs and defending them from injustice. To-day that advocacy is universal. . . . There are many bright, earnest, thoughtful women who would fill the positions created at Richmond with honor to themselves and benefit to those for whom they labored.[60]

Barry-Lake's words are hardly those of one who believed women ought to be confined to the domestic sphere. Nor did her subsequent actions give that impression. Before her letter reached the general assembly, Barry-Lake had once again mounted the lecturer's podium, this time on behalf of temperance. Until her death from mouth cancer in 1930, she toiled on behalf of the Women's Christian Temperance Union and the Catholic Total Abstinence Society. She also worked on Colorado's 1893 suffrage campaign, lectured on the Chatauqua circuit, and participated in numerous charity organizations. She was dubbed the "mother of the Pennsylvania state factory law" for her work on behalf of factory workers there, and was active in several sororal organizations.[61]

It is abundantly clear that Leonora Barry was forced out of the Knights of Labor. Although she loyally withheld the truth, she was the victim of union sexism and organizational decay.

As George Bennie's remarks and Uriah Stephens's sentiments recall, many male Knights were uncomfortable with the thought of women in the Order. Even in Massachusetts, where women made up almost 15 percent of the membership, leaders like Albert Carlton periodically expressed reservations about "unstable" women leaders. The same was true in New York City, the fortress of universalistic, mixed-assembly sentiment.[62] Powderly once even had to chide Charles Litchman, a man who knew KOL procedure as well as anyone in the Order, that no special dispensation was necessary to admit women into assemblies that previously had none.[63]

In Barry-Lake's case, a chauvinist culprit stands out: John W. Hayes. His relentless campaign to purge Barry, when coupled with other actions on his part, suggests arrogance bordering on misogyny. His telling complaint that the KOL did not have sufficient "control" over Barry demonstrates his reluctance to delegate power, a tendency that was magnified when women were involved. Barry's successor, Mary O'Reilly, lasted but a single term under Hayes's supervision, and Alzina Stevens wisely rejected the woman's department post when it was proffered.

Women around Hayes at KOL headquarters tended to leave their jobs abruptly, not always of their own accord. One staff secretary, Maggie Eiler, complained of sexual harassment and verbal abuse from Hayes. As we will see in the next chapter, Eiler had knowledge of Hayes's shady use of KOL funds. He, in turn, flattered, harassed, and threatened Eiler until potentially incriminating documents disappeared, then he fired her.[64]

Attempting to charm Barry and Eiler was consistent with the reputation Hayes's enemies attributed to him. Though married, Hayes was reputed to be a womanizer, though he clearly had no love for strong women. One by one, Hayes eliminated women of Leonora Barry's ilk from the KOL's power structure. After Mary O'Reilly resigned from the women's department, Hayes dismissed her. He even sacked Mary Stephens, daughter of the KOL's founder, on the grounds that a declining treasury necessitated her dismissal. Hayes's financial arguments pale when one considers he periodically hired new help, including his brother. Perhaps most egregious was his hire of Annie Traphagen, who was reputed to be his mistress.[65]

Hayes also eliminated male challengers to his authority including, ultimately, Powderly. But his treatment of women was so consistently abusive that one suspects he did not care for them beyond their ability to assuage his ego or satisfy his sexual appetite. At the very least, one must conclude that he had little understanding of or respect for women's organizing methods or assembly culture. Hayes was a Gilded Age essentialist of the most pernicious kind.

But Hayes's arguments about the KOL's decaying fortunes were true enough. If Hayes was dipping into the KOL till for dubious purposes, he had far less money with which to speculate. By 1890, the year Leonora

Barry-Lake stepped back from an active KOL role, the Order was in disarray. Loss of the New York Central strike later that year propelled the KOL from decline to crisis.

Hayes was a creation of the Home Club; he was also its last survivor. He was not an ideologue or a deep thinker but an artful bureaucrat who shrewdly assessed which way political winds blew and arranged his alliances accordingly. Once he helped engineer the downfall of Charles Litchman and the amalgamation of the secretary and treasurer offices, it was easier for him to manipulate power. By 1888, Powderly's authority was greatly reduced due to his involvement with the Home Club, his unpopular refusal to support clemency for the eight men arrested in conjunction with the 1886 Haymarket Square bombing, his outspoken denunciation of radicalism, and his abrasive personality. Hayes controlled both the Order's finances and its correspondence. By 1889, Powderly was merely the titular head of a united Knights of Labor. In truth, he was little more than head of one of the Order's most powerful factions. He was certainly in no position to advance already controversial plans to organize women.

How did Hayes get away with his purges? The answer is disarmingly simple: the KOL was faction ridden and Hayes commanded the bureaucratic machinery that facilitated removal of troublesome members. Moreover, he knew that few Gilded Age Knights were willing to tackle a figure as powerful as himself over an issue as seemingly trivial as Leonora Barry's right to define her own duties. Given the pervasiveness of gender essentialism within the KOL, where could Barry, Mary O'Reilly, or Maggie Eiler expect to find allies?

It is striking that even as Jim Crow systems emerged, the KOL was far more successful in organizing African-American men than women of any race or ethnicity. There was no equivalent department to investigate the conditions of black labor or to organize African-American laborers, yet their numbers within the KOL exceeded those of female Knights by one-third.

Female leaders certainly could not assume that women themselves would rush to their defense. Barry's letters and reports are chock-full of complaints that women did not see the need to organize on the shop floor, let alone tackle society-wide bias. Barry herself was prone to inconsistencies, but we must remember that within Gilded Age society she was in the progressive vanguard on questions of gender equality and women's spheres.

The women's movements of the Gilded Age had as much trouble reconciling their various factions as the KOL did. Advocates of feminist/full-equality positions were a small minority even among women. The Knights likely had a disproportionate number of feminists (like Charlotte

Smith) who, as time went on, grew increasingly critical of the KOL and challenged male dominance of the Order's affairs. One who did so was Baltimore's Maggie Weir. She dissolved her assembly when she saw "no benefit in belonging to the order" and could "get no recognition from other women's societies as long as we belonged to the Knights of Labor."[66]

But more typical were women like Linda Slaughter of North Dakota, who cheerfully took direction from General Secretary Hayes. Slaughter organized assemblies without regard to gender, as part of the great "industrial hive" of which Barry spoke in 1889.[67] A sizable group of KOL women accepted this logic without question. Perhaps the most prominent example of this was Mary "Mother" Jones, who joined the KOL in the 1880s. Jones was an outspoken critic of feminist movements and insisted that class, not gender, was the touchstone around which one should organize. At times, she even denounced feminist concepts as frivolous ventures that diverted energies from more important tasks.[68]

The differing perspectives of women like Maggie Weir and Mary Jones remind us that the KOL's efforts on behalf of women require a nuanced assessment. One should neither romanticize nor damn those efforts. The KOL did more to organize women, consider their agendas, and attempt to accommodate a female-centered assembly life than any other male-dominated labor organization of its time. The more than fifty thousand women the KOL brought into its fold swamped the achievements of its predecessors and not even women's labor organizations could boast of the cross-class, cross-skill diversity of its female rank and file. The true tragedy of the Barry case lies in what became of women laborers after she became a temperance lecturer and the KOL languished toward an obscure death, as it would be many decades before other labor organizations did as well as the KOL in organizing women.

Gender has long been a blind spot for labor organizations. Historian Ruth Milkman, though acknowledging that unionized women have historically fared better than their unorganized sisters, nonetheless admits, "There is abundant evidence of women workers' ill-treatment on the part of organized labor. Many unions have a history of excluding women from membership altogether; virtually all have tended to exclude them from positions of power. And unions have often acted to reinforce rather than challenge sexual inequality in the labor market."[69]

Alice Kessler-Harris notes that it was not until 1956 that the AFL-CIO accepted the idea of equal pay for equal work, a concept embraced by the KOL in 1878. In similar fashion, the Department of Labor's Women's Bureau did not offer support for the Equal Rights Amendment until 1970, nearly a century after the KOL endorsed such a measure.[70]

It would be impertinent to suggest a cause-and-effect relationship between the KOL's decline and the subsequent difficulties women experienced with organized labor. But the KOL's fate is suggestive of what was lost when the Order declined. Leonora Barry, for all her faults, contradictions, misplaced optimism, and naiveté, was a pioneering leader who briefly held power in a major labor bureaucracy. The potential for greater gain declined when she was forced out and when the KOL faltered.

Today, Leonora Barry is little remembered. Had she been more successful in educating male and female workers alike, she might have helped the KOL resolve its contradictory views on working women. This would have made the road easier for equality advocates who followed. But Barry was a victim of sexism, a pernicious set of ideals that continues to plague social movements. Marge Piercy complained of it in 1969; five years later the Coalition of Labor Union Women (CLUW) was founded to combat sexism within society and within the union movement. The CLUW's mission statement includes the goal of making "unions more responsive to the needs of all women." It goes on to say, "Full equality of opportunities and rights in the labor force requires the full attention of the labor movement."[71] No one would deny the wonderful accomplishments of the CLUW, but its continued existence a quarter-century later is testament to work left undone. Sexism persists within unions and other social movements. It is a problem that Leonora Barry would have understood all too well.

CHAPTER 7

"We Have to Get Rid of You": The Fall of Terence V. Powderly

This work opened by arguing against a one-to-one identification between the Knights of Labor and Terence Victor Powderly. As my final task, I tell the story of how Powderly himself was booted from the Knights.

It is easy to understand how Powderly and the KOL became so entwined. Powderly was a media sensation, and bourgeois newspapers routinely sang his praises or damned him to political perdition. He could command an audience with tycoons, elected officials, and clergymen. Admiring Knights named sons and local assemblies after him; in Alabama, an entire town was dubbed "Powderly."

But there were also Knights for whom the name Powderly was anathema. As the KOL's public spokesperson, he found himself at the center of nearly every controversy that gripped the Order. There were few neutral assessments of Powderly; to most Knights he was either saint or sinner. In his study of recent worker opposition movements, sociologist Samuel R. Friedman notes that internal factions often attack union bureaucrats with the same ferocity they direct toward employers.[1] As we have seen, this is true also of the KOL. It was assuredly so in Powderly's case.

The Order rose to prominence and declined into irrelevance under Powderly. He took up the grand/general master workman's gavel in 1879 and held it through 1893. In between, threats of resignation were a near-yearly threat. More often than not, Powderly used these to build eleventh-hour general assembly coalitions to counter his enemies and "convince" him to remain in office. In November 1893, his luck ran out. As a face-saving gesture, the Assembly reappointed Powderly as master workman and immediately allowed him to resign. Had he not chosen this course, the coalition of western agrarian radicals and eastern socialists who masterminded his resignation would have voted him out. One year later, Powderly was expelled from the organization he had headed for fourteen years. He was reinstated in 1900, but the only thing Powderly salvaged was a piece of his dignity.

Historian Craig Phelan notes, "Terence Powderly is the most vilified labor leader America ever produced."[2] Phelan is critical of historians who have been quick to side with Powderly's detractors, but he is in the scholarly minority. In 1929, Norman Ware lampooned Powderly with a burst of purple prose:

> He was a windbag whose place was on the street corner rousing the rabble to fever pitch and providing emotional compensation for dull lives. They [the KOL] should have thrown him out, but they did not. Instead, with the stupid loyalty of a dog for an abusive master they clung to him as a savior. He offered, even pleaded, to resign over and over, but they refused to listen. For fourteen years they kept him at the head of their organization in spite of obvious disqualifications for the job.[3]

Ware even blamed much of the KOL's demise on Powderly's inept leadership.

Ware's judgment ought to be tempered by the fact that his major source was Powderly's sworn enemy, John W. Hayes. But this has not prevented subsequent historians from accepting Ware's comments at face value. Philip Foner labeled Powderly part of a "rule or ruin" faction that "became corrupt . . . lost contact with the fundamental problems of the workers . . . [and] was more concerned with winning respectability and of earning applause from the employers and their allies than in gaining basic improvements for the workers."[4] Gerald Grob viewed Powderly's opposition to strikes as a cause of the KOL's decline and noted that he paled in comparison to Samuel Gompers, who exceeded him "in both resourcefulness and determination."[5]

Gregory Kealey and Bryan Palmer accuse Powderly of being more interested in moneymaking schemes than in the health of the Order.[6] Bruce Laurie argues that Powderly grew increasingly provincial, unyielding, and arrogant. To compound matters, he was indecisive, bungled important decisions, and was generally guilty of "ineptitude and dictatorial rule."[7] Kim Voss writes that Powderly "was a vacillating, often ineffective leader, who was more timid and less militant than many of his members."[8]

I would not presume to debate character assessments of Powderly. He was prudish, moralizing, scheming, double-dealing, manipulative, and disloyal even to his friends. His ouster could easily be seen as just desserts for plotting the coups of far better leaders than himself. To conflate personality with the health of the Order, however, is more problematic. As Richard Oestreicher notes,

> Explanations based both on personality and ideology must be tempered by the reality of the difficulties that anyone would have faced who tried to alter

the basic character of a society that was becoming the pacesetter and bulwark of twentieth-century capitalism. Quite simply, no one else did much better than Powderly of the Knights of Labor over the next forty years.[9]

Oestreicher and Phelan are among the few historians willing to reassess Powderly's leadership abilities. Phelan insists that Powderly's inability to "bind . . . the disparate forces under his command" was not due to "poor leadership," but to "the virtual impossibility of harmonizing . . . a working class fractured along the lines of skill, gender, race, ethnicity, and geographical parochialism."[10]

Oestreicher's comment that labor's post-Powderly future was hardly a rosy one returns us to the KOL as a social movement rather than a one-man show. Ware's views notwithstanding, the men who ousted Powderly were radicals and self-servers, not bureaucrats, pragmatists, or tacticians. Sociologist Roberta Ash notes that radical social movements fare poorly in the United States: "[T]he greater [their] threat to class structure, the less likely [they] will be to succeed."[11] William Gamson argues that only those leaders and organizations who respect and leave intact the American pluralist tradition prosper.[12]

Powderly's ouster from the general master workman's chair follows a now familiar scenario: personal vendetta disguised as policy dispute. Someone had to be blamed for the KOL's precipitous decline and Powderly was the scapegoat, though his removal actually came in a year in which the Order may have registered a modest membership gain.[13]

According to Oestreicher, Powderly's demise began at the 1887 assembly where Marxist Knights rallied nearly one-third of the delegates to oppose his policies. At issue were Powderly's condemnation of the Haymarket clemency campaign, his handling of the Chicago stockyards strike, his alliance with the Home Club, organizational finances, and assorted other policies.[14] In addition, Marxists harbored deep grudges against Powderly that dated back to the 1882 Duryea Starch boycott and the subsequent expulsion of Theodore Cuno.

Marginalized Marxists anticipated the error of future historians and assumed that the KOL was a "Powderly machine." In truth, Powderly's power derived largely from commanding sizable subgroups within a faction-riddled organization. Powderly's unstable and shifting coalitions—including several with the Home Club—left him with far less power than is usually assumed and allowed power to accrue to General Secretary-Treasurer John Hayes. Powderly was merely vain, manipulative, and unpleasant; Hayes was a thief, a blackmailer, an extortionist, an embezzler, a womanizer, and an egomaniac. In the clash between the unlikable and the amoral, the latter won.

Terence Powderly. Courtesy of the
Catholic University of America Archives.

Powderly was destined for the same fate as Charles Litchman: both
were purged as much for personality as performance. As the KOL declined,
Powderly's rank of supporters thinned. In such a climate, each pronounce-
ment or decision was a potential public relations nightmare. For example,
Powderly refused to endorse clemency for the Haymarket men on the
grounds that they were anarchists. In his universal condemnation of anarchism, Powderly failed to distinguish between ideology and simple justice,
making him appear mean-spirited and petty in the process.

If Powderly had no stomach for anarchism, he had little for third-
party politics either. When clamor rose to ally the Knights with burgeoning
labor parties during the Great Upheaval, Powderly used his position as a
bully pulpit to advance the KOL's nonpartisan stance. Nor would he consider nascent Populist movements. He admonished Ralph Beaumont, the
KOL's legislative lobbyist and People's Party enthusiast, that it was not
Beaumont's task to make the KOL into a political party, and he complained
to Hayes that Beaumont was trying to "wreck" the KOL.[15] Powderly's
public nonpartisanship put him on a collision course with new Knights like
DA 49's Daniel DeLeon, who hoped to merge the KOL and the Socialist
Labor Party. It was also blatantly inconsistent with Powderly's own flirta-
tion with the Republican Party.

Even more damaging was Powderly's association with the purge of popular Knights like Tom Barry and Joe Buchanan. By mid-1886, when the Order was at its pinnacle, many believed (correctly) that Powderly was the tool of the Home Club; subsequent expulsions of Home Club critics only solidified those suspicions. Soon, the blame for every squabble and policy debate within the KOL was laid at the Home Club's door and Powderly was tainted with guilt by association. Powderly was also associated with strike losses, fractious suspensions, jurisdiction battles with trade unions, political setbacks, and the hanging of four of the Haymarket martyrs.

To compound his image problems, as the Home Club withered Powderly foolishly stole a page from its book and tried to command his own secret ring. From supposedly loyal supporters Powderly fashioned a clique called "The Governor." Its nineteen known members included Beaumont, Hugh Cavanaugh, John Devlin, E. J. Lee, Joseph R. Mansion, John O'Keefe, Morris Wheat, A. W. Wright, and Hayes. Years later Powderly claimed his intention was "to protect the Order from its enemies," but he did not specify from whom or how The Governor intended to shelter the KOL.[16]

Years of double-dealing apparently left Powderly blind to the fragility of The Governor. Hayes and Wright loathed each other, with Wright echoing Litchman's earlier complaints that Hayes undermined his authority as editor of the *Journal of the Knights of Labor.* O'Keefe also despised Hayes and wished to wrest the secretary-treasurer's post from him. Wheat was so discredited from his leadership of the second Gould strike that he was an associative detriment, and Lee suffered the same fate after the 1890 New York Central strike.

Others, like Beaumont and Mansion, easily joined the opposition when Powderly's popularity flagged. By 1890, his reputation was so tarnished that George Detwiler, the editor of Chicago's *Knights of Labor,* quit the Order and changed his paper's name to the *Rights of Labor.* Detwiler told reporters that he "declined to regard the G.M.W. as an autocrat . . . and met the fate usual to such temerity."[17]

An 1891 incident brought Powderly still more headaches. After years of sandbagging the political associations of other Knights, Powderly himself created a controversy through his association with the Republican Party. Pressed by a rising People's Party surge, nervous Republicans and Democrats took up long-ignored but much-needed adjustments to the political system. In Pennsylvania, reform measures like adoption of a secret ballot required changes to the commonwealth's constitution.

A constitutional convention was convened with Powderly serving as an at-large delegate. The man who nominated Powderly to serve was Pennsylvania's junior senator, Matthew Quay, who was no friend to organized labor. Rumors flew that Powderly was a patronage-seeking Republican stooge, à la Charles Litchman.[18] Powderly vigorously defended himself in a *Journal of the Knights of Labor* editorial, but many doubted him. His protests rang doubly disingenuous when he served as a delegate to that fall's Republican state convention.[19]

Both Powderly and the Order were in free fall by 1891. The loss of the New York Central strike gutted the KOL in the industrial East and Midwest, historic strongholds.[20] As the KOL hemorrhaged members, it was left with a bloated bureaucracy and a hefty mortgage on its Philadelphia headquarters purchased during halcyon days. To meet bills, Powderly prevailed upon James Campbell, the head of cash-rich Local 300 (glassblowers) for loans. By 1891, it was clear that these were not likely to be repaid and that the glassblowers were out "many thousands of dollars." Hayes simply blamed the financial mess on his predecessors in office, Turner and Litchman.[21] Under the guise of achieving solvency, Hayes took what amounted to personal control over the Order's finances.

By 1892, Powderly was fed up. In February, he drafted a resignation letter and urged the general executive board to accept it. In it he complained of Hayes's speculative ventures with KOL money and stated that he and the secretary-treasurer "cannot much longer remain friends."[22] Board members John Devlin, Tom O'Reilly, and A. W. Wright urged Powderly to stay on. He did so, though events of the next two years rendered his decision unwise.

Powderly first tried to refocus his energies. Shortly after the board refused his resignation, Powderly immersed himself in a battle against the Reading Combine in his home state of Pennsylvania. The Combine was an illegal pool among the Philadelphia & Reading Railroad, the Lehigh Valley Railroad, and the Central Railroad of New Jersey, freight carriers seeking to apportion lucrative tonnage from the anthracite mines. Particulars of the cartel leaked and Powderly sharpened his pen against it, charging it with dismissing known Knights of Labor. His barbs remained tart and sharp, as seen in a curt missive to Pennsylvania governor Robert Pattison, and another refusing the commonwealth attorney general's summons to give sworn testimony. The Combine was officially dissolved after other corporations complained and the governor of New Jersey ordered an injunction against it. Although Powderly's role was mostly rhetorical, he nonetheless declared personal victory.[23] In reality, the Combine was still very powerful. As one investor put it, "The injunction will have no more effect than if it had been directed against the Sioux Indians."[24]

Powderly could offer little more than moral support for 1892's biggest conflagration: the Homestead Steel strike. He met with William

Weighe, president of the Amalgamated Association of Iron and Steel Workers, and issued warnings for Knights to stay away from the region, but his
major contribution to Homestead was a series of editorials denouncing the
strike-breaking activities of the Pinkerton Detective Agency. Such a response was routine by 1892, and Powderly added little that had not been
said during the 1890 New York Central strike.[25]

Even that modest effort must have seemed enormous when compared
to Powderly's bruising personal battles with Hayes. Several of these centered on KOL finances. The historical record makes it clear that Hayes
attempted to amass a personal fortune by using KOL funds as his own. He
justified each investment scheme as an attempt to replenish the KOL's
sagging coffers.

Powderly himself fell prey to several of Hayes's convoluted plans.
One scheme involved buying land to be subdivided into building lots to the
mutual financial benefit of investors. Powderly sank over two thousand
dollars in this scheme, an amount requested by Hayes in July 1892 as a
second installment.[26] Powderly demurred as he had no more money. By
mid-1892, the Order was hard-pressed to pay Powderly's salary and he
often missed paychecks. He instructed Hayes to sell his shares for what he
paid for them and to let him know when he would be able to draw his
salary.[27]

Hayes also sought Powderly's blessing to invest KOL monies in the
Tintic Smelting Company, a silver mine and smelting operation near Eu-
reka, Utah, which Hayes believed was a bonanza. Powderly refused to invest personally, denied the use of KOL funds, and forbade the use of his
name in association with the project.[28]

Hayes was not deterred. He lobbied hard for the investment, even
though Powderly proclaimed the entire matter a company stock fraud designed to raise working capital.[29] He tried to convince Powderly the scheme
was sound and hoped to raise funds by selling the KOL's Philadelphia
general headquarters. Powderly blocked the sale on the grounds that it
required forty days' advance notice to the entire Order. He also produced
an insider letter substantiating his suspicions about the Tintic venture and
told Hayes in unambiguous language, "I have done with the Tintic and all
other schemes to make money. They don't pan out and cannot unless with
the aid of influential men and capital, particularly capital and that is what
we lack just now."[30]

Letters from John Devlin and Tom O'Reilly reveal that Hayes ignored advice and disobeyed orders. Devlin wrote, "John proposes to run
the Order to suit himself." He suggested that if Hayes "will not listen to
reason and be governed by your advice and the advice of those who are
responsible for the manner in which the affairs of the Order are conducted

John W. Hayes. Courtesy of the Library of
Congress.

then it would be better he retire."[31] In subsequent correspondence, Devlin
accused Hayes of "cooking" KOL account books to hide his illegal investments. He also noted a new Hayes scheme involving a gas company.[32]

But Powderly no longer had the power to deter men as powerful as
Hayes. John O'Keefe discovered Hayes's might firsthand. When O'Keefe
challenged him to account for several doubtful expenditures, Hayes dismissed O'Keefe from his office post in the name of economizing. Tom
O'Reilly charged that O'Keefe was sacrificed because he was too close to
uncomfortable truths and hinted darkly that Hayes had "ruined" one of the
women in the office, probably Maggie Eiler.[33]

As had been done with Litchman, Powderly sought to build a coalition to isolate and vilify Hayes. To that end, he relied heavily on O'Reilly,
Devlin, and A. W. Wright, the editor of the *Journal of the Knights of Labor.*
Powderly also tried to limit Hayes's interference with the *Journal* and use
it to his advantage. When that proved difficult, he leaked a report to the
mainstream press that Hayes might have to resign as his New Brunswick,
New Jersey, local assembly had lapsed.[34] When Philadelphia's DA 1
backed Hayes, Powderly seized upon a minor internal squabble and suspended it.[35]

But Hayes was not inept like Litchman. He countered Powderly's
machinations by recruiting allies from an ever-growing list of Powderly

haters including the pliable Thomas McGuire, who had loathed Powderly since the early 1880s; Daniel DeLeon, the mercurial guiding light of revamped DA 49; and KOL cofounder James L. Wright of suspended DA 1. KOL headquarters degenerated into a den of spying and intrigue. Hayes made life especially miserable for A. W. Wright and O'Reilly as they toiled on the *Journal.*

At the 1892 convention, Powderly was forced to swallow the KOL's official endorsement of the People's Party. He refused nomination the first time his name was offered for reelection as general master workman. Supporters forced him to reconsider, but he probably wished that he had stuck to his guns after Hayes easily defeated O'Keefe and kept his secretary-treasurer post. Hayes proceeded to sack O'Keefe and increase pressure on Wright and O'Reilly. Powderly complained that Hayes "has developed the most remarkable traits of idiocy . . . that I ever heard of . . . I hope I never meet his like again. . . . [His] wings will be clipped after the Board meeting or else [someone] will be called upon to take my place, for I won't stand his insulting treatment of everyone around him any longer."[36]

But Hayes was neither cowed by Powderly's puffed-up righteousness nor inclined to take directives from him. He simply ignored a request to include with the mailing of the quarterly report a circular announcing the reinstatement of the Philosopher's Stone ritual and degree. This prompted an angry response from Powderly and necessitated a special mailing that squandered resources the Order could ill afford to waste.[37]

As 1893 opened, Powderly could see the handwriting on the wall. He told A. W. Wright that he intended to resign and called his current situation "the most painful and humiliating period of my life."[38] He launched a final no-holds-barred war against Hayes. In May, he sent a pointed letter to Hayes insisting it was clear that "the Order was in the throes of dissolution" and pronouncing it useless to continue organization efforts as it "will not be an honest thing . . . while we are preparing to disband." Powderly proclaimed, "[M]y usefulness to the Order is ended," but he also lashed out at Hayes's manipulation of KOL funds. A favorite Hayes ploy was to shift money from earmarked accounts into "trust funds," over which he had discretionary spending power. Powderly charged, "The various funds in your hands are no more to be considered "trust funds" than the tax and other revenue that comes in to you. Were the taxes, or other money, yours the term "trust fund" could not be applied, but all money paid in to a person holding a position of trust, and which is not his own, is money held in trust." He ordered Hayes to spend the remainder of the Homestead relief fund to pay KOL debts and challenged him to open the books so that Knights could see their true plight.[39]

When Hayes shrugged off Powderly's letter, O'Reilly advised the general master workman to press charges against Hayes. By then, Powderly was too dispirited to retaliate. He wrote, "I am heart sick of it all," and advised his friend his immediate concern was to make money, as he had not been paid for some time.[40] Weeks later, Powderly complained that Hayes "is organizing beer Assemblies" and roared that he and his clique "are the most unscrupulous liars I have ever met."[41]

Hayes turned up the heat on Powderly. In June, Powderly advised Wright to

> bundle up and send away every scrap of paper that has the name or initials of the Accident Claims Association upon it. Don't allow a single vestige of that paper to be . . . around the office. . . . Don't allow this paper to remain in the building. You may put it in a steal [*sic*] case and rivet it up, still he will find it and offer it in evidence to whoever comes along. Have no evidence of it around and be able to show receipt for payment of the bill to the office. You will need it at the G.A.[42]

Powderly's panic was over a silly idea that he and Wright concocted to sell shares in an insurance scheme. They hoped to sell insurance shares to employers to cover claims by injured workers, with the KOL benefiting from the investment. The plan was a bust from the start, but Hayes used it to infer that Powderly was corrupt.

When Powderly advised Wright that loose documents were unsafe, he knew whereof he spoke. In July, Powderly ordered Hayes not to open mail addressed to Powderly, Wright, or the *Journal*.[43] Hayes countered by demanding that Wright give an accounting of *Journal* expenses, something the hapless Wright was too disorganized to produce and which allowed Hayes to charge malfeasance. Tom O'Reilly advised Powderly to "suspend Wright on Hayes's charges and then suspend the latter for violations of his constitutional duties. Let the General Assembly see that the fellow isn't amenable to authority." O'Reilly suggested that suspending Hayes would allow Powderly to "regain the personal friendship" of Ralph Beaumont, George Schilling, James Campbell, Frederick Turner, William Bailey, and Charles Litchman, though the latter two might reasonably have rejected his overtures.[44]

As Powderly contemplated O'Reilly's advice, Hayes struck. Both John O'Keefe and Hugh Cavanaugh reported that Hayes planned to expose The Governor if Powderly continued to oppose him. Cavanaugh advised Powderly to call Hayes's bluff and threaten him with exposure of "the woman story," a reference to his alleged involvement with stenographer Maggie Eiler.[45] Tom O'Reilly informed Powderly that if pushed, Hayes was prepared to put the KOL into receivership and destroy it.[46]

All of this presented a quandary for Powderly, as many of the allegations against Hayes appear to have been true. Fresh from his harassment of Leonora Barry, Hayes took up with Eiler, whom he apparently seduced and used as a spy. By late 1892, however, Hayes was aware that Eiler was in contact with his enemies and began to browbeat and threaten her. In a private letter in January 1893, which Eiler turned over to the executive board, Hayes told her, "You and me can't be anything but friends for the reason that you know too much about my business. You see, I am still G.S.T., and I intend to remain G.S.T. in spite of Powderly and the entire General Executive Board trying to get me out." He bragged that his threat to pull down the entire Order caused Powderly to back off, and boasted of how he and Tom McGuire had saved Eiler's job. He warned her, "I once told you I had the power to make you tired of living, didn't I? Well, after [what] the d[am]n Board has done to try and get rid of me don't it prove that I am more powerful than they are? Keep my business to yourself."[47]

Hayes informed Eiler that he intended to keep her at headquarters where he could watch her, warned her three more times to keep his "business" affairs confidential, and complained, "By G[o]d, I trusted you with matters I wouldn't trust anyone else with, and then you turn around and tell the d[am]n Board everything you know. It's all right; no harm done. You see I am still G.S.T. and intend to remain G.S.T. till I get d[am]n good and ready to step down and out." In the next breath he stated that his intention was to run a gas plant in Washington "and when I am ready to do that they can all go to h[el]l."[48]

Hayes must have felt secure as he openly bragged of spying and thievery. He wrote of how he stole a package of letters from John Devlin's coat pocket "while he was in the hotel dining room," and confessed, "I took one letter out of Wright's pocket, too." He boasted of investment dealings that would, in the next five years, give him a half-million-dollar portfolio.[49] He hinted broadly that his investment capital came from the KOL treasury.

It was the only place he could have gotten the money; his $1,500 yearly salary was a mere one-hundredth of what he claimed to have invested in railroads alone. He crowed, "I will be a rich man soon, and they can take their office. . . . I was a good fellow as long as I let them into money-making schemes but as soon as I shut down on them they had no further use for me."[50]

Hayes's letter to Eiler indicates that many of Powderly's most lurid charges against Hayes were probably true. His final remark offers clues as to how he got away with it. If other board members were in on his schemes, they would naturally be reluctant to bring down Hayes and expose their own crimes.

Hayes then played a trump card: he leveled charges against Powderly and filed a lawsuit against the Order, thereby forcing Powderly to suspend him. This allowed the brazen Hayes to accuse Powderly of many of Hayes's own misdeeds, including misusing trust funds. Hayes also leveled allegations concerning The Governor, the Accident Claims Association, secret deals with the Republican Party, neglect of the master workman's office, and Powderly's shady involvement with publishing the 1893 *Labor Day Annual.*

Powderly assured O'Reilly that Hayes was "desperate" and motivated by an "insane desire for revenge."[51] But Powderly had been around too long not to be tainted by innuendo, proven or otherwise. Had he kept his own advice and steered clear of investment plans, his position would have been more tenable. But, as we have seen, he foolishly lent his name to the Accident Claims debacle.

He was in even deeper in the *Labor Day Annual.* The *Annual* was the brainchild of Alexander W. Wright who, like Powderly and Hayes, was obsessed with finding unorthodox ways to make money. Wright introduced Powderly to Colonel G. G. Gray, who offered his services as business agent for the fledgling publication. Gray promised that Powderly stood to make at least $500 profit on a Labor Day venture.[52]

The *Labor Day Annual* was planned to be a yearly program to coincide with the eponymous celebration. Booklets would feature articles on the history of labor, profiles on important reformers, and editorials on pressing social concerns. The timing seemed propitious, coming just one year before President Cleveland officially recognized the first Monday of September as a national holiday. Twenty-five states had already set aside such a day in advance of the federal mandate.

Wright had the tools, but not the means, to produce the *Annual.* The equipment of the *Journal of the Knights of Labor* could be rented, but the cash-strapped KOL could not underwrite a speculative venture. Powderly turned to those he perceived to be benevolent capitalists to buy advertisements or vanity features.

The resulting publication was slick but uneven in its content. Powderly contributed a rambling history of Labor Day, tracing its origins to seven centuries before the birth of Jesus and weaving its way to 1893. He also wrote an article condemning prison labor and penned a synopsis of KOL history. Wright provided pieces on the history of money and the AFL. He also announced an arts and industry competition and edited the overall work. Included in the *Annual* were Phillips Thompson's call for land reform, Robert Watchorn's report on factory legislation, various editorials gleaned from the *Journal of the Knights of Labor,* an article on the silver question, and sketches of the careers of Powderly, Cavanaugh, Hazen Pingree, and Gompers.

But the bulk of the publication consisted of advertisements and stories about manufacturers. Charles Pillsbury wrote an article on cooperation, despite the fact that Minnesota Knights frequently clashed with the baking magnate. Pillsbury was also the subject of a glowing sketch that was equal parts fluff and a promotion of his bid for Congress. Some Knights were no doubt rankled by equally flattering looks at such onetime adversaries as the Northern Pacific Railroad, the Michigan Stove Company, and the *New York Tribune.* And remaining old-timers were horrified by the spate of brewing firms and brew masters who helped underwrite the venture: Anheuser-Busch, C. H. Evans, Pabst, and Christian Moerlein.[53]

When Hayes failed to eliminate Wright by charging that his Toronto local had lapsed, he probed the *Annual.* Had the *Annual* actually made money, certain irregularities might have been forgiven, but it was a bust. Gray's financial backing proved illusory and Wright apparently used unauthorized *Journal of the Knights of Labor* funds to jump- start the project. Powderly knew nothing of Wright's misuse of funds, as is made clear in a series of letters between O'Reilly and him, but he was too close to Wright to avoid fallout.[54] There was plenty Hayes could use against his accusers and Powderly knew it.

At the general assembly, Hayes put forth fourteen charges against Powderly, Wright, and Devlin involving The Governor, improper accounting procedures, unauthorized use of KOL printing presses, diversion of funds into special projects not related to the KOL, false expense-account claims, and malfeasance in the Accident Claims and *Labor Day Annual* ventures. Hayes even resurrected moldy charges that Powderly authorized a secret mission to Rome to seek the Catholic Church's approval of the Order and that he manipulated the KOL into a bulk purchase of his book, *Thirty Years of Labor.*[55]

Powderly addressed each of the charges, opened his correspondence book for assembly inspection, produced travel receipts, offered proof of payment for non-business-related costs, demonstrated he had not profited from any outside venture, and showed he was owed over $3,400 in back salary. He so successfully deflected charges of economic malfeasance that Hayes withdrew most of them in mid-hearing. The assembly completely exonerated him. Even his enemies conceded that Powderly might be a rascal, but he was no crook.

Hayes probably knew that he could not make the charges stick, and that probably was not his intent. Although Powderly and his allies were cleared of any wrongdoing, their reputations were besmirched beyond repair. When Powderly's supporters put forth a resolution to declare all officer positions vacant and to elect a new slate of officers, it failed by nearly three to one and Hayes was free to pursue reelection. From the floor, Daniel DeLeon uttered what would have been unthinkable years earlier. Of Powderly he said, "The K of L under you stands in the way of progress. We have to get rid of you and supplant the order with a more radical form of organization."[56]

Officer elections took place amid animosity. Powderly was reelected as general master workman, though he garnered only twenty-six votes, while James Sovereign got nineteen, and Thomas McGuire one. But delegates also returned Hayes to his post, elected Powderly foe M. J. Bishop as general worthy foreman, and replaced Tom O'Reilly on the executive board with McGuire. In light of this, Powderly resigned.

For once, Powderly was sincere in his offer to quit, wanting nothing more than to return home to Scranton. Instead he had to endure an insult-laden debate over accepting his resignation. McGuire moved to accept the resignation, charging that Powderly "has persistently refused to conform to the views of the majority." J. R. Mansion, an ex-member of The Governor, claimed that Powderly "endeavored to use the Order for the purpose of furthering his personal gain." Newly elected General Worthy Foreman Bishop added, "[Powderly] holds as his enemy every delegate who does not vote in accordance with his views on all questions." Powderly's resignation was upheld by a slim margin and would not have carried had not several of his closest friends been convinced that he really wanted to quit. "Yea" votes were cast by Wright, O'Keefe, and Powderly himself.[57]

Though Powderly was only forty-four when he quit, years of infighting had taken their toll and he needed time to recharge before taking on new battles. He showed a short fit of pique by crossing out the picture of Hayes in a *Philadelphia News* article titled "A Great Federation of Labor Men," but he was uncharacteristically silent as labor and mainstream newspapers printed both charitable and unflattering reports of his resignation.[58] An exchange between O'Reilly and Powderly in late 1893 found the latter in a sullen mood. He wrote, "How a reverse shows who a man's friends are. You would think that letters of regret would be pouring in on me Tom but scarcely half a dozen have taken notice of the affair. . . . With the exception of you, Devlin, Cavanaugh, Quinn, and Bernard Feeney I don't think I have any friends left.[59] In a subsequent letter he announced: "I shall pay no further heed to Sovereign, Bishop, or anything they may say or do against me. I have no organ now and it would do me great injury in the eyes of the laboring people if I entered the capitalistic press to defend myself. I must bear in silence all they choose to lay on me and trust to time and the good sense of the people to vindicate me."[60] He also wrote to both O'Reilly and Wright to beg off future involvement with either the *Labor*

Day Annual or a new labor organization contemplated by Wright.[61] Powderly's one assertive act immediately after his removal was to continue mending his relationship with Joe Buchanan. As noted in chapter 3, Powderly originally sought out Buchanan as an ally against Hayes in 1892, but his apology rings sincere. Powderly swallowed his pride and admitted he had wronged Buchanan:

> I thank God for one thing. I was instrumental in bringing you back to the Order before my term ended. You may not think that this is anything to be proud of but I do. Through all the years of our estrangement there was no man in the labor movement whom I respected and admired more than you and now that I am out of office—never again to accept one—I can say to you unreservedly that I sincerely loved you for your truthful, manly way of dealing with those whom you had occasion to oppose. I would rather hold your esteem than to have a thousand of the others around me. This is no flattery, Joe. I mean it; every word and as you travel round you may meet with those to whom I have on many occasion said the same thing.[62]

Hayes, however, would not let Powderly retire gracefully. No sooner had 1894 opened than Hayes began badgering Powderly to turn over the very Philosopher's Stone degree in which he had previously shown no interest. A few months of solitude had restored some of Powderly's fighting spirit and he was not about to take orders from Hayes. Powderly circulated a letter to numerous districts and locals charging general assembly delegates with various violations.[63] He steadfastly refused to hand over information about the Philosopher's Stone degree, arguing that Uriah Stephens had entrusted it to his care. This time Hayes was forced to file charges.

Powderly's poison pen also came back to him. In a private letter Powderly called his successor, James Sovereign, "an ass." He predicted that the new general master workman "will not be long on the outside of the Iowa State Insane Asylum" and dismissed him as the puppet of Hayes and McGuire. He routinely referred to Sovereign as "Sufferin."[64]

In April, attorney F. W. Wiltbank produced an affidavit filed by Hayes and Sovereign. Powderly was charged with possession of KOL property, and he was presented a bill payable to the KOL for printing fees related to the *Labor Day Annual*. The statement also claimed that Powderly had received $1,800 of his disputed back salary. Powderly huffily replied that there was not a scrap of truth to the affidavit. He told Wiltbank that he accepted no responsibility for any expenditures other than those which bore his signature. He asserted, "I have no books belonging to the defendant organization in my possession," insisting that requested letterbooks were "my own property." He provided Wiltbank with a complete inventory of materials shipped to Sovereign and charged that Sovereign had "perjured himself," as he was not present for any of the matters listed in the affidavit and "knows absolutely nothing about what he is swearing to."[65]

To ensure that he could rid himself of Powderly, Hayes plotted to keep him away from the upcoming general assembly. Redrawing the lines of Powderly's District 16 to reinstate the assembly of one D. J. Campbell, a Hayes ally, did this. Through Campbell, Hayes packed DA 16's delegate list and suspended Powderly's local.[66]

In April 1894, Powderly and Buchanan attended an exploratory convention called by disgruntled Knights and AFL members. At issue was a possible new labor organization. Aside from an intriguing discussion about organizing unskilled workers, little came of the meetings.[67] Nonetheless, the specter of Powderly leading loyalists out of the rapidly deteriorating KOL greatly alarmed Hayes and Sovereign. Luckily for them, Powderly was unconvinced such an organization was viable.

A more concrete concern for Hayes was Powderly's countersuit. Powderly, Devlin, and Wright sued the KOL for back salary, an act that led General Master Workman Sovereign to suspend Powderly. This was humiliating, but Powderly's immediate concern was earning a livelihood. With a Democratic administration in Washington, he had few political chits to cash. Powderly recalled:

> I sought employment as a machinist in a shop where I had formerly worked at my trade. I had saved no money, was in debt, and the organization [KOL] owed me, in salary and unpaid expenses over five thousand dollars. I had received a great deal of praise, adulation, and flattery for the part I played as chief of the Knights of Labor, but . . . I could not realize anything on them in a financial way, and they provided nothing substantial in the matter of supporting my family.[68]

Though rebuffed in his attempt to take up his old trade, Powderly rejected advice to open a saloon or take to the professional lecture circuit. In the end, however, Powderly took a path every bit as hypocritical as it would have been for the old temperance warhorse to open a tavern: he studied law.

Lawyers were one of a few groups of professionals barred from KOL membership. Although that rule was violated on several occasions, Powderly surely realized that studying for the bar would place him beyond the KOL pale.[69] But by mid-1894, his situation was desperate. He could not make his mortgage payments, forcing him to give up his Scranton home and move to more modest quarters. He was admitted to the Pennsylvania Bar in 1894, though, by his own admission, he was not a particularly good lawyer.[70]

Powderly nonetheless displayed a lawyer's ability to feud. Hayes continued to press the suspended ex–general master workman for instructions pertaining to the Philosopher's Stone degree, and Powderly refused with equal vigor. Powderly believed that the KOL's fall general assembly would be its last, and he was determined to neither yield to Hayes nor give him the satisfaction of a reply. In private letters to old friends, however, he spared no bile. In one letter he complained of Hayes's "rascality" and ridiculed his withered arm by calling him a "one-winged saint."[71] He also assembled a defiant letter—made available to Hayes—in which Powderly stated he intended to "make no attempt to comply" with the executive board order.[72]

After fourteen pro-Powderly delegates were denied seats, the 1894 assembly was little more than a Powderly lynch mob. Powderly was charged with failing to turn over official property to the Order, slandering the board, holding up the sale of KOL headquarters through his lawsuit, disrupting harmony with his January secret circular, plotting to set up a rival organization, using the Order's money to prepare the *Labor Day Annual,* and engineering the arrest of a board member who went to Scranton to mediate a dispute between DA 16 and Powderly's local assembly. Powderly himself took little heed of the events in New Orleans, having concluded that the KOL was dead.[73]

Predictably, Powderly was expelled from the very organization he had headed for fourteen years. In 1895, a rival group declared independence from the Order. Powderly lent his name to the so-called Independent Order of the Knights of Labor, but he did not take an active role in it. The absurd dance between Hayes and Powderly continued off and on for several more years.

Powderly's prediction of the KOL's demise was premature but essentially correct. His 1894 expulsion was accompanied by more damaging suspensions of the pro-Powderly National Trade District 135 and LA 300. The first were miners, long the backbone of the KOL, and they soon joined earlier defectors to the United Mine Workers. Picking a fight with LA 300 was even more foolish as the glassblowers had long provided needed cash to the KOL when it was not forthcoming anywhere else.

With Powderly gone from the Order, Hayes and Sovereign proceeded to alienate Daniel DeLeon and his DA 49 comrades. When DeLeon's credentials were denied at the 1895 assembly, his supporters left the KOL for the newly formed Socialist Trade and Labor Alliance. Hayes tried to save face by expelling DeLeon and the socialists, but Philip Foner estimated that this rupture cost the Knights thirteen thousand of its thirty thousand members.[74]

John Hayes did not run off with the Order's money as Powderly had feared. He continued as secretary-treasurer until 1902, when he became general master workman. He was, however, the titular head of a dying organization and wielded little power. Hayes managed to hold the KOL together until 1916, when he closed the Order's central office, by then located in Washington, D.C. From that date until his death in 1942, Hayes was involved in small business ventures, one of which was a gas company. But John Hayes was not destined for the fortune he so craved.

As for Powderly, in 1898 he refiled his suit for back salary, reducing the amount to $4,000. The current general master workman, John W. Parsons, countered that Powderly actually owed the Knights $9,000 in debts accrued from the *Labor Day Annual*. The next year, the suit was settled when Powderly accepted a $1,500 buyout.

The payment seems to have soothed animosity all around. In 1900, Powderly returned to the KOL fold despite Hayes's control of the Order. He was reinstated by acclamation at the 1900 general assembly and dutifully became a dues-paying member of Washington, D.C., Local Assembly 4896. His presence was merely symbolic, however, and he never again took an active role in the Knights.

The following year was spent in mourning when his wife Hannah died. He threw himself into his work and spent much of his time in Washington, where he was President McKinley's commissioner-general of immigration. President Roosevelt removed Powderly in 1902 over a controversy involving one of his underlings.

Powderly was again down on his financial luck and drifted from one modest business venture to another before President Roosevelt determined he was blameless in the 1902 controversy and gave him another post. Until his death in 1924, Powderly worked as a bureaucrat, first for the Bureau of Immigration and finally in the Department of Labor. Instead of exhorting laborers to battle or exchanging vitriolic barbs with enemies like John Hayes, Powderly confined his remaining energy to warning Americans of a rising immigrant tide flooding American shores.[75]

Afterword and Conclusion

Terence Powderly was expelled from the Knights of Labor in 1894 and Daniel DeLeon stormed out the next year. After that, relative calm prevailed in the Order, primarily because there were not many Knights left to quarrel. For his part, DeLeon made a good case for those social movement theorists who argue that overly radical groups that ignore American pluralist traditions tend to fare poorly. For most of its short existence, DeLeon's Socialist Trade and Labor Alliance was weaker than even the truncated Knights.

Powderly allowed his name to reappear on the KOL rolls in 1900, despite the fact that John Hayes still ruled the roost. Why not? By then both he and the Order rested on past laurels. The most significant contribution made by the post-1900 KOL is the portrait it provides of a social movement in the throes of dissolution. Why was that the KOL's fate?

The social movement identity provides a few clues. The KOL, like most groups seeking change, neither entirely determined its own destiny nor survived. As I argued in the introduction to this book, the Gilded Age period in which the KOL struggled was one of the more difficult climates any reform group could have faced. Most of the American power structure was arrayed against the Knights: the political system, the courts, financial institutions, churches, the mainstream press, competing labor groups, and social custom. The KOL did not amass the resources necessary to counter such powerful opposition, and it was done in by its enemies.

But external opposition is not the primary focus of this study because it does not tell the entire story. The KOL dealt itself as many blows as those delivered by its enemies. One could endlessly debate whether internal unity would have made the Knights triumphant; I doubt it, but I am certain that factionalism harmed the Order in major ways. Solidarity is a much-bandied-about subject for unions and other reform groups. The KOL's experience demonstrates that solidarity is much easier to create than to maintain. What lessons can social movement advocates and theorists draw from that difficulty?

First, social movements need to be clear about their goals and build organizational structures to accommodate them. The KOL never determined if it was to be a reform, resistance, or revolutionary group. The focus at any given point in its history largely depended on which faction was dominant and how well it was able to control competing factions. Moreover, the KOL's structure was sufficiently broad to foster all three tendencies but insufficiently rigid to allow one of them to stamp its identity on the Order. The KOL fought many valiant battles and contributed to changes in American society, but drift, indecision, and lack of overall clarity sapped its effectiveness.

A second lesson derives from the Home Club's constant interference in KOL affairs. In its principles and rhetoric, the Knights of Labor assumed the guise of a universal organization open to nearly all comers. The Home Club sacrificed those ideals on the altar of particularism. By imposing ideological tests for Knighthood and by exacerbating tensions with trade unionists, the Home Club undermined its own admirable efforts at solidarity in the areas of race, ethnicity, and gender. Historians may take umbrage with my assessments of how much power the Home Club amassed, but I doubt any would argue that the Home Club's meddling was good for the KOL. It helped create a permanent culture of contentiousness that made the Order an easily sparked tinderbox.

William Bailey and Thomas Barry illustrate the dangers involved in trying to manage multiple and complex tasks within an organization with vague lines of command, an underdeveloped bureaucracy, and a propensity for allowing decentralized decision making in situations requiring coordination. In such situations, the focus invariably shifts to individuals and problem solving is only as good as those improvising the solutions. Single individuals should never be allowed to set agendas for an entire organization. If spurned, they will speak with equal zeal *against* said organization.

Joseph R. Buchanan underscored the damage done by opponents of KOL universalism. He also embodied the tensions any organization must face between holding fast to principles or making pragmatic compromises. Buchanan was simultaneously a prophet, an agitator, and a statesman. When pressed, he even demonstrated skills as an administrator. In all, Joseph Buchanan was about all one could hope for in a leader.

And Charles Litchman was his polar opposite, the sort of simpering, self-serving, meddlesome bumbler that social movements would do well to avoid. The problem with difficult men like Litchman is that they tend to bring out the worst in their enemies as well. In Litchman's case, opponents opened a Pandora's box in ridding themselves of him. Well-oiled movements operate according to procedure, not the whims of personality. Once structures are manipulated to accommodate or ruin an individual based on temperament rather than ability, the floodgates open for all manner of scheming.

Another lesson is that what is done at the top tends to filter down. The case studies of Henry Sharpe, John Brophy, and Daniel Hines bring KOL wrangling out of its Philadelphia headquarters and into local and district assemblies. The test of any movement comes with how decisions made behind closed doors play out among the rank and file charged with implementing policy. The KOL's culture of contentiousness certainly spread. As in the case of Litchman, conflict was personal and it frequently entailed abuse of and damage to organizational structures. KOL courts took a big hit, as did cherished goals like cooperation, harmony with trade unions, and pretensions of converting nonmanual workers to the KOL's vision of reform. The KOL was certainly not, as Norman Ware put it, a study in democracy. One suspects that most social movements would be healthier if they were such paragons, but that is easier asserted than accomplished.

Gender has been an Achilles' heel for many social movements. As Leonora Barry's experience shows, movements must back up rhetoric with action in regard to gender equality. Empty rhetorical commitment can attract women to social movements, but it will not keep them involved. Given the depth of Gilded Age opposition to the Knights of Labor, it could have used many times the number of women it actually organized. The implications today are obvious, as is an extension of the argument to include race, ethnicity, sexual preference, and a host of other categories. Social movements need to define themselves clearly, but those that do so through exclusionary means are doomed to marginality.

It would be deliciously tempting to say that Terence Powderly's ouster proves the proverb that chickens eventually come home to roost. I doubt that many reading this work will shed a tear over his fate. But there are more important lessons. First, Powderly's biggest failing as a leader is one that few have commented upon: he should never have allowed the Order to get into the state it found itself when he was ousted. Those critics who tar Powderly as unprincipled have a point: a more honorable man would have quit rather than be associated with such decay.

But Ware had a point, too: the rank and file failed to boot him out. In my view, social movements probably need to adopt the same logic as sports teams: when failure follows failure, change leaders. Just as a losing record is seldom the sole fault of its coaching staff, it is entirely wrong-headed to blame the KOL's demise on Powderly. Those who would blame him for most (or all) of the KOL's problems face the challenge of explaining away the behavior of men like John Hayes. Nevertheless, the KOL rank and file should have canned most of the group that led it downhill; instead it rewarded muddlement and ignored malfeasance. A leadership shake-up was badly needed within the KOL. Social movements too often fail to do what is routine in the corporate world: make changes when the organization begins to hemorrhage, not wait until it is bloodless.

To end where I began, I would suggest that social movements too closely associated with any single individual probably will not thrive. I have argued that the KOL was far more than Terence Powderly and have chided historians for perpetuating that error. I must concede, however, that Powderly's identification with the Knights was far greater than it should have been among the KOL rank and file and the Gilded Age public. Leaders can be important symbols; they can also be detrimental scapegoats. A healthy social movement ought to be judged on the deeds of its followers, not the press releases of its leaders. Who today can recite the names of the Flint, Michigan, General Motors assembly-line workers who sat down in 1937, or those of the black students who did the same at a Greensboro, North Carolina, Woolworth's counter in 1960? Even good leaders can harm a social movement if they come to embody how others perceive the whole. Several observers have argued that this has hampered recruitment for the Southern Christian Leadership Conference since the murder of Dr. Martin Luther King, Jr., and the United Farm Workers in the wake of Cesar Chavez's untimely death.

Effective social movement leaders are not like Kleenex, where we associate the name with the product. Movements should spawn heroic actions, not media-made heroes. Much of what makes a movement possible is behind-the-scenes work that is hard, unglamorous, and unnoticed. Plans, principles, and tactics get hammered out in decidedly unsexy bureaucratic structures that are the lifeblood of any organization that hopes to be more than a flash in the pan.

Finally, "solidarity" and "movement" need to be seen as action nouns, not postmortem descriptors. When the Knights of Labor was at its best, members rallied to the picket lines, adhered faithfully to boycotts, sang lustily in their local assemblies, and sought commonality. They were too busy to dwell on differences, engage in petty squabbles, or bother to demonize (or lionize) their leaders.

Some degree of factionalism is inevitable in human society and I by no means wish to claim that democratic debate should be stifled. Nonetheless, social movements and their leaders need to distinguish healthy disagreement from the contentiousness that comes from stasis. Solidarity can only be maintained when there is more rank-and-file focus on external enemies than internal ones. More often than not, organizations like the Knights of Labor that reflexively and continually dwell on internal factions are moribund. Above all, a successful social movement must continue to *move,* or it withers and dies.

Notes

Introduction

1. *Scribner's Monthly,* August, 1875. Quoted from Paul Boller and Ronald Story, eds., *A More Perfect Union: Documents in U.S. History, Volume II* (Boston: Houghton Mifflin, 1996), 17–18.
2. Bellamy, *Looking Backward,* 30–31.
3. Ibid., 51.
4. Frederick Douglass, *My Bondage, My Freedom* (Miller and Mulligan, 1885), 310.
5. Powderly, *Thirty Years of Labor,* 35–36.
6. Economic expansion is discussed in Zinn, *People's History,* chapter 11. See also Ratner, Soltow, and Sylla, *The Evolution of the American Economy,* esp. chapters 12–14; and Painter, *Standing at Armageddon,* introduction and chapters 1–2.
7. Zinn, *People's History,* 243.
8. A very readable and useful source documenting living conditions in the Gilded Age is Bettmann, *The Good Old Days.* See chapter 3 on housing.
9. Wallace, *St. Clair,* 248–65.
10. Bettman, *The Good Old Days,* 70–71.
11. Painter, *Standing at Armageddon,* 4; Bettman, *The Good Old Days,* 80.
12. Paul Fatout, ed., *Mark Twain Speaking* (Iowa City: University of Iowa Press, 1976), 75.
13. Zinn, *People's History,* 250.
14. There are scores of good studies highlighting the problems of women and immigrants in the post–Civil War period. One of the best studies on women remains the classic work by Flexner, *A Century of Struggle.* Two stellar surveys dealing with nativism after the Civil War are Higham, *Strangers in the Land,* and Takaki, *A Different Mirror.* One of the most useful studies of

farmer problems for both its factual and theoretical content is Goodwyn, *The Populist Moment.* For African-American farmers, see Ransom and Sutch, *One Kind of Freedom.*

15. For more on the founding, early days, rise, and decline of the KOL, see Ware, *The Labor Movement,* and Weir, *Beyond Labor's Veil.* Traditionally, the KOL's 1886 membership is given as 729,000. This, however, reflects only dues-paying members. In my view, this figure is low and excludes those claiming KOL affiliation. Membership applications came in so rapidly during late 1885 and mid-1886 that the central office simply could not process them quickly enough. The number of workers who self-identified as Knights in mid-1886 certainly exceeded 729,000 and may have numbered as many as one million.

16. See Weir, *Beyond Labor's Veil,* preface.

17. Garlock, *Guide to Local Assemblies of the Knights of Labor.*

18. Birdsall, "The Problem of Structure in the Knights of Labor," 532–46.

19. Historian Craig Phelan has been nearly alone in his defense of Powderly, and his forthcoming biography of Powderly promises to be a much-needed reassessment. Some measure of the historical community's antipathy toward Powderly came at the 1998 North American Labor History Association's annual meeting in Detroit. When Phelan unveiled pieces of his work in a paper titled "Terence Powderly and the Great Upheaval," many of his favorable comments on Powderly were greeted with skepticism, as were my own comments in support of Phelan.

20. Workforce data from Stanley Lebergott, "Labor Force and Employment, 1800–1960," *Output, Employment, and Productivity in the United States after 1800* (New York: National Bureau of Economic Research, 1966), 118–19. The strike statistics are from Bettmann, *The Good Old Days,* 82.

21. Marx and McAdam, *Collective Behavior and Social Movements,* 17.

22. There are scores of fine social movement theory studies, the bulk of which have been done by sociologists. Most sociology textbooks contain concise overviews of past and recent work on the subject, and the American Sociological Association maintains a superb bibliography on its official website.

    Some of the works consulted in preparing my remarks include Herbert Blumer, "Collective Behavior," in *Principles of Sociology,* ed. Alfred Lee (New York: Barnes and Noble, 1965), 65–121; Davies, "Toward a Theory of Revolution," 5–19; Kornhauser, *The Politics of Mass Society;* Marx and McAdam, *Collective Behavior and Social Movements;* Mauss, *Social Problems and Social Movements;* McCarthy and Zald, "Resource Mobilization and Social Movements," 1212–41; Piven and Cloward, *Poor People's Movements;* Smelser, *Theory of Collective Behavior;* Tilly, *From Mobilization to Revolution.*

    One of the few historians to adapt social movement theory to his own use is Lawrence Goodwyn, *The Populist Moment.* I have resisted adopting Goodwyn's typologies simply because I wish to draw on broader applications than he used in his look at the Populists.

23.   These terms are borrowed from a summary found in Macionis, *Sociology,* 623–24.
24.   Kealey and Palmer, *Dreaming of What Might Be.*
25.   Marx and McAdam, *Collective Behavior and Social Movements,* 97.
26.   Powderly, *The Path I Trod,* 102.

Chapter One

1.   For more on revolts within the Knights of Labor, see Powderly, *Thirty Years of Labor,* esp. the chapter titled "Improvements?" Earlier versions of some material that follows have been published. See Robert Weir, "Powderly and the Home Club: The Knights of Labor Joust among Themselves," *Labor History* 34:1 (Winter 1993): 84–117. See also Weir, "Here's to the Men Who Lose."

2.   For a list of the Reading delegates, see Powderly, *Thirty Years of Labor,* 127.

3.   *The Industrial West* (Atlantic, Iowa), January 6, 1887.

4.   For more on McGuire, see Galenson, *The United Brotherhood of Carpenters.*

5.   For the content of Drury's articles, see *The Socialist,* April 22–August 5, 1876. See also Drury, *The Polity of the Labor Movement, Volume I.* For more on Drury's life and career, see Weir, "Here's to the Men Who Lose."

6.   Local 1562 had as few as twenty-one members (1883) and as many as forty-eight (1881) during this period. These numbers come from Garlock, *Guide to Local Assemblies of the Knights of Labor.*

7.   *New York Herald,* April 23, 1882. Powderly was prone to flights of rhetorical excess. In August 1880, he got caught up in a heated debate over strikes, which he bitterly opposed. Accounts differ as to what Powderly actually said. Powderly claims he said, "As a representative to the General Assembly, I for one shall vote against the rifle and Gatling gun." Powderly gave that account in his December 1882 report to the *Journal of United Labor* (hereafter cited as *JUL*) on the Cuno matter. It cannot be considered a verbatim rendering of the events as the term "General" was only in effect since the September 1882 KOL convention. In all likelihood, Powderly made one of his sarcastic remarks that so frequently got him into trouble. By some accounts, including Cuno's, Powderly said he was "for" the purchase of weapons, but meant it ironically and delivered the statement in a satirical tone of voice. It is scarcely possible that Powderly could have ever made such a statement seriously.

8.   *Proceedings of the General Assembly of the Knights of Labor,* 1882; *JUL,* December 1882. Once again, accounts differ over the exact words uttered. The *JUL* account quotes Cuno as saying, "All employers are robbers and thieves, and should be boycotted on general principles." See also Powderly to Cuno, June 28 and July 3, 1882; Powderly to Robert Layton, July 26, 1882; Gilbert Rockwood to Powderly, July 3, 1882. All letters located in the Papers of Terence V. Powderly (University Microfilms) hereafter cited as PP.

The Socialist Labor Party was a moderate organization dedicated to victory through the ballot box, not through socialist revolutionary upheaval. Although Powderly made sweeping condemnations of all socialist and anarchist views, he was briefly a card-carrying member of the SLP, having been recruited by Van Patten.

9.   *JUL,* December 1882. John Elliott spelled his name in a number of ways, sometimes adding or deleting an "l" or a "t." This was not atypical in Gilded Age America. Standardization was not yet de rigeur for grammar and spelling.

10. Cuno to Powderly, December 5 and 30, 1882, PP.

11. Layton to Powderly, December 11, 1882 and January 21, 1883; Phillip Van Patten to Powderly, December 28, 1882 and February 15, 1883; John Caville to Powderly, April 27 and June 11, 1883, all in PP.

12. J. Mulhane to Powderly, September 29, 1882, PP.

13. Powderly's renewed attack on LA 1562 can be read in the *JUL,* January 1883. Accounts of the Cook affair were taken up at the 1883 general assembly. See *Proceedings of the General Assembly of the Knights of Labor,* 1883.

14. Powderly to Caville, August 27, 1883, PP. Caville requested commissions for Thomas McGuire, George Lloyd, and a man named Krueckel. Powderly politely advised that he could not grant commissions until the general assembly took up the matter of DA 49's suspension.

15. *Proceedings of the General Assembly of the Knights of Labor,* 1883. Despite the assembly's caution, there was nonetheless an oath-bound splinter group that formed after the convention adjourned. The Independent Order of the Knights of Labor remained small, however, and was largely confined to Excelsior Assembly of Binghamton, New York.

16. *JUL,* January 1884; *John Swinton's Paper,* January 27, 1884.

17. For examples of Powderly/Cuno correspondence, see Cuno to Powderly, 3/29/86 and 8/9/86, PP. Powderly ignored most of Cuno's correspondence.

18. Galenson, *The United Brotherhood of Carpenters,* 1–95.

19. *JUL,* January 1883.

20. For more on the cigarmakers' struggles, see Ware, *The Labor Movement,* 258–79; Foner, *History of the Labor Movement,* 1:512–24; Foner, *History of the Labor Movement,* 2:132–45.

21. Dyer Lum to Joseph Labadie, January 27, 1884, Joseph Labadie Papers, Special Collections, University of Michigan, Ann Arbor (hereafter cited as *JLP*).

22. John McClelland to Powderly, July 7, 1884, PP. (emphasis in original).

23. *Proceedings of the General Assembly of the Knights of Labor,* 1884.

24. Early allies of the Home Club outside of New York City included William Bailey of Shawnee, Ohio; Thomas Barry of East Saginaw, Michigan; Ralph Beaumont of Addison, New York; Hugh Cavanaugh of Cincinnati; John Elliott of Baltimore; David Gibson of Hamilton, Ontario; John Hayes of New Brunswick, New Jersey; William Mullen of Richmond; and Frederick Turner of Philadelphia. Each man had his own reasons for taking part in the plot

and several of them did not share Drury's ideological predisposition. Hayes, for example, was motivated mostly by a quest for power and quickly turned against the Club. Similarly, both Bailey and Barry became enemies of the Home Club because of its anti–trade unionism. Gibson and Mullen quickly distanced themselves for the same reason.

25. Home Club allies elected to the auxiliary board were Cavanaugh, Gibson, Mullen, and DA 49 Master Workman James Quinn. Those existing board members sympathetic to the Home Club were Hayes, Turner, and DA 49's Caville and Homer McGraw. Again, the commitment of Mullen and Gibson was shallow and based more on opposition to Powderly than ideological precepts.

26. Powderly's role was crucial. For four years the Home Club plotted to get rid of him and it now held the power to do so if it wished to fight the ugly battle that would have ensued. Had Powderly resigned, he could have commanded an anti–Home Club faction. In all likelihood it would have split the Order in half, which neither he nor the Home Club wished to happen. It is possible that Powderly's motives were altruistic, but I doubt it. Powderly was always uncomfortable in airing the Knights' dirty linen in public and he shared Victor Drury's love of behind-the-scenes plotting. It is most likely that Powderly's first thought was to hold on to his power base and try to undermine the Club from the inside; subsequent actions are consistent with such a conclusion. In any event, Powderly's refusal to assist anti–Home Club factions in 1886 or 1887 doomed their efforts. This much is also clear: in those years, he was not in control of the Knights of Labor.

The much-ballyhooed assassination attempt against Powderly involved an incident where there was an alleged plot to dump the general master workman in New York harbor. Those who put stock in such things pointed to a Powderly ride on the Staten Island Ferry—probably in 1883—on which he was jostled by another passenger. Rumors abounded that Powderly was saved from a watery grave at the last moment when someone grabbed him by his topcoat. Powderly consistently denied everything except being bumped and insisted his life was never in jeopardy. There is no reason to doubt him on this score, especially given that he could have used such a rumor to his advantage if he had thought it would stand up.

27. Knights of Labor, *Labor: Its Rights and Wrongs* (1886), 227–28.

28. C. Haas to Powderly, April 1, 1886; Peter Kearney to Powderly, May 8, 1886, PP.

29. *New York Times,* June 10, 1886; *Chicago Tribune,* June 7, 1886; *The Boston Knight,* September 18, 1886; *Labor Leaf,* June 9, 1886; *New York Morning Journal,* August 15, 1886; Powderly to David Pascoe, September 28, 1886, PP.

30. *Proceedings of the General Assembly of the Knights of Labor,* 1886, 1887. The Ferrell incidents are also recorded in Philip Foner, *American Socialism and Black Americans: From the Age of Jackson to World War I* (Westport, CT: Greenwood, 1977); Peter Rachleff, *Black Labor in Richmond, 1865–*

1890 (Philadelphia: Temple University Press, 1984); *Frank Leslie's Illustrated,* October 16, 1886; *Montgomery Advertiser,* October 6, 1886; *The New York Freeman,* October 16 and November 20, 1886.

31. For more on Chinese assemblies, see *The Boycotter,* May 12, 1887; *John Swinton's Paper,* June 26, July 10, and July 15, 1887.

32. *Labor Enquirer* (Chicago), June 11, 1887; Buchanan, *Labor Agitator; The Labor Leaf,* June 9, 1886. The *Leaf* names Drury as the head of the Home Club. Throughout 1886 and 1887, Labadie kept up a steady attack on the Club and on Powderly's inept leadership. See Labadie's editorial column "Cranky Notions." For a sample of other attacks, see Milwaukee's *Daily Review,* esp. August 15, 1887. See also such papers as the *Labor Enquirer* (both the Denver and Chicago editions), Philadelphia's *Labor Herald and Tocsin* and *John Swinton's Paper.* By late 1886, most KOL papers printed rumors and accusations about the Club.

33. Buchanan, *Story of a Labor Agitator,* 310–18; *Labor Enquirer* (Chicago) January 26, 1887, August 11, 1888; *Daily Review,* August 15, 1887.

34. See issues of *The Boycotter,* Telegraphers Local 6's newspaper. In late 1886, the paper changed its name to *The Union Printer,* dropped the KOL's slogan from its banner, and discontinued its regular KOL column. By 1887, it printed articles critical of the Knights. See also Edwin Gabler, *The American Telegrapher: A Social History, 1860–1900* (New Brunswick, NJ: Rutgers University Press, 1988).

35. Matthew Maguire to Powderly, February 27, 1887; Patrick Grogan to Powderly, March 9 (?), 1887, PP (exact date on the Grogan letter is smudged); *John Swinton's Paper,* April 24, May 1, May 15, and June 5, 1887. For more on the carpet weavers' strike, see Levine, *Labor's True Woman.*

  John Morrison's hatred of the Home Club and the subsequent debacle surrounding settlement of the carpet weavers' strike led Morrison to publicize Home Club machinations. Morrison and his followers were so vociferous that some historians have concluded that much of what has been attributed to the Club is, in fact, the product of exaggeration on the part of Morrison. That is the position of Craig Phelan in a recent article for *Labor History.*

  I agree with Phelan that the Home Club made a convenient enemy around which trade unionists and others could rally. I also concur that many of the comments concerning Home Club power were fanciful. Phelan, however, goes on to deny that the Home Club ever wielded significant power within the KOL. In my view, Phelan's focus on Morrison is too restrictive and the Club's influence over KOL policy was real, not fictive.

36. *John Swinton's Paper,* April 10, 1887; *Knights of Labor* (Chicago), May 14, 1887; *Labor Enquirer,* December 10, 1887.

37. *The Union Printer,* July 2 and 23, 1887; *Labor Enquirer,* July 9, 1887.

38. Thomas O'Reilly to Powderly, August 8 and 22, 1887; John Mahoney to Powderly, October 3, 1887, PP.

39. *Proceedings of the Knights of Labor General Assembly,* 1887.

40. Ware, *The Labor Movement*, 115–16; *Labor Enquirer*, October 29 and December 10, 1887, January 21, February 11, and February 18, 1888.

41. "Decision of the G.M.W. in the Case of D.A. 49 vs. James E. Quinn"; Quinn to Powderly, May 29, 1888; John Hayes to Thomas O'Reilly, May 31, 1888; Powderly to Edward Kunze, May 31, 1888; and Hayes to Powderly, July 2, 1888, all in PP.

42. *Proceedings of the Knights of Labor General Assembly*, 1888.

43. Hayes to Powderly, January 15, 1889; Powderly to Hayes, September 15, 1888; Powderly to Victor St. Cloud, February 27, April 2 and 20, 1889; St. Cloud to Powderly, February 24, April 16, and October 18, 1889; and Powderly to Leonora Barry, February 7, 1889, all in PP. See also Ware, *The Labor Movement*, 115; Powderly, *Thirty Years of Labor*, 295–300; *The Critic*, February 9, 1889.

44. *Irish World*, January 12 and August 3, 1889; *Journal of the Knights of Labor* (hereafter cited as *JKL*), February 27, September 18, and September 25, 1890, June 4, 1891.

45. Seretan, *Daniel DeLeon.*

46. See Tim Curry, Robert Jiobu, and Kent Schwiran, *Sociology for the Twenty-First Century* (Upper Saddle River, NJ: Prentice Hall, 1999), 412.

47. For more on the meaning and significance of KOL rituals and their impact on those who practiced them, see Weir, *Beyond Labor's Veil*, chapter 1, "The Knights in Ritual: A Culture of Fraternalism."

48. *JKL*, July 17, 1890 and February 8, 1894; *The Irish World*, August 27, 1892; *The Weekly People*, 1891–94; *Proceedings of the Knights of Labor General Assembly*, 1895.

49. Galenson, *The United Brotherhood of Carpenters*, 89–95.

50. The few papers of Drury's that are known to survive are located in *Papers of the Women's Trade Union League and Its Principal Leaders: Leonora O'Reilly* (Radcliffe College: Special Collections). Most of the writings contained therein are from the last two decades of Drury's life.

51. For more on how historians have handled the Home Club question, see Weir, "Powderly and the Home Club." A recent work that downplays the power of the Home Club is Craig Phelan, "The Warp of Fancy: The Knights of Labor and the Home Club Takeover Myth," *Labor History* 40:3 (August 1999), 283–300. In my view, Phelan overstates his case but is correct in pointing out the ways in which Home Club opponents exaggerated its reach. In a sense, both the Home Club and its detractors were focal points for anti-Powderly sentiment. It is also important to note that I agree with Phelan that the Home Club's "control" of the KOL was never complete. But the controversy generated by and toward the ring meant that Powderly and his allies could not control the Order either. Mine is a portrait of internal conflict and turmoil, not a claim that a cabal clandestinely set the KOL agenda. As I argue throughout this work, Home Club machinations were all too public. So too were the battles engendered over policy.

52. *Advance and Labor Leaf* (Detroit), June 9, 1886.

Chapter Two

1. Ware, *The Labor Movement.*
2. Marx and McAdam, *Collective Behavior and Social Movements,* 5.
3. Gamson, *The Strategy of Social Protest,* 99–101.
4. Samuel Friedman, "Worker Opposition Groups," Research in *Social Movements, Conflicts and Change: A Research Annual,* Volume 8: (1985): 133–70; Gamson, *The Strategy of Social Protest,* 99–101.
5. Ware, *The Labor Movement,* 111.
6. Joseph Buchanan complained that Bailey, along with John Hayes and Frederick Turner, did little except "look out" the window and "daydream" during the negotiations with Gould. Buchanan claims to have done most of the work. See Ware, *The Labor Movement,* 142; Buchanan, *Labor Agitator.*
7. Scanty biographical details of Barry's early life can be found in several undated newspaper clippings. The best of these appears under the heading "Heads of the Knights of Labor" and is contained in the Thomas Barry Scrapbooks (hereafter cited as TBS), a microfilmed edition collection of which is owned by the Harlan Hatcher Library of the University of Michigan. A shorter, less useful profile is found in *The Advance and Labor Leaf,* December 8, 1886. Barry is also listed in G. Fink, *Biographical Dictionary,* 103. Barry appears to have been a drummer boy in the Civil War.

    I am exceedingly grateful to Richard Oestreicher, who kindly provided me with a copy of an unpublished paper, "The Limits of Labor Radicalism." Oestreicher has done a masterful job of piecing together materials from the Barry Scrapbooks.
8. For information on the founding dates of KOL assemblies, see Garlock, *Guide to Local Assemblies of the Knights of Labor.*
9. Gilbert Rockwood's letter to Powderly is dated July 17, 1882, just weeks after the formal chartering of New York DA 49. It is located in PP.
10. "Heads of the Knights of Labor," "Men and Politics," "Barry Will Accept," TBS. Barry refused renomination to the general executive board in 1884 at the behest of his family, who felt he needed to contribute more in the way of wages. Either family finances improved by 1885, or the call to serve was greater than Barry's powers to resist.
11. *The Labor Leaf,* January 27, 1886; "Call It Persecution," "Barry Not Guilty," undated clippings in TBS. Carlotta Anderson dubs Barry a "hero" in her *All-American Anarchist,* 113. Anderson also charges that Powderly undercut the settlement by ordering Knights back to work. Anderson overstates the case in this charge. Barry's agreement was more of a face-saving gesture than a real victory. Under it, millworkers accustomed to a twelve-hour day went to eleven, but under the old wage rate. All parties understood that this was a temporary measure that would only remain in effect if other mill owners adopted the new standard. They did not, and the compromise was quietly scrapped.
12. "Fight against the Knights," "A Mammoth Mass Meeting," "Tom Barry

Here," "The Settlement Falls Through," "Another Hitch," "How Amsterdam Mill Owners Reply to Mr. Donovan," "The Knitting Mills," "The Knights of Labor Gain Their Point," undated clippings, TBS.

13. Ibid.

14. Cobble, "Organizing the Postindustrial Work Force," 420–21.

15. Samuel Gompers, *Seventy Years of Life and Labor: An Autobiography,* ed. Nick Salvatore (Ithaca, NY: ILR Press, 1984), 75–80; Ware, *The Labor Movement,* 275–76; Stuart Kaufman, ed., *The Samuel Gompers Papers, Volume II: The Early Years of the American Federation of Labor, 1887–1890* (Urbana: University of Illinois Press, 1987), 18 (hereafter cited as SGP).

16. Ware, *The Labor Movement,* 181–84.

17. Ibid., 213–16; Aurand, *From the Molly Maguires to the United Mine Workers,* 115–45.

18. Ware , *The Labor Movement,* 214.

19. "Knights and Open Unions," "T. B. Barry's Views," undated clippings, TBS.

20. Kealey and Palmer, *Dreaming of What Might Be,* 120.

21. Ware repeated these charges, though he softened them. See Ware, *The Labor Movement,* 153–55. Bruce Laurie calls Powderly's actions "indecisive" and "nervous." See Laurie, *Artisans into Laborers,* 167, 170, 173. Richard Oestreicher says Powderly "betrayed" Barry during the strike. See Oestreicher, *Solidarity and Fragmentation,* 202. Carlotta Anderson calls Powderly "erratic" and his handling of the stockyards strike a "betrayal." See Anderson, *All-American Anarchist,* 134. Their comments are typical of observers' judgments of Powderly's handling of the strike.

22. *Knights of Labor* (Chicago), December 23, 1886.

23. Schneirov, *Labor and Urban Politics,* 193.

24. Ibid., 220; Wade, *Chicago's Pride,* chapter 14. Butler was correct to fear the eight-hour agreement was fragile. It applied only in Chicago, with packinghouses in locales such as Milwaukee, Omaha, Kansas City, and Omaha retaining a ten-hour schedule.

25. Wade, *Chicago's Pride,* 208–11.

26. Ibid., chapter 14.

27. Powderly, *The Path I Trod,* 145.

28. Wade, *Chicago's Pride,* 250.

29. This cable is contained in "Address of the General Master Workman," *Proceedings of the General Assembly of the Knights of Labor,* 1887, PP.

30. Ibid. It is interesting to speculate how those same "headstrong men" would have reacted to still another secret Barry plan under which they would have returned to work under an eight-hours scheme in which their wages would have been slashed by 10 percent.

31. Ibid.

32. More information on the Chicago packinghouse strikes can be found in Foner, *History of the Labor Movement,* 2: 86–88; Ware, *The Labor Movement,* 151–54; Powderly, *The Path I Trod,* 140–62; Oestreicher, *Solidarity*

and Fragmentation, 262–63; Schneirov, *Labor and Urban Politics,* 220–22, 250. See also *Proceedings of the General Assembly of the Knights of Labor,* 1887, PP; "Barry's Last Conference," "The Packers and the Strikers," "Officially Declared Off by Mr. T. B. Barry," "Powderly Not Responsible," "The Big Strike Is Over," undated clippings, TBS. The best secondary account of the strike is Wade, *Chicago's Pride.* Barry and Carlton were responsible for many strikers' losing their jobs. They waited several days before implementing the back-to-work order, and some one thousand workers were fired. Some of them lost their places to scabs.

33. Wade, *Chicago's Pride,* 254. When Gaunt's remarks surfaced again at the 1887 general assembly, an angry Barry denounced Gaunt as "the Powderly of the stockyards." See *Proceedings of the General Assembly of the Knights of Labor,* 1887, PP.

34. Schneirov, *Labor and Urban Politics,* 221. Schneirov notes that Griffiths was more inclined to blame George Schilling, whom he felt was a dangerous anarchist, than Barry.

35. Oestreicher, "The Limits of Labor Radicalism," unpublished paper.

36. Wade, *Chicago's Pride,* 251.

37. Powderly, *The Path I Trod,* 147–48.

38. *Proceedings of the General Assembly of the Knights of Labor,* 1887, PP. "The Big Strike Is Over," "Powderly Not Responsible," "Is There Any Punishment for Barry?" undated clippings, TBS. Michael Butler of DA 57 also found it convenient to blame Powderly, but it was Chicago's radical community that most despised him. Both George Schilling and Charles Seib opposed Powderly at the 1887 convention, and they were among Barry's ardent defenders.

39. For more on the carpet weavers, see Levine, *Labor's True Woman.* See also "The Knights at War, Mr. Barry Said," undated clippings, TBS.

40. Kaufman, *SGP,* 2:18, 339–40.

41. Powderly to Bailey, March 30 and 31, 1887, PP; Ware, *The Labor Movement,* 230; Aurand, *From the Molly Maguires to the United Mine Workers,* 120–24.

42. Powderly to Charles Litchman, July 29, 1887; "Why the General Officers Should Be Deposed," circular from DA 126 dated July 23, 1887, PP. For Bailey's early attacks on Morrison and District 126, see Bailey to Powderly, March 29, 1887, PP.

43. Bailey to Powderly, July 18, 1887; Powderly to Litchman, July 20, 1887, PP.

44. "Labor's Great Chance," undated clipping, TBS.

45. *Proceedings of the General Assembly of the Knights of Labor,* 1887, PP; Powderly, *Thirty Years of Labor,* 338–40; "An Investigation," "The Knights at War," "Messieurs Bailey and Barry," "Powderly's Enemies," "Powderly's Election," TBS.

46. "An Investigation," "The Knights at War," "Messieurs Bailey and Barry," "Powderly's Enemies," "Powderly's Enemies."TBS. Litchman conveniently avoided telling delegates that both Bailey and Barry had traveled more than other board members.

47. Thomas O'Reilly to Powderly, December 20, 1887, PP.

48. Powderly, *The Path I Trod,* 165; Powderly to John Hayes, February 7, 1888, PP.

49. For more on the strike, see Aurand, *From the Molly Maguires to the United Mine Workers,* 120–30.

50. *Office of the Provisional Committee of New York and Vicinity,* January 14, 1888, PP.

51. Bailey to Powderly, December 22, 1887, February 23 and 28, 1888; Hayes to Powderly, February 20, 1888; and Powderly to Bailey, February 23, 1888, all in PP.

52. *Labor Leader,* January 7, 1888; Powderly to Hayes, February 11, 1888.

53. Powderly to Hayes, June 29, 1888; Powderly to Bailey, July 8, 1888, PP.

54. "John Morrison, Decision of the General Master Workman," PP; "Only One Side Told," undated clipping, PP.

55. *East Saginaw Morning Herald,* August 31, 1888, TBS; "Hot Shot at Powderly," circular, PP.

56. Barry to Joseph Labadie, September 6 and 29, October 5, 1888, Joseph Labadie Collection, Department of Rare Books and Special Collections, University of Michigan Library, Ann Arbor (hereafter cited as JLC).

57. Hayes to Powderly, October 27, 1888, PP.

58. Barry to Labadie, October 5, 1888, JLC; "The Fight in the General Assembly," "The One-Armed Veteran Resigns from the Executive Board," undated clippings, TBS.

59. Hayes to Powderly, October 6, 1888, PP; "Barry's Hot Shot," October 11, 1888, TBS; *National Labor Tribune,* October 13 and 27, 1888; *Grand Rapids Times,* October 13, 1888; Thomas O'Reilly to Powderly, October 23, 1888, PP.

60. *JUL,* October 18, 1888.

61. "The Knights in Distress," November 14, 1888; "Before and Aft," November 20, 1888, TBS. Even Powderly's supporters took to calling the Order's headquarters in Philadelphia the "Palace of Poverty." A few even whispered that the Order was so far behind on the mortgage that it would torch the building and collect an insurance settlement.

62. "To the Honorable Body, Officers & Members of the General Assembly, K. of L. Minneapolis, Minn.," PP.

63. "An Account of How the Knights of Labor Made It the Concern of All to Injure One Because Rights of Man Advocated Free Thought, Free Speech, and a Free Press," pamphlet, PP. "Rights of Man" was a pen name Barry employed from time to time.

64. "The Knights in Distress," November 14, 1888, TBS; "To the Officers and Members of International District Assembly 154," PP; "Raked Fore and Aft," November 20, 1888, TBS; "Powderly Re-Elected," *The Critic,* November 24, 1888.

65. The rise of the UMWA is an often-told story for which many excellent accounts exist. Among others see Aurand, *From the Molly Maguires to the United Mine Workers;* Corbin, *Life, Work, and Rebellion in the Coal Fields.*

66. "Where Will Barry Speak," "Powderly Was Expected," "Barry's Big Bomb," undated clippings, TBS; "Boss Powderly Defied," December 24, 1888; "Away from the Knights," December 24, 1888; "Barry's New Order," January 8, 1889; "Barry Loses the Fight," January 8, 1889, all in TBS.
67. "Away from the Knights," December 24, 1888, TBS.
68. "Explanatory Circular to the Working People of America," TBS.
69. Barry to Labadie, February 5, 1889, JLC.
70. Barry to Labadie, February 25, 1889, JLC.
71. Barry to Labadie, May 24, 1889, JLC; "Powderly Arraigned By a Former Clerk in the General Office," October 18, 1889, TBS.
72. Barry to Labadie, 1907, JLC (exact month and day unknown).
73. One of the biggest complaints voiced among KOL officers was how to force locals and districts to submit to general executive board directives. This was especially the case in Chicago, where Powderly tried to use old friend Richard Griffiths to enforce discipline. He was often unsuccessful. District 24, for example, defied Powderly's directive not to take part in the May 1, 1886, strike for the eight-hour day. It also ignored his plea to rid the district of anarchist members and directly disobeyed his order not to take part in the clemency movement for the condemned Haymarket men. Not only did it raise thousands of dollars for their defense, the district's *Knights of Labor* journal published biographical sketches of each man.

    Both Bailey and Barry were well aware of DA 24's independence. Barry's subsequent complaint that Powderly and the board handcuffed his efforts in Chicago does not wash. Both he and Bailey had made their careers out of acting without board control.

Chapter Three

1. Turner and Killian, *Collective Behavior,* 253–56.
2. Powderly, *The Path I Trod,* 162.
3. Ibid., 161.
4. Buchanan, *Labor Agitator,* chapter 1.
5. Ibid., 47.
6. Ibid. See also G. Fink, *Biographical Dictionary.*
7. Buchanan, *Labor Agitator,* 52.
8. Ibid., 66.
9. Ware, *The Labor Movement,* 310; Foner, *History of the Labor Movement,* 2:34–36.
10. *Labor Enquirer,* September 29, 1883. Unless otherwise noted, all references to the *Labor Enquirer* refer to the Denver edition. Papers published in Chicago under the same name after 1887 will be so noted.
11. Buchanan, *Labor Agitator,* 78.
12. Ibid.; Ware, *The Labor Movement,* 136; Brundage, "The Producing Classes and the Saloon," 36.

13. Stromquist, *A Generation of Boomers,* 12.
14. Ibid., 67–68.
15. Buchanan, *Labor Agitator,* 106.
16. Ibid., 106–16.
17. Ibid., 129–32.
18. Ibid., 128.
19. Ibid.,127–213; Foner, *History of the Labor Movement,* Volume II, 250–53; Ware, *The Labor Movement,* 140–45.
20. Buchanan, *Labor Agitator,* 127–213, 251–52.
21. Ibid., 218.
22. Buchanan, *Labor Agitator,* 142–63; Foner, *History of the Labor Movement,* Volume II, 50–53; Ware, *The Labor Movement,* 140–45.
23. Buchanan, *Labor Agitator,* 253.
24. Buchanan to Powderly, June 21, 1887, PP. For more on Buchanan's temperance activities, see Brundage, "The Producing Classes and the Saloon."
25. Buchanan, *Labor Agitator,* 301.
26. Ibid., 301–2.
27. Ibid., 303.
28. J. Ryan to Powderly, May 5, 1886, PP.
29. Buchanan to Powderly, July 31, 1886, PP.
30. Powderly to Buchanan, August 13, 1886, PP.
31. Buchanan, *Labor Agitator,* 298. "Propaganda of the deed" was a common nineteenth-century expression for anarchists who espoused violence, as opposed to a peaceful evolution to anarchism. The latter course was often called "propaganda of the word."
32. *Labor Enquirer,* August 7, 1886.
33. Ware, *The Labor Movement,* 145–54.
34. "Report of Jos. R. Buchanan, Delegate to 10th General Assembly, K. of L.," PP.
35. Ibid.
36. Ibid.
37. Ibid.
38. Buchanan, *Labor Agitator,* 318.
39. Ibid., 361.
40. For Buchanan's charges concerning the stockyards strike, see *Labor Agitator,* 320–22. For more on Catholic/Protestant disputes, see Browne, "The Catholic Church and the Knights of Labor." For more on the Protestant/ Catholic tensions within the KOL, see Weir, *Beyond Labor's Veil,* 92–99. The roots of this tension stem from requests to alter the KOL's original ritual to remove an oath the Catholic church found objectionable. In addition, the Order's heavy concentration of Irish Americans exacerbated the problem.
41. Buchanan, *Labor Agitator,* 316–25.
42. Ibid., 316. In the interest of fairness it should be noted that Buchanan exaggerated Powderly's position. Powderly wanted the Order as a whole to remain officially nonpartisan, but he had fewer objections to Knights *as individuals* engaging in politics. He himself campaigned on Henry George's

behalf and spent election day in New York City traveling from precinct to precinct with George. In Powderly's view, the KOL as an organization should refrain from endorsements, a leftover sentiment from the Masonic principles upon which the Order was founded. Discussions of religion and politics were deemed disruptive of fraternal brotherhood and should be banned from assembly-hall discussion. Moreover, Powderly thought it unwise for the KOL to identify with a given political party as such affiliations both made the organization beholden to office seekers and invited reprisals of nonendorsed election winners.

43.   In 1888, Buchanan supported Henry George for president in his quixotic third-party run for the White House.

44.   For more on the electoral successes of the Knights of Labor, see L. Fink, *Workingmen's Democracy.*

45.   Brundage, "The Producing Classes and the Saloons."

46.   Nelson, *Beyond the Martyrs,* 213–14.

47.   *Labor Enquirer* (Chicago), March 25, 1887.

48.   Nelson, *Beyond the Martyrs,* 214.

49.   *Labor Enquirer* (Chicago), July 16, 1887.

50.   Neasham to Powderly, April 24, 1887, PP.

51.   Buchanan to Powderly, April 25, 1887, PP.

52.   *Labor Enquirer* (Chicago), May 7 and July 16, 1887; Litchman to Powderly, May 4, 1887, PP.

53.   *Labor Enquirer* (Chicago), May 7, 1887.

54.   This information comes from a collection of reports and documents titled "Concerning the Visit of G.M.W. Powderly to Denver," PP.

55.   Neasham to Powderly, May 22, 1887, PP.

56.   *Labor Enquirer* (Chicago), May 14 and 21, 1887.

57.   Buchanan to Powderly, June 11 and 21, 1887, PP.

58.   *Labor Enquirer* (Chicago), July 9 and 16, 1887.

59.   *Daily Review* (Milwaukee), July 21, 1887; *Labor Enquirer* (Chicago), October 29, 1887.

60.   Buchanan, *Labor Agitator,* 361–63.

61.   Ibid., 363.

62.   Ibid., 364.

63.   Ibid., 364–68.

64.   *Labor Enquirer* (Chicago and Denver), October 29, 1887.

65.   Griffiths to Powderly, November 22 and December 1, 1887; O'Reilly to Powderly, November 23, 1887, PP.

66.   For example, see *Labor Enquirer* (Chicago), December 10, 1887.

67.   Powderly, *Thirty Years of Labor,* 340.

68.   Avrich, *The Haymarket Tragedy,* 357–58, 369–70. Louis Lingg committed suicide on November 10, while Samuel Felden, Oscar Neebe, and Michael Schwab had their sentences commuted.

69.   *Labor Enquirer* (Chicago), December 3, 1887.

70.   Ibid., December 10, 1887.

71. Ibid., January 21 and February 18, 1888.
72. Ibid., May 5, June 2, and June 23, 1888.
73. Buchanan, *Labor Agitator,* 371–72.
74. Ibid., 437–38.
75. Foner, *History of the Labor Movement,* Volume II, 249
76. Buchanan, *Labor Agitator,* 442–48.
77. Ibid., 426–32. Richard Schneirov argues that Buchanan and the *Labor Enquirer* briefly provided Chicago's English-speaking socialists with a forum and a voice. This is doubtless true, but I am less inclined to see Buchanan's move to Chicago as positive. He made few inroads among non-English-speaking radicals for whom he was insufficiently doctrinaire, and he was too much of a broad reformer for even the English-speakers, who expelled him. See Schneirov, *Labor and Urban Politics,* 223–24, 244–46.
78. G. Fink, *Biographical Dictionary.*
79. Powderly to Buchanan, September 27, 1892, PP.
80. Powderly to Buchanan, December 1, 1892, PP.
81. Buchanan, *Labor Agitator,* 369–70.
82. Ibid., 439; Foner, *History of the Labor Movement,* Volume II, 245–46.
83. Buchanan, *Labor Agitator,* 434–37.
84. Kealey and Palmer, *Dreaming of What Might Be,* 273.
85. Foner, *History of the Labor Movement,* Volume II, 413.
86. Montgomery, *The Fall of the House of Labor,* 445; G. Fink, *Biographical Dictionary.*
87. Kealey and Palmer, *Dreaming of What Might Be,* 383.

Chapter Four

An earlier version of this chapter appears under the title "When Friends Fall Out: Charles Litchman and the Role of Personality in the Knights of Labor," in *Labor in Massachusetts: Selected Essays,* ed. Kenneth Fones-Wolf and Martin Kaufman (Westfield, MA: Institute for Massachusetts Studies, 1990). Thanks to Professors Fones-Wolf and Kaufman for their comments and suggestions.

1. Weber, *Essays in Sociology;* Weber, *The Theory of Social and Economic Organization.*
2. Parkinson, *Parkinson's Law.*
3. Peter and Hull, *The Peter Principle.*
4. Birdsall, "The Problem of Structure in the Knights of Labor," 532–46.
5. Weber, *Essays in Sociology.*
6. Van Tine, *The Making of a Labor Bureaucrat.*
7. Turner and Killian, *Collective Behavior.* See esp. 253 passim, 377–82.
8. A biographical sketch detailing Litchman's career to 1880 can be found in the *JUL,* June 1880.

9. Much of the KOL's early history is discussed in Ware, *The Labor Movement.* See also Powderly, *Thirty Years of Labor.*

10. Charles Kenyon to Powderly, April 7, 1881, PP.

11. *Proceedings of the Grand Assembly of the Knights of Labor,* Detroit, 1881.

12. Litchman's correspondence to Powderly is too voluminous to list. He knew he was in trouble by mid-1881 and kept up a steady stream of "Dear Terry" letters until the grand assembly convened. See PP.

13. Layton to Powderly, December 13 and 20, 1881, PP.

14. For examples, see Litchman to Powderly, March 10 and June 2, 1882, PP. Litchman first blamed "enemies" in 1880, when he was not nominated to run for reelection to the Massachusetts General Court. This became such a frequent tactic that it is difficult to know whether Litchman was mildly paranoid or just vain.

15. This photo is enclosed in the archive edition of the Powderly Papers housed at the Catholic University of America in Washington, D.C.

16. Powderly's suspicions had merit. Layton made no secret of his socialist sympathies or his fondness for Marxist-style trade unions.

17. Litchman to Powderly, March 13, 1882, PP. In the same letter Litchman also offered to serve in the prestigious but largely ceremonial post of grand worthy foreman if Richard Griffiths declined renomination.

18. Litchman to Powderly, June 5, 1882, PP.

19. Powderly to Litchman, August 16, 1882, PP.

20. *Proceedings of District Assembly 30,* 1882, PP.

21. Unfortunately, not many issues of the *Statesman* have yet come to light. The best known collection is owned by the Wisconsin Historical Society and is available in their labor papers collection.

22. For examples of allegations against Litchman's involvement in the *Statesman,* see Litchman to Powderly, December 7, 1885; *Labor Enquirer* (Chicago), September 29, 1887; *Labor Herald,* October 1, 1887.

23. *JUL,* June, 1880.

24. Ware, *The Labor Movement,* 358.

25. Powderly to Litchman, April 17, 1886, PP.

26. Litchman to Powderly, July 27, 1886, PP.

27. Hayes to Powderly, August 9, 1886, PP.

28. *Haverhill Laborer,* June 5, 1886; *Labor Leader,* July 30, 1887.

29. Hayes to Powderly, September 8, 1886, PP.

30. George McNeill to Powderly, November 25, 1886; Powderly to McNeill, December 29, 1886; Powderly to McNeill, April 12, May 26, and May 30, 1887, PP.

31. *Labor Leader,* July 23, 1887.

32. Powderly to Litchman, February 28, 1887, PP.

33. Litchman to Powderly, February 28, 1887, PP.

34. Powderly to Hayes, March 29, 1887, PP.

35. Powderly to Litchman, May 1, 1887, PP.

36. Powderly to Litchman, July 30, 1887, PP.

37. Litchman to Powderly, August 15, 1887; Powderly to Litchman, August 19, 1887, PP.

38. *Labor Herald and Tocsin,* October 1, 1887.

39. Litchman to Powderly, November 11, 1887, PP.

40. Litchman to Powderly, December 2, 1887, PP.

41. Powderly to Thomas O'Reilly, November 14, 1887, PP.

42. Litchman to Powderly, December 2, 1887, PP.

43. Litchman to Powderly, February 20, 1888, PP. Emphasis in original.

44. Powderly to Layton, April 12, 1888; Hayes to Powderly, April 27, 1888, PP.

45. Powderly to Rockwood, April 18, 1888, PP. Given the emphasis that the Knights put on the very concept of manhood, Powderly could not have chosen more provocative phrasing. For a longer discussion of manhood and the Knights, see Weir, *Beyond Labor's Veil,* esp. chapter 1.

46. Powderly to Litchman, July 15, 1888; Litchman to Powderly, July 19, 1888, PP. Litchman quoted from the July 19 letter.

47. Powderly to Litchman, July 15, 1888, PP.

48. Litchman to Powderly, July 19, 1888, PP.

49. Litchman to Powderly, August 25, 1888, PP.

50. Hayes to Powderly, September 9, 1888; O'Reilly to Powderly, September 10, 1888; Powderly to Hayes, September 12, 1888, PP.

51. A collection of comments from KOL journals was reprinted in the *Labor Leader,* September 15, 1888. See also *The Daily Review,* September 21, 1888.

52. Hayes to Powderly, September 14, 1888, PP.

53. Powderly to Litchman, October 26, 1888; Litchman to Powderly, November 1, 1888, PP.

54. Litchman to Powderly, February 2 and March 15, 1889; Powderly to Litchman, March 21, 1889, PP.

55. Unattributed clipping dated October 18, 1889, PP.

56. P. F. Derby to Powderly, August 29, 1892, PP.

57. Derby to Powderly, August 29, 1892, PP. There are also several unattributed clippings pertaining to Litchman's ouster found in Powderly's scrapbooks. These are located in the PP.

58. Litchman to Powderly, October 11 and 31, 1892, PP.

59. Van Tine, *The Making of a Labor Bureaucrat,* 144.

60. Thomas McGuire's obituary can be found in the *New York Times,* July 1, 1916.

61. Powderly's first wife, Hannah Drever, died in 1901. In 1919, he married Ms. Fickenscher. She survived him, and died in 1940.

Chapter Five

1. Garlock, "The Knights of Labor Courts," 18.

2. Ibid., 32.

3. Ibid., 20; McLaurin, *The Knights of Labor in the South,* 155.
4. Ware, *The Labor Movement,* 325–26.
5. Ibid., 320.
6. Curl, *History of Work Cooperation,* 7, 14.
7. Overviews of cooperative experiments can be found in Curl, *History of Work Cooperation.* Regional studies can be found in Edward Bemis et al, *Coöperation.* 2 vols. (1888; reprint, 2 vols. in 1, New York: Johnson Reprint Corporation, 1973).
8. By the time Henry Sharpe took over KOL cooperative efforts he could look back at plenty of examples in which individualist impulses undermined collective efforts. Brook Farm communities were a casualty of this.
9. Powderly, *Thirty Years of Labor,* 233.
10. Ware, *The Labor Movement,* 323.
11. Quoted in McNeill, *The Labor Movement,* 411.
12. Ware, *The Labor Movement,* 120–21; Powderly, *Thirty Years of Labor,* 236.
13. *Proceedings of the Grand Assembly of the Knights of Labor,* 1881; Ware, *The Labor Movement,* 120–23; Grob, *Workers and Utopia,* 44–48.
14. Ware, *The Labor Movement,* 120–23.
15. Ibid., 326–27. Sharpe's cooperation column ran regularly in the *JUL* in 1884.
16. Grob, *Workers and Utopia,* 45.
17. Perlman, *A History of Trade Unionism,* 125.
18. *JUL,* July 25, 1884; Ware, *The Labor Movement,* 329–33.
19. *JUL,* September 25, 1884. Also included on the board were Peter Cattanoch of Troy, New York; Hugh Cameron of Lawrence, Kansas; Henry Meant of Ithaca, New York; and O. M. Boyer of Louisville, Kentucky. Boyer was the only holdover from Sharpe's tenure. Only Cameron represented rural concerns.
20. Marx and McAdam, *Collective Behavior and Social Movements,* 32.
21. Ibid., 33–34.
22. Sharpe to Powderly, September 10 and 20, 1884, PP.
23. Sharpe to Powderly, November 19 and December 30, 1884, PP; *New York World,* June 2, 1886.
24. Turner to Powderly, January 15, 1885, PP.
25. Sharpe to Turner, February 27, 1885, PP.
26. Sharpe to Powderly, March 6, 1885, PP.
27. Rockwood to Powderly, March 22, 1885, PP.
28. Sharpe to Powderly, June 9, 1885, PP.
29. *JUL,* June 19, 1885.
30. Powderly to Turner, June 26, 1885. See also Powderly to Barry and Caville, June 18, 1885; and Powderly to Sharpe, June 18 and 25, 1885, PP.
31. Rockwood to Powderly, June 24, 1885, PP.
32. Powderly to Sharpe, June 28, 1885, PP.
33. Sharpe to Powderly, June 26, 1885, PP.
34. Sharpe to Powderly, June 25, 26, and 27 (two letters), 1885, PP.

35. Powderly to Sharpe, July 7, 1885; Powderly to Rockwood, July 10, 1885, PP.

36. Sharpe to Powderly, September 27, 1885; Rockwood to Powderly, October 7, 1885, PP.

37. Perlman, *A History of Trade Unionism,* 126.

38. Ware, *The Labor Movement,* 329–33.

39. Perlman, *A History of Trade Unionism,* 126.

40. Bemis, *Coöperation;* Kealey and Palmer, *Dreaming of What Might Be.*

41. McLaurin, *The Knights of Labor in the South.*

42. Kealey and Palmer, *Dreaming of What Might Be.*

43. Bemis, *Coöperation,* 88–89, 326.

44. Ibid., 402–5.

45. Ibid., 162–67.

46. Powderly, *Thirty Years of Labor,* 238.

47. *John Swinton's Paper,* September 21, 1884. Like many KOL songs, Brophy's verses were more topical than poetic. Verse two reads: "My mother's maiden name was Toil / My sister's name is Slavery / And though I never share the spoil / I'm famed in war for bravery." John Donnelly Brophy should not be confused with the John Brophy who was a key official in the United Mine Workers and the Congress of Industrial Organizations. The latter was not born until 1883. I was unable to determine whether the two Brophys were related.

48. Brophy, "Equality among Men."

49. *JUL,* April 25, 1885. This information was printed a year later as a summary of events in Troy.

50. *John Swinton's Paper,* June 4, 8, and 15, July 13, and August 24, 1884.

51. *John Swinton's Paper,* February 1 and 22, 1885.

52. *JUL,* July 10 and November 25, 1885.

53. *John Swinton's Paper,* July 5, 1885; *JUL,* July 10, 1885.

54. Ibid.

55. *JUL,* August 23, 1885.

56. *JUL,* March 10, 1886. For material predating the victories, see *John Swinton's Paper,* February 14 and 28, 1886. For another report on the strikes, see *John Swinton's Paper,* March 14, 1886.

57. The five were: J. R. Mansion, Peter Cattanoch, Joseph Hogan, John Hickey, and Edward O'Brien.

58. *JUL,* September 10, 1886; *John Swinton's Paper,* October 31 and November 10, 1886.

59. Brophy, "Equality among Men," 1, 14.

60. Ibid., 2.

61. Ibid., 3–4.

62. Ibid., 8.

63. Ibid., 9.

64. Ibid., 10. Emphasis in original.

65. Ibid., 10–12.

66. Ibid., 15.
67. Ibid., 14.
68. Garlock, *Guide to Local Assemblies of the Knights of Labor.*
69. Kealey and Palmer, *Dreaming of What Might Be,* chapter 5. Dudden, "Small Town Knights," 307–27. Dudden does note tension between large employers and the Knights, but sees cooperation between small shopkeepers and the Order.
70. For a discussion of employers in KOL ranks, see Kealey and Palmer, *Dreaming of What Might Be;* Oestreicher, *Solidarity and Fragmentation;* L. Fink, *Workingmen's Democracy.*
71. Thomas Hines, "The Anarchist's Conspiracy, or The Blight of 3770: True History of Daniel Hines as a Knight of Labor," 7, 9. Booklet owned by the Wisconsin Historical Society.
72. Ibid., 16–18.
73. Ibid., 20–21.
74. Ibid., 45–46.
75. Ibid., 56–58.
76. Ibid., 61–65.
77. Ibid., 67.
78. Ibid., 69.
79. Ibid., 82–88.
80. For examples of local disputes, see L. Fink, *Workingmen's Democracy;* Kealey and Palmer, *Dreaming of What Might Be;* McLaurin, *The Knights of Labor in the South;* Oestreicher, *Solidarity and Fragmentation;* Voss, *The Making of American Exceptionalism.* Another instructive exercise is to peruse incoming correspondence in the Powderly Papers. Powderly was inundated by disputes whose substance was no greater than that of the Hines matter.
81. For more on the structural deficiencies of the Knights of Labor, see Birdsall, "The Problem of Structure in the Knights of Labor," 532–46.
82. For more on the battle over fraternalism, see Weir, *Beyond Labor's Veil,* esp. chapter 1.
83. Tilly, "Social Movements Old and New," 1–18.
84. Marx and McAdam, *Collective Behavior and Social Movements,* 32.
85. Garlock, "The Knights of Labor Courts," 21–27.
86. Students for a Democratic Society is often evoked by sociologists as a model for organizations that grew, but did not manage growth, ideological differences, or bureaucratic exigencies. Frederick Miller has studied the group. A concise summary of his work is found in Macionis, *Sociology,* 623–25. William Gamson highlights other groups for which these factors have been divisive in his *Strategy of Social Protest.*

Chapter Six

1. Alzina Stevens to Powderly, February 3, 1991, PP.
2. Ibid. Charlotte Smith's article was attached to Alzina Stevens's letter to Powderly.

3. Marge Piercy, "The Grand Coolie Damn," in *Sisterhood Is Powerful*, ed. Morgan, 473, 475.
4. Goldman, *Living My Life*, 1:53–54, 105–6, 151–54. In the first two sections Goldman reveals that Johann Most was a sexual predator and that he often belittled the views of women, a tendency that led Goldman to horsewhip him. She also tells of her relationship with anarchist Ed Brady, who held conventional views about women and wanted Goldman to become a dutiful housewife and mother. See also Flynn, *The Rebel Girl*, esp. the section titled "Woman's Place," 55–58.
5. Quoted in Baxandall and Gordon, *America's Working Women*, 162–64.
6. Quoted in ibid., 164.
7. For example, see Sarah Rozner's antisexism letter directed to the CIO in Baxandall and Gordon, *America's Working Women*, 216–19. In 1955, Emma Murphy angrily told UAW convention delegates to stop paying "lip service to the women in industry" by passing hollow resolutions unsupported by action. For her comments, see Lerner, *The Female Experience*, 312. The convention debate on women is found on 309–16.
8. The KOL's preamble and principles can be found in most issues of its official journal, the *Journal of United Labor*. In addition, numerous local and allied newspapers frequently printed these.
9. For more on the association between male ideals and fraternalism, see Carnes, *Secret Ritual and Manhood in Victorian America;* Clawson, *Constructing Brotherhood;* Weir, *Beyond Labor's Veil*.
10. Flexner, *Century of Struggle*, 193.
11. *Proceedings of the Grand Assembly of the Knights of Labor,* 1881, PP.
12. Foner, *Women and the American Labor Movement*, 185.
13. George Bennie to Powderly, January 24, 1887, PP. Also quoted in Levine, *Labor's True Woman*, 111.
14. Levine, *Labor's True Woman*, 132.
15. *JUL*, July 5, 1888.
16. For a superb look at women's work cultures in American labor history, see the wonderful collection of essays in Baron, *Work Engendered*.
17. Biographical sketches of Leonora Barry can be found in *The Irish World and Industrial Liberator,* April 7, 1888, and in the Leonora Barry folder housed in the American Reformers section of the Sophia Smith Collection, Smith College, Northampton, Massachusetts.
18. Powderly to Barry, June 2, 1886, PP.
19. *Proceedings of the General Assembly of the Knights of Labor,* 1886.
20. *JUL*, December 25, 1886.
21. For another look at the differences between men's and women's experiences at home and work in the Gilded Age, see Smith-Rosenberg, *Disorderly Conduct*.
22. Flexner, *Century of Struggle*.
23. Kealey and Palmer, *Dreaming of What Might Be*, 143–44; Weir, *Beyond Labor's Veil*, 51–55.

24.	*Labor Enquirer,* February 10, 1883; Buhle, "The Knights of Labor in Rhode Island," 29–52; Levine, *Labor's True Woman;* Weir, *Beyond Labor's Veil.*

25.	Barry to Powderly, December 31, 1886, PP.

26.	Levine, *Labor's True Woman,* 117.

27.	Wertheimer, *We Were There,* 187.

28.	*Report of the General Investigator for Woman's Work,* 1887. Barry's reports are located in the Powderly Papers. They can also be found in the Barry folder in the Sophia Smith Collection.

29.	Ibid.

30.	*JUL,* April 16, 1887.

31.	*Report of the General Investigator for Woman's Work,* 1887.

32.	Phily Sallon to Powderly, December 19, 1886; Barry to Powderly, July 26, 1887, PP.

33.	*JUL,* February 5, 1887.

34.	*Report of the General Investigator for Woman's Work,* 1887.

35.	*JUL,* February 5, 1887, quoted from Wertheimer, *We Were There,* 188.

36.	Barry to Powderly, July 26, 1887; Powderly to Barry, July 29, 1887, PP.

37.	*Report of the General Investigator for Woman's Work,* 1888.

38.	*JUL,* December 31, 1887.

39.	Powderly to Barry, May 21 and June 25, 1887, PP.

40.	Frances Willard to Powderly, September 2, 1887, PP.

41.	*Report of the General Investigator for Woman's Work,* 1888.

42.	Ibid. Note that Barry used the singular noun "woman's" to refer to her department, not the collective term "women's." The KOL was inconsistent on this score. Both terms appear in official documents. For the sake of current convention I use the collective noun, except when direct quotations are involved.

43.	Powderly to Barry, February 15 and 17, 1888, PP.

44.	Powderly to Barry, March 7, 21, and 23, 1888. For Powderly's own struggles with Catholic clerics, see his autobiography *The Path I Trod,* chapter xxvii.

45.	Powderly to Barry, September 28, 1888, PP.

46.	Powderly to O'Reilly, December 11, 1888, PP.

47.	Powderly to Barry, December 27, 1888, PP.

48.	Powderly to Hayes, December 27, 1888, PP.

49.	*JUL,* January 3, 1889.

50.	Particularly bleak letters were printed on February 18, March 21, and March 28, 1889.

51.	Powderly to Barry, June 14, 1889, PP.

52.	Hayes to Powderly, September 24, 1889, PP. Emphasis in original.

53.	Powderly to Barry, September 25, 1889, PP.

54.	Hayes to Powderly, October 26, 1889, PP. Emphasis in original.

55.	*Report of the General Investigator for Woman's Work,* 1889; *Proceedings of the General Assembly of the Knights of Labor,* 1889.

56.	*Report of the General Investigator for Woman's Work,* 1889; *Proceedings of the General Assembly of the Knights of Labor,* 1889.

57. *Report of the General Investigator for Woman's Work,* 1889; *Proceedings of the General Assembly of the Knights of Labor,* 1889.
58. Hayes to Powderly, February 26, 1890, PP.
59. Powderly to O. B. Lake, April 17, 1890, PP.
60. Barry-Lake's letter was read before the 1890 general assembly and can be found in *Proceedings of the General Assembly of the Knights of Labor,* 1890.
61. This information is gleaned from an obituary in the Leonora Barry file located in the Sophia Smith Collection.
62. Albert Carlton to Powderly, August 11, 1885; C. Haas to Powderly, April 1, 1886, PP.
63. Powderly to Litchman, April 27, 1887, PP.
64. A. W. Wright to Powderly, December 5, 1892, February 14, and 19, 1893; Thomas O'Reilly to Powderly, December 7, 1892, May 15, and July 29, 1893, PP. According to Wright, Hayes bragged to Eiler of his "money-making schemes." Charges of misappropriation of funds were frequent under Hayes's tenure at the helm of the KOL treasury. My research suggests that the charges were accurate, but Hayes was far more skillful than the woeful Charles Litchman in covering his financial trail and no charges against Hayes were ever substantiated.
65. Many of the more outrageous charges against Hayes came during his battles with Powderly before the latter's 1893 ouster. In fairness to Annie Traphagen, I have not found conclusive evidence that she was indeed Hayes's mistress.
66. *Baltimore Sun,* April 7, 1891. For the record, Weir is no known ancestor of mine.
67. Hayes to Linda Slaughter, May 5, 1890, August 7, 1891, April 15, 1892, and May 8, 1893, PP.
68. For Mary "Mother" Jones's views, see her *Autobiography.*
69. Milkman, *Women, Work & Protest,* xi.
70. Kessler-Harris, *Out to Work,* 315–17, 298.
71. The full document can be viewed on CLUW's superb website: http://www.cluw.org/about/mission.htm.

Chapter Seven

1. Friedman, "Worker Opposition Movements," 133–70.
2. Phelan, "Terence Powderly."
3. Ware, *The Labor Movement,* xvi.
4. Foner, *History of the Labor Movement in the United States,* 2:169.
5. Grob, *Workers and Utopia,* 120.
6. Kealey and Palmer, *Dreaming of What Might Be.*
7. Laurie, *Artisans into Workers,* see chapters 5, 6. Quote from p. 183.
8. Voss, *The Making of American Exceptionalism,* 239.

9. Richard Oestreicher, "Terence Powderly, the Knights of Labor, and Artisanal Republicanism," in *Labor Leaders in America,* ed. Dubofsky and Van Tine, 59.

10. Phelan, "Terence Powderly."

11. Quoted in Gamson, *The Strategy of Social Protest,* 41.

12. Gamson, *The Strategy of Social Protest,* 12.

13. No official membership figures were reported for 1891 or 1892. Membership was probably between 55,000 and 60,000 in 1892. There were nearly 75,000 dues-paying Knights in 1893. Even that figure may be lower than those actually identifying themselves with the KOL. By 1893, the Knights' strength had shifted to rural America. There, the KOL was so thoroughly fused with Populism that it was not always easy to distinguish between the two. There is no extensive study of the Knights after the New York Central strike of 1890.

14. Oestreicher, "Terence Powderly."

15. Powderly to Beaumont, April 14, 1890; Powderly to Hayes, April 20, 1890, PP.

16. Untitled document pertaining to the governor is located in PP. Joseph R. Mansion is the same individual who dogged J. Donnelly Brophy. See chapter 5 of this work.

17. *National Labor Tribune,* January 25, 1890.

18. Powderly's critics were probably correct in this allegation. Senator Quay later nominated Powderly for the post of commissioner general for immigration. See Powderly, *The Path I Trod,* 298.

19. *JKL,* September 10, 1891; Powderly, *The Path I Trod,* 241–42.

20. For more on the New York Central strike, see Weir, "Dress Rehearsal for Pullman," 21–42.

21. *Philadelphia Times,* January 19, 1891; *Philadelphia Record,* January 19, 1891. Clippings located in PP.

22. Powderly to the General Executive Board, February 20, 1892, PP.

23. Powderly, *The Path I Trod,* 235–60.

24. Ibid., 255.

25. Ibid., 261.

26. Hayes to Powderly, July 25, 1892, PP.

27. Powderly to Hayes, July 25, 1892, PP.

28. Powderly to Hayes, July 21, 1892, PP.

29. Powderly to Hayes, September 11, 1892, PP.

30. Powderly to Hayes, September 20, 1892, PP.

31. Devlin to Powderly, October 1, 1892, PP.

32. Devlin to Powderly, October 19, 1892, PP.

33. Hayes to Powderly, December 2, 1892; O'Reilly to Powderly, December 2, 1892, PP.

34. O'Reilly to Powderly, January 9, 1892; Undated clipping from the *New York World* filed on August 21, 1892, PP.

35. Powderly to Hayes, November 3, 1892, PP.

36. Powderly to O'Reilly, December 8, 1892, PP.
37. Powderly to Hayes, December 26, 1892, PP. The Philosopher's Stone degree was a relic from the KOL's pre-1882 secret period in which it was as much a ritual-bound fraternal organization as a labor union. The Knights abandoned the specialized Philosopher's Stone degree as inconsistent with its rhetoric on equality. But the more KOL ritual declined, the louder the clamor among some Knights to revitalize it. As the Knights grew desperate in the 1890s, renewed emphasis on ritual was seen as a "reform." These matters are discussed in greater detail in Weir, *Beyond Labor's Veil,* chapter 1.
38. Powderly to Wright, January 6, 1893, PP.
39. Powderly to Hayes, May 10, 1893, PP.
40. Powderly to O'Reilly, May 14, 1893, PP.
41. Powderly to O'Reilly, June 13, 1893, PP.
42. Powderly to Wright, June 14, 1893, PP.
43. Powderly to Hayes, July 10, 1893, PP.
44. O'Reilly to Powderly, July 27, 1893, PP.
45. O'Keefe to Powderly, September 12, 1893; Cavanaugh to Powderly, August 9, 1893, PP.
46. O'Reilly to Powderly, September 1, 1893, PP. Apparently, Hayes received some of his damaging information from none other than Thomas Barry.
47. Hayes to Maggie Eiler, January 1893, PP.
48. Ibid.
49. Ibid. Among other investments Hayes spoke of a six-figure railroad stock scheme.
50. Ibid.
51. Powderly to O'Reilly, September 14, 1893, PP.
52. Kealey and Palmer, *Dreaming of What Might Be,* 268–71.
53. A copy of the 1893 *Labor Day Annual* is housed at the Wisconsin Historical Society in Madison.
54. O'Reilly to Powderly, July 20, 22, 27, and 29, 1893; Powderly to O'Reilly, July 11, 18, and 20, 1893, PP.
55. Details of Hayes's charges can be found in the *Proceedings of the General Assembly of the Knights of Labor,* 1893. Also see A. W. Wright's *Report to D.A. 125,* and an unnamed document written by Powderly in which he defends himself against the charges. All documents are located in PP.
56. Powderly, *The Path I Trod,* 262; *Proceedings of the General Assembly of the Knights of Labor,* 1893.
57. *Proceedings of the General Assembly of the Knights of Labor,* 1893.
58. For examples of press coverage, see the *Labor Leader,* November 25, 1893, and the *Brooklyn Citizen,* December 3, 1893. Clippings are located in PP.
59. Powderly to O'Reilly, December 6, 1893, PP.
60. Powderly to O'Reilly, December 15, 1893, PP.
61. Ibid.; Powderly to Wright, December 16, 1893, PP.
62. Powderly to Buchanan, December 20, 1893, PP.
63. *Proceedings of the General Assembly of the Knights of Labor,* 1894.

64. Powderly to Hugh Greenan, February 3 and March 9 (?), 1894, PP. The date on the latter letter is smudged.
65. Powderly to F. W. Wiltbank, April 14, 1894, PP.
66. *Scranton Republican,* April 2, 1894.
67. Kealey and Palmer, *Dreaming of What Might Be,* 272. There are also cryptic references in Powderly's personal correspondence that suggest some individuals were discussing a merger between the American Railway Union, pro-Powderly Knights of Labor, and several renegade AFL constituent unions.
68. Powderly, *The Path I Trod,* 286–87.
69. For more on lawyers in the KOL, see Weir, *Beyond Labor's Veil,* 219–20.
70. Powderly, *The Path I Trod,* chapter 25.
71. Powderly to Cavanaugh, September 21, 1894, PP. The "one-winged saint" refers to the fact that Hayes had lost the use of his right arm in a railway accident in 1878.
72. Unaddressed, undated letter in PP.
73. *JKL,* November 8, 1894; *Proceedings of the General Assembly of the Knights of Labor,* 1894.
74. Foner, *History of the Labor Movement,* 2:292–96.
75. See Powderly, *The Path I Trod,* pp. vii–xii.

Select Bibliography

Primary Sources: Knights of Labor Manuscripts and Published Materials

Adelphon Kruptos. Microfilm editions, University of Massachusetts, Amherst.

Barry, Thomas. Thomas Barry Scrapbook. Joseph A. Labadie Collection, Harlan Library Special Collections, University of Michigan, Ann Arbor.

Brophy, J. Donnelly. "Equality among Men: As She Works North of the Mason-Dixon Line, Not Far from District 49." Pamphlet housed at the Wisconsin Historical Society, Madison.

Buchanan, Joseph R. *The Story of a Labor Agitator.* 1903. Reprint, Freeport: Books for Libraries, 1971.

Drury, Victor S. Papers. In Papers of the Women's Trade Union League and Its Principal Leaders: Leonora O'Reilly. Special Collections, Schlesinger Library, Radcliffe College.

———. *The Polity of the Labor Movement, Vol. I: A Synopsis.* Philadelphia: Frederick Turner, 1885.

Hayes, John W. Papers. Microfilm. University of Massachusetts, Amherst.

Hines, Thomas. "The Anarchist's Conspiracy, or, The Blight of 3770: True History of Daniel Hines as a Knight of Labor." Booklet, Wisconsin Historical Society, Madison.

Knights of Labor. *Labor: Its Rights and Wrongs.* Washington, DC: Knights of Labor, 1886.

Knights of Labor. *Labor Day Annual.* Philadelphia: Knights of Labor, 1893. Housed at Wisconsin Historical Society, Madison.

McNeill, George C. *The Labor Movement: The Problem of To-Day.* New York: Augustus M. Kelley, 1887.

Powderly, Terence V. Papers. Catholic University of America, Washington, D.C. Microfilm edition, University of Massachusetts, Amherst.

———. *Thirty Years of Labor, 1859–1889.* 1889. Reprint, New York: Augustus M. Kelley, 1967.

———. *The Path I Trod: The Autobiography of Terence V. Powderly.* Ed. Harry
     Carman, Henry David, and Paul Guthrie. 1940. Reprint, New York: AMS
     Press, 1968.
Wright, Carroll. "An Historical Sketch of the Knights of Labor." *Quarterly Journal
     of Economics* (January 1887): 137–68.

Knights of Labor Journals, Newspapers (includes affiliated papers)

Advance and Labor Leaf. Detroit, 1884–89
The Boycotter. New York, 1886–87
The Critic. Baltimore, 1888–93
The Daily Review. Milwaukee, 1887–89
The Industrial Leader. Dubuque, Iowa, 1885–89
The Industrial West. Atlantic, Iowa, 1882–87
Irish World and American Industrial Liberator. New York, 1882–95
John Swinton's Paper. New York, 1883–87
Journal of the Knights of Labor. Philadelphia, Washington, 1889–1901
Journal of United Labor. Haverhill, MA, Philadelphia, 1880–89
Knights of Labor. Chicago, 1886–89
Knights of Labor. Lynn, MA, 1885–86
Labor Enquirer. Chicago, 1887–88
Labor Enquirer. Denver, 1883–87
Labor Herald and Tocsin. Philadelphia, 1887–88
The Labor Leader. Boston, 1887–97
The Laborer. Boston, 1886–87
The Laborer. Haverhill, MA, 1884–87
National Labor Tribune. Pittsburgh, 1870–90
The People. New York, 1891–96
Solidarity. New York, 1892
Toledo Industrial News. 1887–88

Primary Source Materials Not Specifically Related
to the Knights of Labor

American Federation of Labor Records. Microfilm edition. University of Massa-
     chusetts, Amherst.
The Baltimore Sun. 1891.
Bellamy, Edward. *Looking Backward: 2000–1887.* 1888. Reprint, New York: Sig-
     net, 1960.
Ely, Richard T. *The Labor Movement.* New York: Thomas Y. Crowell, 1886.
Garraty, John, ed. *Labor and Capital in the Gilded Age: Testimony Taken by the
     Senate Committee upon Relations Between Capital and Labor.* Boston: Little,
     Brown and Company, 1968.

Jones, Mary. *The Autobiography of Mother Jones.* 1925. Reprint, Chicago: Charles H. Kerr, 1980.
Kaufman, Stuart, ed. *The Samuel Gompers Papers, Volume I: The Making of a Union Leader.* Urbana: University of Illinois Press, 1986.
———. *The Samuel Gompers Papers, Volume II: The Early Years of the American Federation of Labor, 1887–1890* Urbana: University of Illinois Press, 1987.
Montgomery Advertiser. 1886
The New York Freeman. 1886
New York Herald. 1882
New York Times. 1884–95, 1916
New York World. 1890–94
Philadelphia Record. 1891
Philadelphia Times. 1891
The Socialist. 1876
The Union Printer. 1887
The Weekly People. 1891–94

Secondary Works Relating Substantially to the Knights of Labor

Anderson, Carlotta. *All-American Anarchist: Joseph Labadie and the Labor Movement.* Detroit: Wayne State University Press, 1998.
Bemis, Edward W., Albert Shaw, Daniel Randall, Charles Shinn, and Amos Warner. *Coöperation.* 2 vols. 1888. Reprint, (2 vols. in 1), New York: Johnson Reprint Corporation, 1973.
Birdsall, William C. "The Problem of Structure in the Knights of Labor." *Industrial and Labor Relations Review* 6 (July 1953): 532–46.
Browne, Henry. "The Catholic Church and the Knights of Labor." Ph.D. diss., Catholic University of America, 1949.
Brundage, David. *The Making of Western Labor Radicalism: Denver's Organized Workers, 1878–1905.* Urbana: University of Illinois Press, 1994.
———. "The Producing Classes and the Saloon: Denver in the 1880s." *Labor History* 26 (Winter 1985): 29–52.
Buhle, Paul. "The Knights of Labor in Rhode Island." *Radical History Review* 17 (Spring 1978): 39–73.
Cassity, Michael J. "Modernization and Social Crisis: The Knights of Labor and a Midwest Community, 1885–1886." *Journal of American History* 66 (June 1979): 41–61.
Dudden, Faye. "Small Town Knights: The Knights of Labor in Homer, New York." *Labor History* 28 (Summer 1997): 307–27.
Fink, Leon. *Workingmen's Democracy: The Knights of Labor and American Politics.* Urbana: University of Illinois Press, 1983.
Fones-Wolf, Elizabeth, and Kenneth Fones-Wolf. "Knights versus Trade Unionists: The Case of the Washington, D.C. Carpenters, 1881–1886." *Labor History* 22 (Spring 1981): 192–212.

Gabler, Edward. *The American Telegrapher: A Social History, 1860–1900.* New Brunswick, NJ: Rutgers University Press, 1988.

Garlock, Jonathan. *Guide to Local Assemblies of the Knights of Labor.* Westport, CT: Greenwood, 1982.

———. "The Knights of Labor Courts: A Study of Popular Justice." In *The Politics of Informal Justice Volume I,* ed. Richard Abel. New York: Academic Press, 1982, 17–33.

Goldberg, Judith L. "Strikes, Organizing and Change: The Knights of Labor in Philadelphia, 1869–1890." Ph.D. diss., New York University, 1985.

Kealey, George S., and Bryan D. Palmer. *Dreaming of What Might Be: The Knights of Labor in Ontario, 1880–1890.* Toronto: New Hogtown Press, 1987.

Kessler, Sidney. "The Organization of Negroes in the Knights of Labor." *Journal of Negro History* 37 (1952): 248–76.

Landon, Fred. "The Knights of Labor: Predecessors of the C. I. O." *Quarterly Review of Commerce* (Summer–Autumn 1937): 133–39.

Levine, Susan B. *Labor's True Woman: Carpet Weavers, Industrialization, and Labor Reform in the Gilded Age.* Philadelphia: Temple University Press, 1984.

McLaurin, Melton. *The Knights of Labor in the South.* Westport, CT: Greenwood, 1977.

———. "The Racial Policies of the Knights of Labor and the Organization of Southern Black Workers." *Labor History* 17 (Fall 1976): 568–85.

Oestreicher, Richard. "The Limits of Labor Radicalism: Tom Barry and the Knights of Labor." Unpublished paper.

———. *Solidarity and Fragmentation: Working People and Consciousness in Detroit, 1875–1900.* Urbana: University of Illinois Press, 1986.

Palmer, Bryan. *A Culture in Conflict: Skilled Workers and Industrial Capitalism in Hamilton, Ontario, 1867–1917.* Montreal: McGill University Press, 1979.

Phelan, Craig. "Terence Powderly and the Great Upheaval." Unpublished paper delivered at the North American Labor History Conference, Detroit, 1998.

———. "The Warp of Fancy: The Knights of Labor and the Takeover Myth." *Labor History* 40:3 (August 1999): 283–300.

———. *Grand Master Workman: Terence Powderly and the Knights of Labor.* Westport, CT: Greenwood, 2000.

Rachleff, Peter J. *Black Labor in the South: Richmond, Virginia, 1865–1890.* Philadelphia: Temple University Press, 1984.

Stromquist, Shelton. *A Generation of Boomers: The Pattern of Railroad-Labor Conflict in Nineteenth-Century America.* Urbana: University of Illinois Press, 1987.

Voss, Kim. *The Making of American Exceptionalism: The Knights of Labor and Class Formation in the Nineteenth Century.* Ithaca, NY: Cornell University Press, 1993.

Ware, Norman J. *The Labor Movement in the United States, 1860–1895: A Study in Democracy.* 1929. Reprint, Gloucester, MA: Peter Smith, 1959.

Weir, Robert E. *Beyond Labor's Veil: The Culture of the Knights of Labor.* University Park: Pennsylvania State University Press, 1996.

———. "Dress Rehearsal for Pullman: The Knights of Labor and the New York Central Strike." In *The Pullman Strike and the Crisis of the 1890s: Essays on Labor and Politics,* ed. Richard Schneirov, Shelton Stromquist, and Nick Salvatore. Urbana: University of Illinois Press, 1999.

———. "Here's to the Men Who Lose: The Hidden Career of Victor Drury." *Labor History* 36:4 (Fall 1995): 530–56.

———. "Tilting at Windmills: Powderly and the Home Club." *Labor History* 34 (Winter 1993): 84–113.

———. "When Friends Fall Out: Charles Litchman and the Knights of Labor." In *Labor in Massachusetts: Selected Essays,* ed. Kenneth Fones-Wolf and Martin Kaufman. Westfield, MA: Institute of Massachusetts Studies, 1990.

Selected Secondary Sources Pertaining to the Gilded Age

Aurand, Harold. *From the Molly Maguires to the United Mine Workers: The Social Ecology of an Industrial Union, 1869–1897.* Philadelphia: Temple University Press, 1971.

Avrich, Paul. *The Haymarket Tragedy.* Princeton: Princeton University Press, 1984.

Barth, Gunther. *City People: The Rise of Modern City Culture in Nineteenth-Century America.* Oxford: Oxford University Press, 1980.

Bettmann, *The Good Old Days—They Were Terrible!* New York: Random House, 1974.

Buhle, Mari Jo. *Women and American Socialism, 1870–1920.* Urbana: University of Illinois Press, 1983.

Buhle, Paul, Scott Molly, and Gail Sansbury, *A History of Rhode Island Working People.* Providence, RI: Regini Printing Company, 1983.

Commons, John R., D.J Saposs, H.L. Sumner, E.B. Mittelman, H.E. Hoagland, J.B.Andrews, and S. Perlman, eds., *History of Labour in the United States.* New York: Augustus M. Kelley, 1966.

Corbin, David, *Life, Work, and Rebellion in the Coal Fields: The Southern West Virginia Miners, 1880–1922.* Urbana: University of Illinois Press, 1981.

Curl, John. *History of Work Cooperation in the United States.* Berkeley: Homeward Press, 1980.

Dubofsky, Melvyn, and Warren Van Tine, eds. *Labor Leaders in America.* Urbana: University of Illinois Press, 1987.

Flexner, Eleanor. *A Century of Struggle: The Woman's Movement in the United States.* New York: Atheneum, 1974.

Foner, Eric. *Politics and Ideology in the Age of the Civil War.* New York: Oxford University Press, 1980.

Foner, Philip S. *American Socialism and Black Americans: From the Age of Jackson to World War II.* Westport, CT: Greenwood, 1977.

———. *History of the Labor Movement in the United States, Volume I: From Colonial Times to the Founding of the American Federation of Labor.* 1947. Reprint, New York: International Publishers, 1982.

————. *History of the Labor Movement in the United States, Volume II: From the Founding of the American Federation of Labor to the Emergence of American Imperialism.* New York: International Publishers, 1955.

Foner, Philip S., ed. *The Autobiographies of the Haymarket Martyrs.* New York: Monad Press, 1969.

Galenson, Walter. *The United Brotherhood of Carpenters: The First Hundred Years.* Cambridge: Harvard University Press, 1983.

Goodwyn, Lawrence. *The Populist Moment: A Short History of the Agrarian Revolt in America.* New York: Oxford University Press, 1978.

Gordon, David, Richard Edwards, and Michael Reich. *Segmented Work, Divided Workers: The Historical Transformation of Labor in the United States, I.* Cambridge: Cambridge University Press, 1982.

Greenberg, Brian. *Worker and Community: Response to Industrialization in a Nineteenth Century City: Albany, New York, 1850–1920.* Albany: State University of New York Press, 1985.

Grob, Gerald N. *Workers and Utopia: A Study of Ideological Conflict in the American Labor Movement, 1865–1900.* Evanston, IL: Northwestern University Press, 1961.

Gutman, Herbert. *Power & Culture: Essays on the American Working Class.* New York: Pantheon Books, 1987.

————. *Work, Culture & Society in Industrializing America.* New York: Knopf, 1966.

Halker, Clark D. *For Democracy, Workers, and God: Labor Song-Poems and Labor Protest, 1865–95.* Urbana: University of Illinois Press, 1991.

Harris, William H. *The Harder We Run: Black Workers since the Civil War.* New York: Oxford University Press, 1982.

Harvey, Katherine. *The Best-Dressed Miners: Life and Labor in the Maryland Coal Region, 1835–1910.* Ithaca, NY: Cornell University Press, 1969.

Higham, John. *Strangers in the Land: Patterns of American Nativism 1860–1925.* New York: Atheneum, 1978.

Hoxie, Robert F. *Trade Unionism in the United States.* New York: D. Appleton, 1936.

Laurie, Bruce. *Artisans into Workers: Labor in Nineteenth-Century America.* New York: Noonday Press, 1989.

May, Henry F. *Protestant Churches and Industrial America.* New York: Harper Torchbooks, 1967.

Montgomery, David. *The Fall of the House of Labor: The Workplace, the State, and American Labor Activism, 1865–1925.* Cambridge: Cambridge University Press, 1989.

National Bureau of Economic Research. *Output, Employment, and Productivity in the United States after 1800.* New York: 1966.

Nelson, Bruce. *Beyond the Martyrs: A Social History of Chicago's Anarchists, 1870–1920.* New Brunswick, NJ: Rutgers University Press, 1988.

Painter, Nell Irwin. *Standing at Armageddon: The United States, 1877–1919.* New York: W. W. Norton, 1987.

Perlman, Selig. *A History of Trade Unionism in the United States.* New York: Augustus M. Kelly, 1950.

Ransom, Roger, and Richard Sutch. *One Kind of Freedom: The Economic Consequences of Emancipation.* Cambridge: Cambridge University Press, 1983.

Ratner, Sidney, James Soltow, and Richard Sylla. *The Evolution of the American Economy: Growth, Welfare, and Decision Making.* New York: Basic Books, 1979.

Rosenzweig, Roy. *Eight Hours for What We Will: Workers and Leisure in an Industrial City, 1870–1920.* Cambridge: Cambridge University Press, 1983.

Schneirov, Richard. *Labor and Urban Politics: Class Conflict and the Origins of Modern Liberalism in Chicago 1864–1897.* Urbana: University of Illinois Press, 1998.

Seretan, L. Gene. *Daniel DeLeon: The Odyssey of an American Marxist.* Cambridge, MA: Harvard University Press, 1979.

Sorge, Frederich. *Labor Movement in the United States: A History of the American Working Class From Colonial Times to the Present,* ed. Philip Foner and Brewster Chamberlain. Westport, CT: Greenwood, 1977.

Takaki, Ronald. *A Different Mirror: A History of Multicultural America.* Boston: Back Bay Books, 1983.

Thelen, David. *Paths of Resistance: Tradition and Dignity in Industrializing Missouri.* New York: Oxford University Press, 1986.

Thompson, Edward P. *The Making of the English Working Class.* New York: Vintage Books, 1966.

Wade, Louise. *Chicago's Pride: The Stockyards, Packingtown, and Environs in the Nineteenth Century.* Urbana: University of Illinois Press, 1987.

Wallace, Anthony F. C. *St. Clair: A Nineteenth Century Coal Town's Experience with a Disaster-Prone Industry.* New York: Knopf, 1987.

Wiebe, Robert. *The Search for Order, 1877–1920.* New York: Hill and Wang, 1967.

Zinn, Howard. *A People's History of the United States.* New York: Harper, 1980.

Selected Works on Social Movement Theory

Davies, James. "Toward a Theory of Revolution." *American Sociological Review* 27:1 (February 1962): 5–19.

Fantasia, Rick. *Cultures of Solidarity: Consciousness, Action, and Contemporary American Workers.* Berkeley: University of California Press, 1988.

Friedman, Samuel. "Worker Opposition Groups." *Research in Social Movements, Conflicts and Change: A Research Annual,* ed. Louis Kreisberg, Volume 8, 133–70. Greenwich, CT: JAI Press, 1985.

Gamson, William. *The Strategy of Social Protest.* Homewood, IL: Dorsey, 1975.

Kornhauser, William. *The Politics of Mass Society.* New York: Free Press, 1959.

Lee, Albert, ed. *Principles of Sociology.* New York: Barnes and Noble, 1965.

Marx, Gary, and Douglas McAdam. *Collective Behavior and Social Movements: Process and Structure.* Englewood Cliffs, NJ: Prentice Hall, 1994.

Mauss, Armand. *Social Problems and Social Movements*. Philadelphia: Lippincott, 1975.

McCarthy, John, and Mayer Zald. "Resource Mobilization and Social Movements; A Political Theory." *American Journal of Sociology* 82:6 (May 1977): 1212–41.

Piven, Francis, and Richard Cloward. *Poor People's Movements: Why They Succeed, How They Fail*. New York: Pantheon, 1977.

Smelser, Neil. *Theory of Collective Behavior*. New York: Free Press, 1962.

Tilly, Charles. *From Mobilization to Revolution*. Reading, MA: Addison-Wesley, 1978.

———. "Social Movements Old and New." *Research in Social Movements, Conflict and Change: A Research Annual*, ed. Louis Kreisberg, Bronislaw Miztal, and Janus Muda, Volume 10, 1–18. Greenwich, CT: JAI Press, 1988.

Turner, Ralph, and Lewis Killian. *Collective Behavior*. 3rd ed. Englewood Cliffs, NJ: Prentice Hall, 1987.

Zald, Mayer, and John McCarthy. "Social Movement Industries: Competition among Movement Organizations." *Research in Social Movements, Conflict and Change: A Research Annual*, ed. Louis Kreisberg, Volume 3, 1–20. Greenwich, CT: JAI Press, 1980.

Other Works Consulted

Baron, Ava, ed. *Work Engendered: Toward a New History of American Labor*. Ithaca, NY: Cornell University Press, 1991.

Baxandall, Rosalyn, and Linda Gordon, eds. *America's Working Women: A Documentary History, 1860 to the Present*. New York: W. W. Norton, 1995.

Carnes, Mark. *Secret Ritual and Manhood in Victorian America*. New Haven: Yale University Press, 1989.

Clawson, Mary Ann. *Constructing Brotherhood: Class, Gender, and Fraternalism*. Princeton: Princeton University Press, 1989.

Cobble, Dorothy Sue. "Organizing the Postindustrial Work Force: Lessons from the History of Waitress Unionism." *Industrial and Labor Relations Review* 44:3 (April 1991), 419–36.

Fink, Gary, ed. *Biographical Dictionary of American Labor*. Westport, CT: Greenwood, 1984.

Flynn, Elizabeth Gurley. *The Rebel Girl: An Autobiograpy, My First Life (1906–1926)*. New York: International Publishers, 1955.

Foner, Philip. *Women and the American Labor Movement: From the First Trade Unions to the Present*. New York: Free Press, 1979.

Goldman, Emma. *Living My Life: Volume One*. New York: Dover, 1971.

Kessler-Harris, Alice. *Out to Work: A History of Wage-Earning Women in the United States*. Oxford: Oxford University Press, 1982.

Lerner, Gerda, ed. *The Female Experience: An American Documentary*. New York: Oxford University Press, 1992.

Macionis, John. *Sociology.* Upper Saddle River, NJ: Prentice Hall, 1998.

Milkman, Ruth, ed. *Women, Work & Protest: A Century of U.S. Women's Labor History.* London: Routledge, 1991.

Morgan, Robin, ed. *Sisterhood Is Powerful: An Anthology from the Women's Liberation Movement.* New York: Vintage, 1970.

Parkinson, C. Northcote. *Parkinson's Law and Other Studies in Administration.* Boston: Houghton Mifflin, 1957.

Peter, Laurence, and Raymond Hull. *The Peter Principle.* New York: Morrow, 1969.

Smith-Rosenberg, Carroll. *Disorderly Conduct: Visions of Gender in Victorian America.* New York: Oxford University Press, 1985.

Wertheimer, Barbara. *We Were There: The Story of the Working Women in America.* New York: Pantheon Books, 1977.

Van Tine, Warren. *The Making of a Labor Bureaucrat: Union Leadership in the United States, 1870–1920.* Amherst: University of Massachusetts Press, 1973.

Weber, Max. *Essays in Sociology,* ed. H. H. Gerth and C. Wright Mills. New York: Oxford University Press, 1946.

———. *The Theory of Social and Economic Organization,* ed. Talcott Parsons. Glencoe, IL: Free Press, 1947.

Index

Accident Claims Association, 172, 173
Adelphon Kruptos, 25, 29, 41, 43, 100, 101, 102, 110, 143, 152
Allyn, Fannie C., 125, 146
Amalgamated Association of Iron and Steel Workers, 167
American Federation of Labor, 13, 18, 24, 37, 68, 82, 83, 93, 96, 176
American Railway Union, 77, 93, 210 n.67
American Reform Party, 91
American Statesman (Marblehead, MA), 104, 200 n.21
Anheuser-Busch brewers, 173
Anthony, Susan, 143
Armour Corporation, 56, 57, 58
Arthur, Peter, 91
Asch, Roberta, 163
Aylsworth, Ira, 80

Bailey, William, 19, 40, 41, *54,* 70–71, 73, 79, 87, 110, 111, 113, 114, 130, 170, 180, 188 n.24, 192 n.6, 194 n.46, 196 n.73; early career, 48; expelled from KOL, 47, 66–67; fight with executive board, 62–66; Home Club and, 52–53, 62–66; knitting mill strikes, 50–51, 60, 61; national trade district views, 51–52, 61; occupational unionism, 51–52; post-KOL activities, 67–68; stockyards strike, 53–60

Bakunin, Mikhail, 75
Barry, Leonora, 19, 141, 141–59, *150,* 171, 181; advocates separate spheres, 154; Department of Women's Work and, 145, 149–51, 152–54, 155; family life, 144–45, 155; harassment of, 148–49, 152–55; joins KOL, 145; lecturer, 146–47, 155; organizer, 148; resigns Department of Women's Work, 153–54; resigns KOL, 154–55; suffrage and, 155; temperance and, 149, 155
Barry, Thomas, 19, 41, 44, 47–71, *54,* 73, 79, 87, 95, 107, 111, 113, 114, 116, 130, 152, 165, 180, 188 n.24, 192 n.11, 196 n.73; anarchism and, 62–63, 69; early career of, 48–50; expelled from KOL, 66–67; fight with executive board, 62–66; Home Club and, 52–53, 62–66; knitting mill strikes, 50–51, 60, 61; legislative career, 49–50; lumber mill strikes and, 50; national trade district views, 51–52; occupational unionism of, 51–52; post-KOL career, 67–69; stockyards strike, 53–60, 193 n.30, 193 n.32, 194 n.46
Barry, William, 144, 145
Bates, James, 135
Beaumont, Ralph, 100, 120, 122, 164, 165, 170, 188 n.24
Bellamy, Edward, 9–10; nationalism, 13

Bennie, George, 143, 155
Birdsall, William, 15, 97, 98, 115
Bishop, Maurice, 112, 174
Boston Globe, 112
Boyer, Oliver, 120, 202 n.19
Breslin, Michael, 66, 68
Brisbane, Arthur, 26, 44, 118, 119
Brophy, John, 19, 117, 118, 139, 140,
  180; and KOL court, 129–31; as au-
  thor, 125, 126, 203 n.47; organizer,
  127–28
Brotherhood of Locomotive Engineers,
  63, 78, 90–91, 93
Brotherhood of Locomotive Firemen,
  91
Brotherhood of United Labor, 68–69
Brown, Edward E., 133, 134, 135
Buchanan, Joseph, 19, 60, 61, 66, *77,*
  107, 111, 113, 114, 116, 139, 165,
  175, 176, 180, 192 n.6; anarchism
  and, 75–76, 82, 94–96; C, B, & Q
  line strike, 90–91; eclectic beliefs
  of, 73–74, 82, 94–96; executive
  board and, 77–80; expelled, 88;
  Haymarket and, 84, 85, 86, 89; miners and, 78, 88; Montclair, NJ,
  92–94; opposes Home Club, 38, 40,
  41, 45, 81–83; organizing ability,
  76–77, 85, 86; Provisionals and,
  87–90; reinstated to KOL, 92–93,
  175; runs for Congress, 94; Southwest strike, 78–79; temperance and,
  79, 84, 87; Union Pacific strike and,
  77–78
Buchanan, Mary Ellen (Holt), 74
Bureau of Immigration, 178
Bureau of Labor Statistics, 104, 111,
  145
Butler, Michael, 55, 56, 60, 194 n.38

Callahan, James, 84
Cameron, Hugh, 202 n.19
Campbell, D. J., 176
Campbell, James, 94, 166, 170
Cannellsburg coal strike, 120, 124

Canon City Coal Company, 78
Carlton, Albert, 56, 58, *59,* 60, 65, 67,
  104, 105, 106, 156, 194 n.32
Catholic Total Abstinence Society, 155
Cattanooch, Peter, 127, 202 n.18
Cavanaugh, Hugh, 44, 165, 170, 173,
  174, 188 n.24
Caville, John, 29, 34, 35, 105, 122
Chavez, Cesar, 182
C. H. Evans Brewery, 173
Chicago Ethical Society, 91
Chicago Packing Company, 57, 58
Chicago stockyards strike (1886), 38,
  51, 53–60, 62, 70, 83, 86, 163, 192
  n.11, 193 n.21, 193 n.30, 193 n.32
Chicago Tribune, 36, 59
Christian Merlin Brewery, 173
Churchill, I. T., 134, 136
Cigarmakers International Union, 33,
  36, 38, 41, 51, 81, 82, 83, 86
Cleveland, Grover, 111, 112, 172
Coalition of Labor Union Women, 159
Cobble, Dorothy Sue, 51
Colorado Coal and Iron Company, 78
Colorado Prohibition Party, 84
Congress of Industrial Organizations,
  142
Cook, R. H., 30
Corbin, Austin, 63
Cowen, William, 29
Crowne, Thomas, 24
Cudahy and Company, 56
Cuno, Theodore, 25, 31, 44, 45, 86,
  102, 163; Duryea boycott, 28–29,
  43; expulsion of, 30, 32; Home Club
  and, 32, 33; Marxism of, 24, 26, 29,
  32, 42–43, 163; reinstatement of,
  31, 42

Daily Star (Chicago), 84
Davis, John, 52
Debs, Eugene, 91
Degnan, William, 58
DeLeon, Daniel, 42, 92, 164, 169, 174,
  176

Denton, Perly, 132, 133
Denver & Rio Grande Railroad, 78
Denver Democrat, 74
Department of Labor, 94, 158, 178
Derby, P. F., 111–12
Detwiler, George, 165
Devlin, John, 164, 166, 167, 168, 171,
    173, 174, 176
Donnelly, F. F., 67
Donovan, Florence, 51
Douglass, Frederick, 10
Drury, Victor, 24, *28,* 29, 38, 39, 64,
    66, 82, 95, 96, 119, 121, 122, 125,
    189 n.24, 189 n.26; dealing with rac-
    ism, 37; organization of Home Club,
    30–32, 34, 40; political views 24,
    26–27, 41–45; secrecy and, 27,
    35–36; trade union views, 32–33
Dudden, Faye, 131
Dunne, George, 40, 68, 148
Durkheim, Émile, 17
Duryea Starch Company, 28, 29, 32, 43,
    86, 102, 163

Eiler, Maggie, 156, 157, 168, 170–71,
    207 n.64
Elliott, John, 29, 44, 188 n.24
Engel, George, 89
Evans, Chris, 52
Evans, George Henry, 119

Federation of Organized Trades and
    Labor Unions, 51, 80, 82
Ferrell, Frank, 37
Fischer, Adolph, 89
Flannigan, Father P. M., 60
Flynn, Elizabeth Gurley, 142
Foner, Philip, 143, 177
Foster, Frank, 105, 106, 111, 112, 116
Foster, William H., 82
Founders Order of the Knights of
    Labor, 41
Fourier, Charles, 26, 44, 118, 119
Fowler Brothers Corporation, 57, 58
Friedman, Samuel, 47, 70, 161

Fuller & Warren boycott, 125, 126–28,
    131

Gaffney, William, 136
Gamson, William, 47, 163
Garlock, Jonathan, 14, 117, 138
Gaunt, Sylvester, 59, 194 n.32
George, Henry, 26, 83, 84, 86, 92, 94,
    197 n.42
Gibson, David, 44, 188 n.24
Gilded Age, 20; agrarian ideals,
    118–19; business practices, 12, 13;
    economic conditions, 11–13, 99,
    179; farmers, 13; social movements
    in, 13; women workers and, 142–44,
    146–47, 149–50, 152, 157–58, 185
    n.14
Goldman, Emma, 142, 205 n.4
Gompers, Samuel, 13, 32, 36, 37, 51,
    69, 82, 93, 105, 162, 173
Gould, Jay, 34, 38, 78, 79, 80, 81, 90,
    105, 165
Grange movement, 13, 91
Gray, Col. G. G., 172
Great Upheaval, 20
Greeley, Horace, 119
Greenback movement, 13, 49, 91, 94,
    99, 100, 104, 115
Griffiths, Richard, 54, 55, *55,* 59, 103,
    196 n.73
Grob, Gerald, 162

Hanafin, Mary, 143, 145
Hardison, Nellie, 145
Harrison, Benjamin, 110, 111, 112
Haskell, Burnette, 38, 75, 84–88, 92
Hayes, John, 45, 62, 64, 65, 66, 71, 79,
    87, 105–11, 115, 148, 151, 152, 157,
    162, 163, 165, *168,* 173–77, 179,
    182, 192 n.6; disobeys direct orders,
    167–68, 169–70; files lawsuit vs.
    KOL, 172; General Master Work-
    man, 178; harassment of Leonora
    Barry, 148–49, 153–55; KOL fi-
    nances and, 166–68, 170, 171, 207
    n.64; sexism of, 156–57, 168,

170–71; suspended, 172; thievery of, 171
Haymarket Square incident (1886), 38, 53, 60, 80, 81, 84, 85, 89, 107, 163, 164, 165, 196 n.73
Hines, Daniel, 19, 118, 131–38, 139, 140, 180
Hines, Thomas, 132
Hocking Valley coal strike, 78
Holcobe, George, 120
Holmes, William, 85
Home Club, 23–46, 47, 52, 61–62, 66, 80–82, 86–88, 92, 95, 105, 106, 107, 111, 114, 115, 121, 122, 123, 126, 127, 128, 130, 138, 148, 157, 163, 165, 180, 188 n.24, 189 n.26, 190 n.35, 191 n.51; attacks against, 38–41; Chinese and, 37, 66; collapse of, 40–41; impact of, 42–47; organization and recruitment, 27–32; politics of, 30, 32–34; reorganization of, 40–41, 61–62, 64, 68, 70; strikes and, 34; trade unions and, 27, 32–33, 36, 39
Homestead Steel strike, 166–67
Horan, William, 24–31 passim, 34, 41, 42, 95, 124
Howes, John, 105, 106, 134

Illinois Bureau of Labor Statistics, 56
Illinois National Guard, 58
Independent Order of the Knights of Labor (1883), 94,
Independent Order of the Knights of Labor (1895) 177, 188 n. 15
International Typographical Union, 74, 75
International Workingmen's Association (Red International), 75–76, 85
International Working Peoples' Association (Black International), 75–76

John Swinton's Paper, 32, 125, 126, 127, 128
Jones, C. W., 127
Jones, Mary, 143, 158

Jones, Rev. Jesse, 136
Journal of the Knights of Labor. See Journal of United Labor
Journal of United Labor/Journal of the Knights of Labor, 32, 34, 66, 101, 102, 104, 107, 108, 111, 113, 114, 120, 122, 123, 125, 127, 147, 148, 152, 165, 166, 168, 170, 172, 173
Joyce, John, 55, 59

Kealey, Gregory, 18, 94, 131, 162
Keen, Robert, 41
Kennedy, Joseph, 41
Kessler-Harris, Alice, 158
Killian, Lewis, 73, 98, 114
King, Rev. Martin Luther, Jr., 182
Knights of Labor, Noble and Holy Order of: anarchists and, 24, 30, 44; boycotts and, 28; Chicago, 53–60, 81, 85, 92; Chinese and, 37, 66, 75; cigarmakers and, 32–33, 41, 81–83, 86; Colorado, 75–78, 82, 83, 85–87; cooperatives and, 118, 120–25; courts of, 122, 123, 124, 129–31, 139–40, 181; culture of contentiousness, 180; decline of, 15–16, 19–20, 152, 195 n.61, 208 n.13; employers as members, 131, 132, 133–36, 137; growth of, 13, 23, 24, 34, 79, 100, 105, 140, 186 n.15; Marxists and, 26, 29, 32, 42–43; Massachusetts, 100, 104–06, 107, 132–37, 146, 156; national trade districts, 36, 52, 61, 63, 68; New York City, 23–46; religious turmoil in, 83, 86, 173, 197 n.40; ritual and, 25, 27, 34, 42, 129, 130, 169, 175, 177, 209 n.37 (see also Horan, William); shoemakers and, 99–100, 106, 107, 135; social movement (KOL as), 16–18; strikes and, 34, 38, 39, 55, 90 (see also under specific strikes); structure of, 14–15, 26, 27, 45, 47–48, 51–52, 67, 70, 97–99, 138, 180, 196 n.73; trade unions and, 25, 32–33, 36, 43,

80–82, 86, 106, 111, 177; women and, 76, 141–48, 149, 155–56, 158–59, 181
Knights of Labor (Chicago), 84, 165
Knights of St. Crispin, 99, 100, 113
Kunze, Edward, 30

Labadie, Joseph, 33, 38, 45, 65, 69
Labor Day Annual, 172–75, 177, 178
Labor Enquirer (Denver and Chicago), 75, 76, 80, 84, 85, 86, 87, 88, 92
Labor Leader (Boston), 106
Lake, Obadiah, 155
Lassalleanism, 24–34, 42–45, 94, 127, 138, 148
Lasters Protective Union, 135
Laughlin and Junction Steel strike (1886), 61
Laurell, Ferdinand, 33
Laurie, Bruce, 162
Laverty, Samuel, 75
Layton, Robert, 28, 102, 103, 105, 109, 113, 200 n.16
Lease, Mary, 143
Lee, E. J., 165
Levine, Susan, 143, 146
Lewis, William, 61, 63, 68
Litchman, Annie (Shirley), 99, 110
Litchman, Charles, 19, 62, 65, 86, 111, *103,* 117, 120, 132, 148, 156, 157, 164, 166, 168, 170, 180–81, 194 n.46, 207 n.64; and bureaucracy, 97–99, 112–16; dropped from KOL, 112; early career, 99; editor of *Journal,* 101–02, 107–09; Grand/ General Secretary, 100–02, 106–10, 112; politics of, 99–100, 103, 104, 110; post-KOL career, 112
Lum, Dyer, 33

Maguire, Matthew, 39
Mansion, J. R., 127, 128, 165, 174
Martin, William, 39
Marx, Gary, 17, 47, 70, 127, 138
Marx, Karl, 75, 118
McAdam, Douglas, 17, 47, 70, 121, 138

McBride, John, 52
McCartney, John, 121
McCauley, Robert, 41
McClelland, John, 33, 34
McEnroe, Father Peter, 151
McGlynn, Father Edward, 83, 86
McGraw, Homer, 105
McGuire, Peter J. 24–45 *passim,* 69, 82; Brotherhood of Carpenters and Joiners and, 32, 43; Home Club and, 30–32
McGuire, Thomas, 27, 30, 31, 34, 40, 41, 62, 64, 66, 115, 169, 174
McKinley, William, 178
McLaughlin, Daniel, 52
McLaurin, Melton, 117
McNeill, George, 40, 76, 86, 104, 105, 106, 107, 112
McVicar, Katie, 146
Meant, Henry, 202 n.19
Michigan Federation of Labor, 69
Michigan Stove Company, 173
Milkman, Ruth, 158
Mines and Mine Laborers union, 61
Montauk Assembly, 39–40, 61, 86
Morley, William, 78
Morris and Company, 56, 57
Morrison, John, 39, 40, 41, 43, 45, 60, 61, 63, 65, 81, 88, 107, 128, 129, 138, 190 n.35
Mulhane, J., 30
Mullen, William, 36, 38, 44, 188 n.24
Murphy, John, 133, 134
Murray, George, 39, 40–42, 64, 88, 89
Murray, Joseph, 84
Mutual Mining Company, 124

National Amalgamated Iron and Steel Workers, 61
National Association of Knit Good Manufacturers, 50
National Butchers Protective Association, 56
National Cattle Growers Association, 56

National Federation of Miners and Mine
   Owners, 52
National Labor Union, 13
National Protective Tariff League, 124
National War Labor Board, 94
Neasham, Thomas, 77, 85, 86, 91
Nelson, Bruce, 84
New York Central strike, 157, 165, 166
New York Herald, 28, 29
New York State Board of Mediation, 51
New York Times, 36
New York Tribune, 173
Northern Pacific Railroad, 173
Noyes, John Humphrey, 119

occupational unionism, 51–52
O'Donnell, Edward, 142
Oestreicher, Richard, 59, 162–63
Oglesby, Richard, 89
O'Keefe, John, 165, 168, 169, 170, 174
O'Reilly, Leonora, 44, 143
O'Reilly, Mary, 145, 154, 156, 157
O'Reilly, Thomas, 40, 108, 110, 151–
   52, 166, 167, 168, 169, 170, 172,
   173, 174
Owen, Robert, 118

Pabst Brewing Company, 173
Palmer, Bryan, 18, 94, 131, 162
Parkinson, C. Northcote, 97
Parsons, Albert, 55, 69, 80, 86, 89
Parsons, John, 178
Pattison, Robert, 166
Perlman, Selig, 124
Perry, Everett, 134, 135
Peter, Laurence, 97, 113, 115
Phelan, Craig, 162, 163, 186 n.19, 190
   n.35, 191 n.51
Philadelphia and Reading strikes
   (1887–88, 1892), 63, 166
Philadelphia News, 174
Piercy, Marge, 141, 142, 159
Pillsbury, Charles, 173
Pingree, Hazen, 173
Pinkerton detectives, 58, 167
Plummer, J. D., 132, 133, 134, 136, 137

Populists (People's Party), 92, 93, 95,
   125, 164, 165, 169
Powderly, Hannah, 178
Powderly, Terence, 10, 15, 16, 19, 20,
   23, 27, 30, 34, 35, 42, 53, 56, 61–70,
   73, 76, 81–86, 88, 90, 92, 93, 96,
   100, 102, *103*, 105, 117, 119, 120,
   122, 123, 125, 135, 136, 145, 146,
   149, 151, 152, 154, 156, 157, *164*,
   181, 182, 187 n.7; assassination attempt rumors, 189 n.26; Charles
   Litchman and, 106–15; cooperates
   with Home Club, 35, 40–41, 66, 86,
   107, 163, 165, 189 n.26; countersues
   KOL, 176, 178; expelled, 161, 176,
   177; Haymarket and, 89–90; historians' views on, 162–63; John Hayes
   and, 167–74; insurance scheme and,
   170, 173; *Labor Day Annual* and,
   172–75; Leonora Barry and, 145,
   146, 148–49, 152–53; politics and,
   164–66, 169, 172, 176, 197 n.42;
   post-GMW career, 176–78; resigns
   as GMW, 174; returns to KOL, 178;
   stockyards strike and, 53–60, 86–
   87, 192 n.11, 193 n.21; sued by
   KOL, 175; The Governor and, 165,
   170, 172–74
Powers, Henry, 133, 134
Price, F. F., 127
Progressive Cigar Makers Union, 33, 51
Progressive Labor Party, 91
Provisional Committee of the Knights
   of Labor, 41, 63–66, 87–90, 91, 108

Quay, Matthew, 165
Quinn, James, 27, 29, 30, 31, 34, 41, 64,
   66, 82, 174
Quinn, Timothy, 30, 37

Reed, Rev. Myron, 84
Robb, Ralph, 39, 64
Robinson, A. C., 104
Rochdale movement, 119
Rockwood, Gilbert, 29, 49, 109, 122,
   123

Rocky Mountain News (Denver), 75
Rocky Mountain Social League, 80, 81,
    84, 92
Rodgers, Elizabeth, 55, 59
Roosevelt, Theodore, 112, 178

St. Louis Globe Democrat, 155
Sallon, Philly, 147
Samuel, John, 121, 122, 124
Sanial, Lucien, 43
Schilling, George, 55, 60, 62, 63, 170,
    194 n.38
Schimkowitz, Samuel, 33
Schonfarber, J. G., 93
Scribner's Monthly, 9
Seib, Charles, 62, 63, 87, 194 n.38
Sharpe, Henry, 19, 117, 118–25, 129,
    138, 139, 140, 180, 202 n.19
Skeffington, Henry, 111, 112, 143
Skidmore, Thomas, 119
single tax, 13
Slaughter, Linda, 158
Smelser, Neil, 17
Smith, Charlotte, 141, 142, 143, 158
Smith, Patrick, 136
The Socialist, 26, 69, 85
Socialist Labor Party, 29, 32, 85, 86,
    92, 143, 164, 188 n.8
Socialist Trade and Labor Alliance,
    177, 179
social movement theory, 17–18, 23,
    179–83, 186 n.22
Southern Christian Leadership Confer-
    ence, 182
Southwest strikes (1885, 1886), 34, 38,
    78–79, 81, 165
Sovereign, James, 174, 175, 176
Spies, August, 69, 89
Staats-Zeitung, 28
Stephens, Mary, 156
Stephens, Uriah, 25, *25,* 82, 100, 103,
    120, 142, 145, 155, 175
Stevens, Alzina, 141, 156
Stirling, Mary, 143
Stove Manufacturers Association, 126

Stove Mounters Defence Association,
    129
Strasser, Adolph, 33, 36, 37, 51, 82, 105
Stromquist, Shelton, 77
Swift and Company, 56, 57

Thompson, Phillips, 172
Tilly, Charles, 138
Tintic Smelting Company, 167
Tönnies, Ferdinand, 17
Traphagen, Annie, 156
Truth (San Francisco), 75
Tubon, William, 133
Turner, Frederick, 34, 44, 63, 65, 79,
    105, 106, 107, 122, 166, 170, 188
    n.24, 192 n.6
Turner, Ralph, 73, 98, 114

Union Pacific Employees Association,
    76
Union Pacific Railroad, 76, 77, 79, 91
United Auto Workers, 142, 182, 205 n.7
United Farm Workers, 182
United Labor Party, 85, 89, 91
United Mine Workers of America, 68,
    177

Vale, William, 120, 122
Van Patten, Phillip, 29, 30, 32, 143
Van Tine, Warren, 98, 114–15
Voss, Kim, 162

Wade, Louise, 57
Wallace, T. J., 68, 69, 111
Wannamaker, John, 145
Ward, Henry, 133
Ware, Norman, 15, 47, 48, 51, 118, 162,
    163, 181
Watchorn, Robert, 172
Waugh, Henry, 136
Weber, Max, 97, 98, 113, 114
Weighe, William, 167
Weir, Maggie, 158
Western Federation of Miners, 69
Willard, Frances, 143, 149
Wiltbank, F. W., 175–76

Woman's Journal, 141
Women's Christian Temperance Union,
    149, 155
Wright, Alexander, 165, 166, 168–72,
    174–76, 207 n.64

Wright, Carroll, 104, 111
Wright, Frances, 119
Wright, James L., 41, 169

Zinn, Howard, 11